PACIFIC SAIL

PACIFIC SAIL

FOUR CENTURIES OF WESTERN SHIPS IN THE PACIFIC

ROGER MORRIS

IM

International Marine Publishing Company
Camden, Maine 04843

For Kathleen

Copyright © Roger Morris 1987

Published by International Marine Publishing Co., a
division of Highmark Publishing, Ltd., 21 Elm Street,
Camden, Maine 04843

in association with David Bateman Ltd
'Golden Heights', 32-34 View Road
Glenfield, Auckland, New Zealand

Printed and bound in Hong Kong

10 9 8 7 6 5 4 3 2 1

Library of Congress Cataloging in Publication Data

Morris, Roger, 1935-
Pacific Sail.

Includes index.
1. Sailing ships—Pacific Ocean. 2. Pacific Ocean—
Navigation. I. Title.
VK18.M67   1987   387.2'2'09164   87-2943

ISBN 0-87742-248-6

Typeset in 10/11 Schneidler medium by
Typeset Graphics Ltd, Auckland
Printed in Hong Kong by Everbest Printing Co. Ltd

Design—Errol McLeary

CONTENTS

PREFACE

The Pacific covers one-third of the Earth's surface, spanning nearly half the circumference at the equator. It is greater in area than all the continents combined. Nearly five and a half centuries have passed since three small ships thrashed their lonely way into this vast sea, named by their commander 'Mare Pacifico'. Much has been written about the exploration of the Pacific, from Magellan to Cook, but the ships have to some

extent been neglected. As I have had a lifetime interest in sailing ships and a certain ability as a marine artist, I started work on this book with the idea of focussing attention on the individual ships and types of ships used by the Europeans during the age of exploration and continuing until this century. I soon found, however, that I could not entirely divorce a study of the ships from the voyages they made. Also, research made it apparent that very little positive detail is known about the early ships. Explorers rarely describe their ships in detail, no more than a modern traveller would describe the car in which he tours. Illustrations from those far-off days are often stylised and drawn by inexperienced landsmen, so little reliance can be placed on them. The few expertly draughted examples by artists such as Peter Brueghel are invaluable sources, and by extracting detail from texts, a composite idea of the ships can be put together. Nevertheless, I must admit to a certain amount of conjecture in my paintings and descriptions.

Although I have been as careful as possible to be accurate, this is not a treatise. I am an artist and have tried to add colour to description not only with the paintings but by the occasional use of verse and poetry of the period. Whenever possible, first-hand accounts have been used.

Each type of ship included in this book would require a volume in itself if I was to describe its structure, rig, fittings, crew and management. I can only provide an outline covering the more interesting, unusual or innovative aspects of the ships, for the subject is as vast as the ocean on which the vessels sailed.

The voyages of the navigators have been well

recorded, but some are more well known than others. In my country everyone knows of the superb voyages of Cook and is acquainted with Drake and Magellan. Fewer have learned of the tribulations of Anson, the voyages of the Manila galleons or the hardships of the eighteenth-century Russians.

Rather than repeat a detailed account of Captain James Cook's three voyages, I have only briefly outlined his achievements and concentrated on the ships which served him so well. Others have been omitted – for example, Byron, Wallis, Carteret and Vancouver are only referred to in passing. The type of ship in which they sailed has elsewhere been described, and to include an account of the entire voyages of every navigator would broaden the scope of the book to a point where it would become unmanageable.

The book falls into three sections: the first covers the age of exploration, dwelling on ventures which are not necessarily the most well known or important; the second comprises a more detailed study of the colliers of Cook and Bligh, a type of ship in which I have some experience, having sailed a replica of the *Bounty*; the third part highlights a few of the host of ships which sailed the Pacific during the nineteenth and twentieth centuries.

Not included owing to the restriction of space are the large American schooners, the blackbirders and missionary ships in the South Pacific, Australian ketches, pearlers, the eighteenth-century Welsh ships carrying coal out to and copper ore home from South America, the early Pacific Island traders in search of sandalwood and shell, and so on, which I realise some could judge as being intrinsic to a comprehensive account of sailing ships in the Pacific.

EARLY NAVIGATION

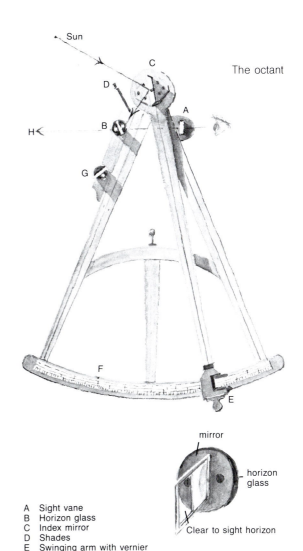

The octant

Unless one has crossed the Pacific in a slow ship it is difficult to visualise the distances involved. The North Atlantic is considered a sizable ocean and a voyage from New York to the United Kingdom is less than 3000 miles. Consider the Pacific. From Sydney to Tahiti is 3300 miles and by no means half way across; Hobart to Panama, 7640 miles; San Francisco to Valparaiso, 5940, and Honolulu to San Diego, 2270. Imagine crawling across these distances at a speed of about four knots – nearly three months from Hobart to Panama for an old sailing ship. But hold on! That is a great circle distance or the shortest route. Our old sailing ship could add possibly another 2000 miles to this in keeping to regions which would give her favourable winds. If she tried the direct route, she might not get there at all.

It was the winds that to a large extent dictated the way in which the Pacific was opened up. From the north and south strong westerlies merge through the variables to the northeast and southeast trades, between which lie the doldrums. Along the immense American coastline the winds blow generally towards the equator. In the northwest Pacific, monsoons dictate the movement of sailing ships, and in the southwest, around New Zealand and Australia, anything goes; there changes can occur within hours and last days.

For 250 years after Magellan, whole vast regions of the Pacific remained unexplored. Practically none of the southwest Pacific was ever ploughed by a European keel, and the Hawaiian Islands were only put on the chart in 1779 in spite of the annual passage of the Manila galleons across the north Pacific. Magellan, when he struck out from the

mirror

horizon glass

Clear to sight horizon

A Sight vane
B Horizon glass
C Index mirror
D Shades
E Swinging arm with vernier
F Scale to 90°
G Horizon glass for back observations

South American coast, could only be certain of two topographical facts: the latitude of his departure and the latitude of his destination in the Spice Islands. All else was conjecture. The size of the earth was disputed; only 30 years before, Columbus thought he had reached outriders of the East Indies when he arrived in what are now known as the West Indies. Longitude could only be estimated by dead reckoning, using primitive instruments to measure course and distance.

To understand the task that faced the European navigator in the Pacific, we should take a brief look at the resources available to him at different periods. Along with the weatherliness of his ship and the favouring winds, the art of navigation would bring the mariner safely to his destination.

Magellan would have had with him a few basic instruments to assist in finding his way. In those early days, when charts as we know them did not exist, one's position at sea was not so necessary. What mattered most was to arrive at one's destination, and to do this it was necessary to know the point of departure, the course to make good, and the distance. The latitude of the destination was also of prime importance.

Latitude

Simply, *latitude* is the distance of a position north or south of the equator. It is measured in degrees and can easily be found by measuring the angular distance above the horizon of any celestial body when it is on the meridian; in other words, due north or south. Early navigators used the Pole Star in the Northern Hemisphere but as in those days it was up to 3½° away from the pole, it could only be 'shot' when the stars around it were aligned in a certain way. In the Southern Hemisphere the top and bottom stars of the Southern Cross, when aligned vertically, were on the meridian. By measuring the altitude of the lower star, α Crucis, and subtracting 30°, a southern latitude could be obtained.

To work a latitude from other celestial bodies on the meridian, it was necessary to possess tables of declination, or the angular distance of the body north or south of the equator. For instance, the sun varies from about 23½°N to 23½°S in the course of a year. The stars stay more or less constant; a planet, as its name tells us, is a wanderer and the moon is all over the place, recycling her movements every 19 years. Tables of declination for the sun were available to mariners from about 1485. Tables for certain stars were gradually introduced, but it appears that the use of a star on the meridian to obtain a latitude was rare until the late eighteenth century. Tables for the moon were not compiled until the mid eighteenth century. Therefore, from Magellan almost to the time of Cook, celestial navigation depended almost entirely on the observation of the poles or the sun, which could give no more than a latitude. For much of this period it is my opinion that if the navigator could get within half a degree with his instrument he was doing very well. (Half a degree is 30 nautical miles.)

Early instruments

The quadrant

This was simply a 90° arc on which degrees were marked, with sights on one radius and a plumb-bob suspended from the centre. The observer held the instrument vertically, sighted the star, nipped the string of the plumb-bob with his thumb and read off the altitude. Most of these very early instruments were not marked in degrees but with either the names of, or symbols for, various ports. The navigator then could tell when he was on the latitude of his destination by sighting the pole star. If we were to the south, the altitude would be less, if to the north, greater. Degrees only came into use among seamen when the art of navigation improved to cope with ocean voyaging and the need to apply declinations.

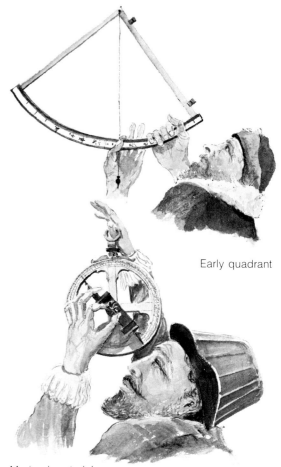

Early quadrant

Mariner's astrolabe

The astrolabe

Originally an astronomer's instrument, the astrolabe was simplified for use at sea. It consisted of a heavy brass circle, in the centre of which was pivoted a rule or *alidade* with a sight at each end. The observer held the instrument over his head by means of a ring and sighted the star by rotating the rule. The altitude was then read off at the end of the rule on a scale inscribed on the circle. The

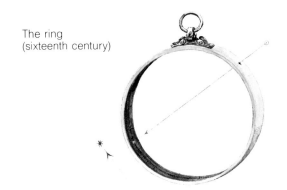

The ring
(sixteenth century)

Cross staff
(sixteenth century)

First Davis backstaff (first described 1594)
Below: modified version used until the end of the
eighteenth century.

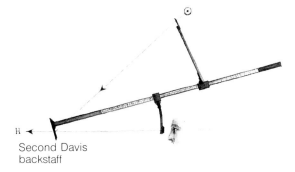

Second Davis
backstaff

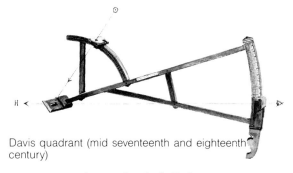

Davis quadrant (mid seventeenth and eighteenth
century)

altitude of the sun could be taken by holding the instrument low and turning the alidade until the sun shone through both sights.

Note that with both the quadrant and the astrolabe, the 'levelling' of the instrument to get an horizon depended on it hanging vertically – difficult to achieve on a rolling, pitching ship.

The ring

The simplest instrument of all, with no moving parts and popular through most of the seventeenth century, was the *ring*. It consisted of a heavy ring or band with a suspension ring on top. A small hole was drilled 45° from the top and a scale was inscribed inside the ring and opposite to the hole. The instrument was held by the suspension ring so that sunlight shone through the hole on to the scale.

The cross-staff

Magellan would probably have had one of these with him as they were then just coming into general use. A long wooden shaft was held to the bone beside the observer's eye and a cross-piece slid into a position where the star or sun rested on top of the cross-piece and the horizon 'touched' the bottom. The angle was then read off on.a scale on the shaft. On the earlier instruments, four cross-pieces had to be carried, suitable for different altitudes. This necessity was overcome by providing adjustable pegs on the cross-piece which matched

appropriate scales on the shaft. Refinements were made to the cross-staff until about the last decade of the sixteenth century which saw the instrument superseded by the back-staff.

The back-staff

One of the disadvantages of the cross-staff was that one needed to look directly at the sun. The back-staff was used by sighting the horizon away from the sun and lining up the shadow cast on the horizon vane by a vertical arm. The first back-staff was not suitable for angles over 45°, but modifications soon followed and a refined version continued to be used into the eighteenth century.

The Davis quadrant

More sophisticated than the back-staff, which had also been developed by John Davis in the mid sixteenth century, was this quadrant. Like the back-staff, it depended on a thrown shadow and was thus no use for stars. There were many variations to the basic instrument, some simple and others much more complicated.

The octant

In 1730 two independent inventors, Thomas Godfrey in America and John Hadley in England, produced instruments that used mirrors to measure angles. These were the forerunners of the modern sextant but only used an arc of 45°, or one-eighth of a circle. On this arc, due to the properties of

9

reflection, angles of up to 90° could be measured. Godfrey's and Hadley's first instruments were held with the arc towards the observer, but in 1734 Hadley made an instrument with the arc held downward. With this instrument altitudes of both stars and sun could be measured with a degree of accuracy hitherto not possible.

The sextant

The sextant is identical in conception to the octant except that it possesses an arc of 60° and is capable of measuring angles of up to 120°. This was useful in taking lunar distances, a method of computing longitude, back angles and horizontal angles.

Direction, or the compass

By the sixteenth century the *mariner's compass* was in general use, although it remained comparatively primitive until the mid 1700s, when permanent magnets were produced and, later, correctors placed around the compass. Up until this time the needle was made of soft iron or sheet steel in a variety of shapes designed to enable it to balance on the pivot. As these needles lost their magnetism in time, they had to be re-magnetised by means of a *lodestone*. At first the lodestone, at an increasing rate, was passed round and round the outside of the compass bowl, the needle following. The lodestone was then snatched away, leaving the needle re-magnetised without the stone having come into contact with the needle. Later, in various ways, the needle was rubbed with the lodestone.

The *card,* with the standard 32 points, was mounted on the needle. The accepted colouring was blue for the cardinals and red for the half-cardinals. North was indicated, as it is now, with a fleur-de-lys and sometimes the east point with a cross. A dark card was popular; this had the points marked white on a black background and had the advantage that it could be seen better in a bad light. In the late

sixteenth century and on into the eighteenth, the centre and the eight triangles marking the cardinals and half-cardinals were often highly embellished with symbolic figures and ships.

From the fifteenth century, northern Europeans offset the cards from true north to allow for variation in their home waters. They continued to do this until the eighteenth century, although the English took to carrying another compass with the needle set north on the card, and had by the eighteenth century dispensed with the offset card. The Dutch combined the two by mounting two cards on the same pivot, the one applying to variation being adjustable. Most compasses were mounted in wooden bowls, but brass bowls began to be used in the seventeenth century and gradually came into more general usage.

Variation

This is the amount by which the compass needle is offset by the Earth's magnetic field. It varies throughout the world and can range to a considerable amount. Where I am now writing the variation is about 19° East. Before navigators were able to observe their longitudes, the variations in particular localities were often used as an aid to position finding. This change with location was soon appreciated by the early navigators and methods to measure it developed. The Pole Star of course provided the best check, but when tables of declination came into use, *amplitudes,* or the bearing of the rising or setting sun, were used. There was no reason why the amplitudes of stars could not be used, but this was not common practice. To take these bearings, *azimuth compasses,* or compasses with sights of some form or other, were employed from early in the sixteenth century. From the mid eighteenth century, when time-keeping became more reliable, an azimuth or bearing of any celestial object for which hour angle and declination was tabled, could be calculated and compared with the compass bearing.

Deviation

It is often claimed that until the building of iron ships, seamen knew little about deviation. This, in my opinion, can hardly be true. *Deviation* is the compass error produced by the needle being deflected by nearby ferrous metals or by the induced magnetism of the ship itself. Surely those sailors of old would have been observant enough to see a compass needle deflect if they rested their sword across the bowl, and would have taken care not to leave cutlasses, arquebuses and crossbows leaning against the compass house? I have read that some ships were run ashore by similar mismanagement and this was claimed as proof that the navigators were not aware of deviation. One ship I was in was steered for 24 hours way off course because of a torch left in the binnacle. That was carelessness, not ignorance. It is true that until ironwork became more common, deviation was not a consistent error to be allowed on each course steered.

Speed and distance, or the log

It is possible to guess the speed of a ship by looking over the side, but this needs experience and can be subject to all sorts of error. Mariners found it was essential to measure their speed more accurately. The *Dutch log,* used in the seventeenth century, involved the timing of a chip of wood passing marks set in the gunwale of the ship. An English invention however, appears to predate the Dutch log. This was the *log-ship,* and the apparatus remained basically unchanged and in use until early this century.

Initially the log was a wooded segment of a circle. The curved edge was weighted and a bridle was attached to the three corners. The log-ship was dropped over the stern on a line which was allowed to run out until a minute glass had expired. The length of line run out was measured in rough fathoms by an arm's stretch. The number of fathoms was multiplied by 60 and divided by 2500 to get leagues per hour. The English reckoned 5000 feet to one mile, three miles to a league and 20 leagues to a degree. The Iberians also worked 5000 feet to a mile, but made four miles a league and 17½ leagues to a degree. In 1635 Richard Norwood, in measuring the distance from London to York, came up with 6120 feet to the mile; this was closer as the true measurement is 6080 feet.

The log was soon modified, first by having knots put into the line to eliminate the need to measure it each time the log was cast, secondly by a stray line which allowed the log to stream clear of turbulence before the glass was turned. Next one of the lines of the bridle was pegged in such a way that the sharp jerk when the reel was stopped disconnected that bridle from the log. This made the log easy to haul in. Lastly, a 30-second glass was used. From the knots marking the log-line comes the expression for nautical miles-per-hour; thus, a ship travels at so many knots. Sailors, being conservative, often stuck to their own methods. The factors used to calculate speed varied and thus so did the distance between knots on the line. Some navigators preferred the old 5000 feet to a mile as it gave them a faster speed which could be a safety factor in making a landfall.

Inaccuracies were inevitable. Among other things, turbulence, judging the time to turn the glass, and stretched line, could all affect the reading. Although many methods were experimented with, not until 1878 was a really satisfactory alternative developed by Thomas Walker, who produced a *rotator* that towed astern and registered the distance on dials at the taffrail.

Sounding

The *lead-line* would be one of the oldest navigational aids, but until about 1600 the line was probably unmarked. Around this time marks began to be placed at suitable intervals to indicate various depths.

Cord, leather and cloth were used so that the marks could be differentiated in the dark. For example, the modern lead-line has ten fathoms marked with a piece of leather with a hole in it. Not every fathom is marked, the unmarked depths being known as *deeps*.

Casting the lead

The leadsman, leaning out from the forechains in a bight of a line, swings the seven-pound lead over and over until he has attained sufficient impetus to hurl the lead well ahead of the ship. As the ship passes over the lead, if it has reached the bottom, he gathers in the slack, observes the markings and sings out the depth. Examples could be 'By the mark seven', or 'By the deep eight', or 'A quarter less ten'. If the lead does not reach the bottom before the line is vertical, the call is 'No bottom at . . . .' (whatever mark shows).

In the base of the lead a hollow filled with tallow picks up material from the seabed. Knowledge of the bottom, whether it is sand, mud or shingle, is useful in ascertaining a position and is shown on charts.

For deep-sea sounding, a heavier lead was used and men, each holding a coil of the line, were ranged along the ship's side. The ship was hove to and the lead cast. As the line ran out from each man's hand, he warned the next by calling 'Watch, there, watch' until the lead reached the bottom.

Charts

The very early charts, known as *portolans,* were hand-drawn on sheepskin. Directions were indicated by *wind-roses* or *compass-roses*, with lines extending from their centres through all 32 points of the compass. As three or four roses would be positioned on the portolan, the lines, or *loxodromes,* formed a lattice, conventionally coloured according to whether the loxodrome represented a cardinal, half-cardinal, or intermediate by-points. All these portolans ignored the fact that the Earth's surface is curved, and they could be termed 'plane' charts. In fact, throughout the sixteenth century all charts showed the Earth as a plane and although Mercator had by the end of the sixteenth century produced a chart ideal for navigation, plane charts continued to be used. At the beginning of the eighteenth century probably half the charts in use were still plane charts. Mercator's projection, which is still used in charts today, is ideal for navigation, having latitudes and longitudes represented as straight lines intersecting at right angles. Thus compass directions and rhumb line courses can be laid off with a rule.

Portolans were soon superseded in the sixteenth century by engraved charts. Of course, in regard to the Pacific, printed charts were probably non-existent at first, for the Spanish would have kept their 'lake' under close wraps.

Much ocean navigation was carried out with the aid of sailing instructions known in England as *Rutters* and later *Wagoners*. It was the Spanish sailing instructions for the Pacific that every foreign captain or pirate prized. They contained descriptions of any local phenomena, winds, currents, recommended courses, drawings of coastlines – in fact all the sorts of information one would expect to find in a modern pilot book, but including the ocean sailing routes for the region.

For the best part of 250 years from the time of Magellan, navigators in the Pacific struggled with these few aids. The estimation of dead-reckoning, depending on inaccurate instruments and being affected by such unknown factors as leeway and currents, was so dubious that the wise captain stood far to the west or east of his destination, so he could find it by sailing along its latitude, keeping course by the altitude of the Pole Star or the sun on the meridian when he could see them. If his goal was a small atoll, he stood a good chance of missing it or running up on it on a dark night. As all the mid-Pacific winds and currents flow generally in the east-west direction, it was important that the anxious navigator find his latitude well to the windward or east of his goal. To go from north or south straight to where he thought it might be would leave him, if he missed it, wondering whether to turn east or west. If you look at Magellan's track you will see how far east he got on to his latitude – something like 3500 miles.

Is it any wonder that the southwest Pacific was untraversed for so long? Most wishing to go that way were baulked by the westerlies in the south. The southeast trades should have given a good slant from South America, but the weeks and weeks of sailing, with stores and water diminishing and scurvy making its appearance, would discourage both captain and crew. If the Tuamotus were raised, the reefs and currents in the maze of atolls would be intimidating and they would suffer the frustration of being unable to anchor. Uncertainty of their distance run westwards and two additional worries would further intimidate the adventurers. First, the winds and currents would be implacably driving them west; they could become embayed or trapped in some vast gulf. Secondly, uncertain of longitude, they would be anxious not to get so far to leeward that it would be impossible to get to windward in

the latitude of any known haven in the north. Not until Tahiti was discovered by Wallis was a suitable place of refreshment and departure available for the exploration of the southwest.

Longitude

Until the eighteenth century, *longitude,* or one's distance east or west of whatever prime meridian was in use, could only be estimated. At the equator one minute of longitude is equivalent to one nautical mile or one minute of latitude. As all meridians intersect at the poles, as soon as the equator is left, a minute of longitude becomes less than a sea mile. As all distances were measured in sea miles and leagues, a ship sailing west for 70 miles at 45°S latitude would change its longitude by 99 minutes. The distance in miles east or west is known as *departure* and the distance in minutes and degrees of longitude *difference of longitude.* This was not always understood or applied by navigators right up to the eighteenth century. Apparently there were East Indiamen as late as 1750 who still reckoned in what is known as *plane sailing* – probably using plane charts. When the difference between departure and difference of longitude is taken into account, the resulting courses and distances are known as *Mercator sailing.* To be fair, we should remember that until the chronometer came into use, longitudes were wildly in error and consequently could not be relied upon. It was safer to ignore the guesses and work on what was known – the latitude and direction.

The need to be able to observe and calculate longitude became so desperate in the eighteenth century that the British Admiralty set up a Board of Longitude which in 1714 offered prizes of up to £20,000 to anyone who could find a method of getting a longitude at sea accurate to within half a degree. The finding of longitude requires that the observer knows his exact time at the prime meridian. Now the prime meridian is Greenwich and this is accepted internationally; in the past there was a multiplicity of prime meridians – each nation using

its own. Only since 1883, when the United States used their growing influence, was Greenwich established as the international prime meridian. To get the time on this meridian anywhere in the world, one solution would be to manufacture a very accurate clock, or at least one which had a regular error which could be applied, and most importantly, withstand the movement and change of temperatures inherent in a ship. A satisfactory clock, or *chronometer* was developed by John Harrison and was tested on a voyage to the West Indies in 1761-2. John Harrison did not receive the last instalment of the Admiralty's reward until 1772.

While Harrison was working on a clock, others sought alternatives. In 1761 Doctor Neville Maskelyne worked out a method of finding longitude by measuring lunar distances. The moon changes its position in the sky so rapidly that it could be used for determining time, if one could observe its position relative to a star. Provided tables were available giving the required data for Greenwich, a time could be ascertained and hence a longitude. The method worked, and in 1767 the first British Almanac was published which gave suitable information for the working of *lunars.* The French had produced a similar almanac as early as 1679. The mathematics in computing lunars was involved, difficult and beyond most masters. In addition, the taking of the necessary sights was difficult, requiring three assistants. The navigator shot the lunar distance, two of the assistants took simultaneously the altitudes, and the third recorded. This was repeated five times. Later a method was worked out using only one assistant. Cook, Bligh and many others used lunars, which could usually get a longitude within one degree.

Once navigators were able to fix their positions, both in latitude and longitude, charts became more accurate and this contributed to a vast expansion in vessels making ocean passages and in some measure advanced the settlement of Europeans around the western Pacific.

THE VOYAGE OF MAGELLAN

Fernão de Magalhães of Portugal, the primordial European navigator of the Pacific, entered the ocean on 28 November 1520. Sailing in Spanish ships financed by a Spain anxious to share in the wealth of the Far East, Magellan himself was inspired by his experiences in the Moluccas (Spice Islands), the widening geographical knowledge of the day (including Balboa's sighting of the 'Great South Sea'), and by his own single-minded determination to find the route westward.

The hazards of Spanish and Portuguese politics through which he had to thread and inveigle his way to mount the expedition were probably more difficult and dangerous for him than the williwaws, rips and rocks of the strait which bears his name. He had surmounted treachery and lost the ships *Santiago* and *San Antonio* by the time Cape Froward, the southernmost tip of South America, was weathered. It was with the small *naos* (carracks) *Trinidada, Vittoria* and *Concepcion* that Magellan cleared Cape Deseado and entered the 'Great South Sea'.

After cruising up the Patagonian coast to the north of 40°S, Magellan made his departure northwest for the Spice Islands. He knew nothing except the latitude of his destination; he knew he must reach this latitude to the east of the islands so as to run westward on that parallel to make his landfall. A glance at his track will show how far to the east he

reached his desired latitude and turned west, graphically illustrating his underestimation of the size of the Pacific. He had to sail west approximately 3500 miles to reach the Philippines. The Spice Islands lay approximately 600 miles south of his

landfall in the Philippines. When Magellan bore away from the South American coast he was ignorant of what might lie on his course, his east-west distances were wild guesswork, and his provisions were badly depleted by the absconding

San Antonio. It would be difficult today to envisage such a nerve-shattering situation.

The weather was kind to Magellan and it was he who described the sea as the 'Mare Pacifico', a title which has stuck in spite of the oceans far from pacific regions. The shortage of provisions and the resultant scurvy took their toll of the crews who, to sustain themselves, ate rats and the leather chafing-pieces from the rig.

Landfall was made on one of the northeastern Tuamotus on 24 January 1521, and 11 days later on another island, named by them Los Tiburones or Shark Island, one of the Line Islands. Landings could be made at neither, and it was only on 6 March, after 98 days, that they were able to refresh themselves at islands they called the Ladrones or Thieves Islands. These were Guam and Rota in the Marianas. Here was sadly initiated the frequent bloodshed caused by the conflict between the inhabitants, with their compulsive thieving habits, and the understandable desire of the voyagers to keep their ships in one piece. In retaliation for the theft of a skiff, Magellan led a shore party, burned 50 houses and some boats, and killed seven islanders.

The ships sailed on to the Philippines and at Cebu Magellan was killed in an ill-conceived affray intended to demonstrate the superiority of European arms. The officers and crews of the three ships, now leaderless, were further depleted in an attack by the local inhabitants, sparked by Magellan's disillusioned ex-slave, Enrique. The *Concepcion* was scuttled, for there were not sufficient men to man her, and the remaining two ships, after roaming the Philippines, found their way to Tidore, their destination in the Moluccas. Under the command of Sebastien del Cano, the *Vittoria* sailed home, arriving at Seville on 28 September 1522. On board were just 31 men, of whom only 18 or 19 were of the complement of 240 of the original five ships. The *Trinidada* tried to sail to Mexico, but failed, and returned to the Moluccas, where she was given up to the Portuguese. Only four of her crew of 41 ever reached home.

Trinidada and Vittoria

The *Trinidada* and *Vittoria* are seen here rounding Cape Froward, the southernmost extremity of the South American continent, in 1520. The *Vittoria*, inshore, has let her sheets fly in a squall. Both ships are shortened down, their spritsails inboard and topsail yards sent down. The courses are without bonnets. I may have depicted the *Trinidada*'s fore course a little too large.

It was these two ships of Magellan's expedition which first turned the continent. After rounding the cape they anchored in a bay named by them the Bay of Sardines. A boat, sent out to explore further, sighted the 'Great South Sea' and named the headland at the end of the strait Cabo Deseado. The success of this reconnaissance was greeted with heartfelt rejoicing, but before they could sail on, the whereabouts of two other ships of the expedition had to be resolved.

The *San Antonio* and *Concepcion* had been despatched to explore a likely looking lead in the labyrinth of channels which form the strait. The *Vittoria* was sent back in search and met the *Concepcion* off Cape Froward. Magellan's close friend João Serrano reported that the *San Antonio* had vanished in a snow squall. The *Vittoria* was again sent back and in her search navigated virtually the whole strait, but no trace of the missing vessel was found. Alvora de la Mesquita, captain of the *San Antonio,* and Estaban Gomez, king's pilot, had had enough. They made their way back to Spain.

The *Trinidada* and *Concepcion* ended their days in the East, but the *Vittoria*, which must have been a handy ship, sailed home under the command of del Cano. She was the first ship to circumnavigate the Earth.

The *Trinidada* and *Vittoria* rounding Cape Froward

THE SPANISH SHIPS

Caravel, carrack, *nao,* galley, galliass, galleon and frigate are some of the evocative names given to the first ships – variations of which were to traverse the Pacific. To overcome the lack of direct sources, I have drawn on the available records of similar ships and hundreds of old illustrations. I do not believe that these ships were as cranky looking as they were often shown in early woodcuts and paintings, for there is no doubt that these vessels made incredible voyages and worked their way through difficult and uncharted waters. On the whole they must have been sea-kindly and enduring, for although many were lost, they generally survived better than their crews, who were decimated by malnutrition resulting in scurvy and other related diseases. Handling the ships became burden enough, not to mention the continual maintenance and make-and-mend demanded by any sailing ship.

To interpret early visual sources I have used principles of seamanship, and the paintings are generally as accurate as I can achieve – although I admit to using a little licence and guesswork, and when this occurs you will be told.

I must comment here on the enormous ensigns, flags, pennants and burgees flown in those days. No doubt they did fly them, but with due caution, especially in battle or when manoeuvring. When sailing in the *Bounty* replica, we tried flying similar bunting, but it snarled itself in the rig and wound itself round spars and jammed blocks. The last straw was when a large pennant flying at the main truck fouled the fore topgallant hounds where it thrashed and banged around in a stiff breeze, whipping the fore and main topgallants to and fro so violently that

the spars were at risk. After a variety of futile attempts to clear it, one of our young monkeys volunteered to lay aloft and cut it adrift. To do this he had to shin up the quaking fore topgallant mast and it was a relief when our proud but truncated pennant was lowered to the deck. If I have painted bunting, it is therefore with a thoughtful eye to its practicality and its murderous tendencies.

Due to the lack of specific information, apart from national and a few other flags, I have unashamedly made up the rest. A study of Spanish heraldry is beyond my resources and a glance at any contemporary painting will show you a vast number and variety of flags, no doubt reflecting the honour of the captains, admirals, the Church, royalty, the sponsors, the local don and his dog.

After the inspired direction of Portuguese Prince Henry the Navigator, the quality of ships provided for the expeditions declined sadly. I suppose this could be attributed to good commercial common-sense, or parsimony, depending on your point of view. The authorities that supplied the ships usually did not have the expedition at heart and were probably more interested in the fast *real* than the survival of the crew, a reflection on naval dockyards which was to hold true over the next three centuries. Privately organised ventures were generally much better equipped and seemed to have suffered less loss of men and ships.

Caravels. During the sixteenth century caravels seem to have come in a variety of shapes, sizes and rigs. Some competed in size with carracks and galleons, although they would not have been as beamy as the former. These are three examples based on contemporary drawings.

The caravel

Originating from small coastal craft dating back well before the fifteenth century, caravels became useful and versatile ships in the initial age of exploration. They were shallow-draft vessels, fast, and with a hollow waterline forward which gave them fine windward qualities. Had they possessed finer lines aft instead of the flat transom stern, they would have been fast indeed. Initially they were lateen-rigged on all masts, but it was found handier to square-rig them for long ocean passages. A variety of combinations of lateen and square-rig are shown in these illustrations. Columbus's favourite ship, *Nina*, was a caravel which he re-rigged with square-sails while at the Canary Islands.

I am inclined to think that the Moors had an influence on the caravel. They have a distinctly Arabic appearance, and the large Arab craft which still sail from the Persian Gulf bear a striking resemblance. Off the Indian coast one fine calm morning I remember gazing in admiration at a large ship I believe was a *kotia*. She was obviously the owner's pride and joy. The low sun glinted from the oiled sides and spars and she carried a multitude of sails such as lateen topsails and others which I could not name. The white cotton was spotless. She stepped four masts, although the aftermast looked as if it was not permanent – as I think the bonaventure was on many sixteenth-century ships. To complete the picture, she had a towering aftercastle which even included quarter galleries; a beautiful ship which could have sailed right out of the past.

Caravela redonda, or square-rigged caravel

Included in this illustration are some commonsense modifications which began to appear during the 1500s, if my interpretation is correct. The rudimentary beakhead would be useful for handling the spritsail. Later it became a structural part of the

A caravela redonda or square-rigged caravel

stem and the bowsprit gammoning and later the bobstays were secured to it. The caravel was originally flush-decked apart from the aftercastle. The demands of space and dryness on long voyages seem to have led to longer and stronger poops and

a low raised forecastle. The fore-tack is boomed out by a luff-spar, probably just a pole pushed out forward.

The lateen sails on southern ships were generally set outside the shrouds. The true lateen is tacked

17

before the mast and the very early mizzens may have been so handled. It became the practice, however, to change the mizzen by bringing it round behind the mast, allowing for a mizzen stay, and the lead of the halliard tie led from the yard forward. As the sail became a steering sail, or a sail set to balance the rig, it would not normally have been set with the wind aft. Northern ships set the yard inside the shrouds. When the change took place in southern ships it is difficult to say. In the painting of Loaysa's *San Lesmes* on page 26, I have depicted the mizzen inside the shrouds as she was a Basque ship and probably subject to northern influences. The small lateen aft, named the *bonaventure,* is no bigger than a boat sail–which it probably was.

Rigging

In this early period the exact details of the vessels are to a large extent guesswork. There would be variations according to the size of the ship, the traditions and usage of its home port and the affluence of its owners. The rigging shown here and on page 20 is based more on northern ships.

Spanish ships of the sixteenth century leaving an imaginary Spanish port. From left: a galleon, a *nao* or carrack, a galliass, another galleon and a small caravel. Note the multiplicity of anchors on the closest galleon. As the ability of these ships to sail to windward was so poor, it was imperative that they had good 'ground tackle' to hold them off a lee shore.

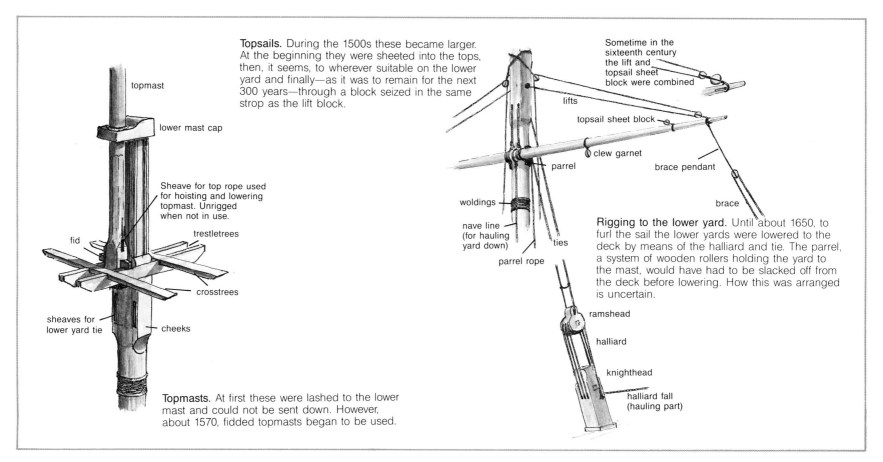

topmast

lower mast cap

Sheave for top rope used for hoisting and lowering topmast. Unrigged when not in use.

fid

trestletrees

crosstrees

sheaves for lower yard tie

cheeks

Topmasts. At first these were lashed to the lower mast and could not be sent down. However, about 1570, fidded topmasts began to be used.

Topsails. During the 1500s these became larger. At the beginning they were sheeted into the tops, then, it seems, to wherever suitable on the lower yard and finally—as it was to remain for the next 300 years—through a block seized in the same strop as the lift block.

Sometime in the sixteenth century the lift and topsail sheet block were combined

lifts

topsail sheet block

clew garnet

parrel

brace pendant

brace

woldings

nave line (for hauling yard down)

ties

parrel rope

Rigging to the lower yard. Until about 1650, to furl the sail the lower yards were lowered to the deck by means of the halliard and tie. The parrel, a system of wooden rollers holding the yard to the mast, would have had to be slacked off from the deck before lowering. How this was arranged is uncertain.

ramshead

halliard

knighthead

halliard fall (hauling part)

Martnets. These were lines which controlled the leech of the sail when taking it in. They were rigged on the fore and after side of the sail and my theory is that not only could they haul the sail to the yard while the yard was still hoisted but probably, more generally, the martnet was left fast and the yard lowered into the martnet legs which would bring the leech to the yard. As the yard was lowered further, the martnets could be eased back as necessary. The buntlines could be handled in a similar manner. From about 1650 the yards remained aloft and martnets were replaced with leechlines.

Footropes. These were not introduced until the second half of the seventeenth century. Most sail handling was done with the yard lowered and the sails themselves were stowed in the bunt, being brought to the central part of the yard. Any work required out on the yards while they were aloft, and the ship at sea, must have been precarious.

Reefing. In a rising wind the topsails came in first, then the area of the courses could be shortened by removing the bonnets. The yards could be lowered by the depth of the bonnet, thus reducing the height, the centre of effort. Ships began to carry a second bonnet called a 'drabbler'. Reef points did not come into use until about 1660.

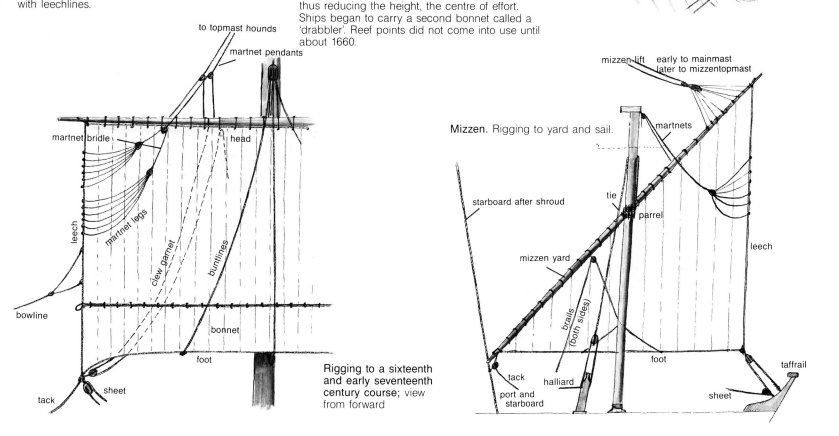

Rigging to a sixteenth and early seventeenth century course; view from forward

Mizzen. Rigging to yard and sail.

The carrack or nao*

The sixteenth-century carrack, as used by Spain and Portugal, was a natural development from the earlier Mediterranean carracks, and the style of ship became the jack-of-all trades throughout Europe. They seem, like the caravels, to have become diversified, and drawings show a variety of sterncastles. They ranged in size from the huge Portuguese *Santa Catarina do Monte Sinai* to Magellan's little *Vittoria*, but there were features common to all.

The stern was usually rounded up to a beam transom and why this superior form of run aft gave way to the flat transoms of later ships is a mystery. It may have been that the flat transom could have been pierced for guns at gun-deck level. I have noticed that ships which were designed mainly as merchantmen retained the rounded stern, an ample being the Dutch fluyt which had its origins in the sixteenth century.

By far the most characteristic and, I might say, ungainly aspect of the *nao* was the towering forecastle, commonly two decks above the waist, but if illustrations can be trusted, I have identified three, four and a skyscraping five on the *Santa Catarina*. This puts the upper forecastle deck on a level with, or higher than, the aftercastles.

A third feature was their broad beam; they would need it. The rule of thumb for Mediterranean carracks was 'tres, dos, yas' specifying a ratio of length, breadth and depth of 3:2:1. With those high forecastles and design ratios, their windward performance would have been miserable, even if they had been given the rig of a modern racing yacht.

I must confess that this representation of a *nao* is very much *my interpretation* of what they really may have been like. She is not a fighting ship, although

*Note: The Iberians seem always to use the word *nao* for the type of ship represented by the carrack. Perhaps 'carrack' was a northern term, as in the Flemish 'kraeck'.

The *Santa Catarina do Monte Sinai*. Detail from a painting made in 1520 of a large Portuguese warship. She has at least six decks and mounts 140 cannon, mostly small railing pieces.
(National Maritime Museum, Greenwich)

An early *nao*

all ships of the period were well armed. The superstructure must have been lightly built for obvious reasons. The aftercastle is two continuous decks and the arched openings on the lower or quarterdeck would allow for the mounting of small cannons, mounted on mikes or swivels. This veranda-like deck must have been pretty draughty and no doubt either canvas or light wooden shutters would have provided for the openings. The waist is part of a continuous weather deck. Right aft, the tiller port in the transom would have been open to the weather, although canvas covers may have been provided, as on later ships. The deck around the tiller and forward to the bulkhead would have contained the officers' quarters and maybe wealthier passengers were berthed here.

In the waist, over the main hatch are the ship's boats, and along each side at quarterdeck level two spars were used for securing the boarding netting which spanned the whole waist. A central spar, or even gangway, may have been rigged, but I have not shown this.

Heavy cannon mounted on carriages were in the process of development. Although guns had started to be placed on the lower deck from the beginning of the century, very few contemporary illustrations show cannon in the waist or at lower or gun-deck level. I have shown four a side in the waist, which would also serve as washports, and have tentatively suggested some on the lower deck. The ports on all ships, and particularly southern ships, were very small.

Fore and main channels are securely strengthened with knees. The mizzen and bonaventure shrouds are still set up inside the poop rail. I must point out that the bonaventure was not stepped on all ships, although it certainly seems to have been widely used up to the end of the century. The rigging for this vessel and for galleons would have been similar to that of the caravel I have described. *Naos* and galleons were all square-rigged, although there may have been exceptions.

The carracks or *naos* evolved into some enormous failures. There are examples of larger ships which never left port; they could not. Smaller versions and less extreme larger ships got around satisfactorily. Magellan sailed in *naos* and they were the workhorses of the century. Although the Portuguese continued to use huge *naos* in the Far East, the end of the sixteenth century saw them largely superseded by a more weatherly and faster ship.

The galleon

Little is known of the origins of the galleon. They begin to appear during the first half of the sixteenth century, and were possibly galliasses re-rigged as primarily a sailing craft capable of carrying guns and working on the Atlantic coasts where the oared galleys were unsuitable. Whatever the origins, they rapidly became a class of vessel in their own right; employed by all nations, and with no radical alterations to the basic hull and rig, they continued to be used right up to the clipper ship era.

The first galleons were warships, fine lined and handy when compared with the lumbering *naos*. The better sea-keeping and sailing qualities of the galleons soon commended them to the merchants and consequently they were modified to carry more freight and the superstructures enlarged.

The most obvious difference between the *nao* and the galleon was in the design of the forecastle. The galleon's forecastle was built aft of the stem and the line of the bulwarks at weather-deck level was continued forward to form a beakhead from which the spritsail, which at this period was hoisted on a parrel, could be handled.

Although aftercastles of two continuous decks were for a while common, these were soon superseded by a quarterdeck and poop. To reduce the height of the aftercastle, a halfdeck was sometimes formed as a poop, or between the quarterdeck and poop. The arrangement of decks varied and were not necessarily continuous, nor did they on later

ships follow the sheer of the wales. Should they have done so, the graceful upsweeping aftercastles would have been decidedly uncomfortable. As the internal arrangements of these early ships are nowhere described, as far as I can gather, one can only come to any conclusions by examining the position of the aftercastle's rails, quarter galleries, windows and gunports.

Quarter galleries begin to appear during the second half of the century. Vessels of the 1580s, the period of the Spanish Armada, display them in profusion, but I cannot find any representations of them in the 1560s; this is not to claim that they were non-existent then. I have shown a quarter gallery in the front-cover painting of Mendana's ships in the Solomons in 1568. Quarter galleries, particularly of the Indiamen of the seventeenth century, became totally enclosed, and although beautifully decorated, served no purpose other than officers' latrines.

The ship I have drawn is a generalised example from the third quarter of the sixteenth century and this basic form was prevalent until well into the seventeenth. The *Mayflower* of 1620 was very similar. Drake's *Golden Hinde*, the Indiamen, the Plate and the Manila ships were all galleons, the latter still being referred to as galleons when the last Manila galleon sailed from Acapulco in 1815.

Steering

How these vessels, and carracks, were steered remains something of a mystery. We know the rudder was operated by a massive tiller, but this was at weather-deck level. Above the tiller were stacked all the aftercastle decks. If the helmsman was steering directly with the tiller, he would have at least one deck above him, and even if there was a hatch over the steering position, his view would be very limited and the only way the ship could be steered would be by conning from above, or, clear of narrow waters, by compass. Now there is nothing wrong with conning, especially on powered vessels. That is how they are directed today. There is nothing

A late sixteenth
century galleon

Elevation of the stern of the *Vasa* showing tiller and whipstaff arrangement
(Statens Sjöhistoriska Museum, Wasavarvet, Stockholm)

Possible means of steering by tiller ropes

wrong with steering by compass if the ship is off the wind, provided the compass is well damped – and the early ones were not. However, anyone who has sailed even a dinghy knows that steering a sailing vessel requires an alertness and response which cannot be given by a helmsman out of sight of the elements around him. Even on the sophisticated and gigantic *Preussen* (see page 175) the helmsmen were placed exposed on the bridge deck where they could see both the sea and the sails. Steering a sailing ship by proxy can be downright dangerous.

Even small ships often need tackles led to the tiller to overcome weather helm, and the shock of seas, and I have no doubt these were used. On the *Bounty* replica we steered for two days using tackles and the helmsmen loved it. They could sit on the tiller with the fall in their hand and found that the ship could be steered even more positively than with the wheel. (I do not recommend sitting on the tiller in fresher weather.) There is no doubt that these early ships were steered with tackles and it would have been a simple step to have led the tiller rope to a more advantageous position where the sea and the sails could be watched. Given the fifteenth-century sailors' increasing ability with rigging, I think this is how the vessels may have been steered.

It was a logical step in the eighteenth century to lead these tiller ropes to a winch or horizontal capstan which was basically all the first wheel steering arrangements were.

During the sixteenth century the whipstaff came into use, but there is still some argument about its efficacy and arrangement. It would appear that any mechanical advantage gained would only have been when the tiller was within say 10° of amidships. The whipstaff would have allowed the helmsman to stand one deck above the tiller and possibly higher. A hatch in the deck above him would have allowed the helmsman to have visibility two decks above the tiller.

Detail of tiller and whipstaff
(Adapted from *Seamanship in the Age of Sail*, by John Harland)

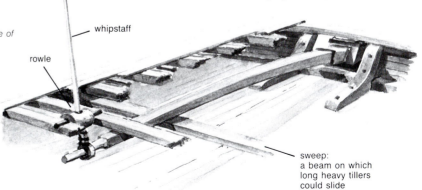

whipstaff

rowle

sweep:
a beam on which
long heavy tillers
could slide

EXPLORING THE SPANISH LAKE

In little *Vittoria's* hold were enough spices to pay for the whole cost of Magellan's expedition. This and the positive results of the Royal Inquiry encouraged Charles V of Spain to put in hand another expedition to sail to the Moluccas. The question remained whether the Spice Islands lay in the Spanish or Portuguese hemisphere. Both nations put forward their own views, but as the means of determining longitude was so vague, no decision could be arrived at. At this time Spain was at the height of her expansion, consolidating her acquisitions in the West Indies and Central America, and Hernando Cortez had recently completed his remarkable conquest of Mexico.

The Loaysa expedition (1525)

As was quite customary in Spanish maritime expeditions, command of the 1525 expedition was given to a soldier, Garcia Jofre de Loaysa, who was to take up the governorship of the Moluccas. With Loaysa, as chief pilot and in command of one of the ships, sailed del Cano of the *Vittoria*, and another officer, Andre de Urdaneta, who was to become closely associated with the Philippines on a later and more successful venture.

Seven ships were prepared at Corunna and Portugalete in north Spain. To avoid the political strife which plagued Magellan, no Portuguese were employed and a large proportion of the crews came from the Basque provinces. On 24 July 1525 the seven ships, manned by about 450 men, sailed from Corunna, bound for the Magellan Strait and beyond.

Arellano and Lope Martin in their tiny *patache* the *San Lucas*, poling her head round with the spritsail yard. Normally a *patache* would be a lateen-rigged, fast, small ship. From reading between the lines in the account of the voyage of the *San Lucas*, it appears she was rigged as shown. (See page 28)

It was May 1526 before they entered the Pacific after one abortive attempt on the strait, the loss of del Cano's ship, the *Sancti Spiritus*, with nine lives, the disappearance forever of the *Annunciada* and the desertion of the *San Gabriel*.

Ships of the Loaysa expedition

Santa Maria de la Vittoria	300 ton
Sancti Spiritus	200
Annunciada	170
San Gabriel	130
Santa Maria del Parral (caravel)	80
San Lesmes (caravel)	80
Santiago (pinnace)	50

After steering northwestward for 500 miles in cold, sunless weather, the four remaining vessels were scattered by a gale. While the other ships could make their own way to the Moluccas, the voyage was impossible for the tiny pinnace *Santiago*. With 50 people in her, she seems to have carried more than her fair share of the survivors of the lost ships; she had no provisions to speak of and little water. To have attempted to cross the Pacific would have been suicide. Instead, she made for Mexico, where she arrived after an appalling voyage of 50 days.

Although Loaysa and del Cano died on the voyage, the *Santa Maria de la Vittoria* reached the Philippines and eventually the Moluccas, where heroic attempts to beat off the Portuguese finally finished her when the concussion of her big guns opened her seams.

In 1527, Cortez, on instructions from Spain, sent out three ships from Mexico with the purpose of ascertaining what had become of Magellan's *Trinidada*, checking on Loaysa's situation and, hopefully, loading a cargo of spices to bring back to

Mexico. Of the three ships, only the *Florida*, under the command of Alonso de Saavedra, reached the Philippines and finally the Moluccas. There Saavedra was able to tell the survivors of the Loaysa expedition the fates of the *Santiago* and the *Santa Maria del Parral*. The latter, Saavedra discovered, had reached the Philippines but most of her crew had been lost to the islanders. Saavedra's other two ships, the *Santiago* and *Espiritu Santo*, had become separated from the *Florida* and were never seen again. Perhaps they finished up in the Carolines where Ruy Lopez de Villalobos, 16 years later, discovered Spanish-speaking people, or perhaps, but less likely, one of them got to Hawaii, where there are legends of a wreck from that time.

Saavedra twice attempted to make the passage back to Mexico, but both times was frustrated by contrary winds. He died on the second attempt and his despondent crew returned to Tidore in the Moluccas, where they joined forces with the remnants of Loaysa's expedition, desperately trying to hang on in the face of Portuguese opposition.

What had become of Loaysa's seventh ship, the *San Lesmes*? After the gale which had separated the expedition, she had been sighted from the *Santiago*, so she had survived the storm and presumably she would have sailed on, hoping to close with the other ships or ultimately to come up with them in the Moluccas. Should she have taken a more westerly track than the *Santa Maria de la Vittoria*, she could easily have come to grief on the Tuamotus. There are, according to Robert Langdon, an Australian author, several indications that this is what happened.

Firstly her cannon and stones, found as they were with no other evidence of a wreck, may have been discharged to lighten the vessel. If she struck the reef and became fast, she would almost certainly have been damaged and repairs would have been necessary once she got off. A safe harbour would have to be found. Langdon's theory is that the caravel either sailed around Amanu and in through one of

the western passes or that she crossed the nine-mile channel to a neighbouring atoll named Hao. In either lagoon they would have found safe careenage. To support the theory that the *San Lesmes* never left the islands, Langdon writes of Quiros's 1606 experiences on Hao, where he found islanders '. . .the colour of mulattos but with well made limbs and good features'. The Spaniards communicated with 'well understood signs', found dogs 'like ours' (referring to spaniels) and half a cedar pole. An old woman wore a ring set with an emerald, and they met a man with curly red hair. Much evidence is put forward in Langdon's book, *The Lost Caravel,* and some interesting theories about the subsequent voyaging of the survivors and their descendants – even to the possibility that they may have reached Easter Island and New Zealand.

There are many mysteries in the Pacific, and the ultimate fate of the multitude of missing ships and their crews are among the most intriguing.

In 1529 Charles V of Spain sold out to the Portuguese any claims Spain may have had to the Moluccas, and subsequently interest in traversing the Pacific waned. Two expeditions were sent out from Mexico. The first, in 1537, was despatched with the aim of discovering the islands in the Western Pacific which were supposed to abound with gold, and ended with the commander of one ship murdered in a mutiny, and the other, under Alvarado, wrecked in New Guinea. The second venture, commanded by Villalobos, sailed for the 'Isles of the West' as the Philippines were known, and ended in the loss of all six ships. The failure of expeditions to return from the other side of the Pacific cooled the exploratory ardour of the Spanish for the next two decades. Interest in the Philippines as a source of spices grew, but until a sailing route back eastwards was charted, any venture westward stood little chance of success.

Legaspi, Arellano and Urdaneta (1537-66)

In the late 1550s the first steps were taken in planning an expedition with the dual purpose of founding a colony in the Philippines and making a serious attempt to find a route back. Miguel Lopez de Legaspi, a wealthy and respected citizen of Mexico City, was appointed commander with the dual task of founding a colony in the Philippines and attempting the first west-east crossing of the Pacific. A kinsman of his, a former Augustinian monk in Mexico and veteran of Loaysa's expedition, Andres Urdaneta, agreed to sail and use his skill in navigation and knowledge of the Philippines for the benefit of the venture.

Two large ships were built at La Navidad, Mexico, taking six years to complete and using local materials as far as possible. The cordage was layed up in Guatamala, using *pita*, a satisfactory substitute for hemp. Local woods were used, and grain was specially grown for the biscuit. However, the heavy ironwork, anchors, guns and the like had to be shipped from Spain. Two smaller vessels, the *San Juan* and *San Lucas*, were completed first and employed in fetching and carrying around the coast. There was always a dearth of craft on the Mexican west coast. The Spanish in Mexico were reluctant to settle in the coastal region as it was distinctly unhealthy, so most trade was carried on overland. Whereas the South American colonies needed ships to transport their silver and produce to Panama, Mexico's wealth exited by the east coast. Later Acapulco became alive only on the arrival or departure of a Manila galleon.

On 20 November 1564 the expedition sailed, led by the flagship *San Pedro*, followed by her sister *San Pablo*, the largest ship until then to sail the Pacific. The *San Juan* and *San Lucas* accompanied them; the latter was a 40-ton *patache*, about 50 ft (15.25 m) in length by 15 ft (4.58 m) beam.

As the result of a long hatched plot by her pilot, Lope Martin, and others scattered about the ships, the *San Lucas* became separated from the rest. It was the intention of Martin, after picking up some of his co-conspirators from the *San Pablo* to sail on his own account to load spices in the western islands for Europe. The plot failed due to the alertness and suspicion of those on the other ships, and the *San Lucas* was henceforward on her own, with her captain, Don Alonso de Arellano, completely unaware of the plot and hoping to rejoin the others in the Philippines.

Martin's scheme resulted in the *San Lucas* sailing south of the usual route and she had a hazardous voyage through the Marshall and Caroline islands. At Pulap, in the Carolines, they lost two sailors to the islanders, reducing their complement of seamen to eight. They anchored in the Davao Gulf, Mindanao on 30 January 1565.

Lightening the *San Lesmes* after she struck a reef in the Tuamotus—one possible explanation for the disappearance of the 80-ton caravel which vanished from Spain's second expedition across the Pacific.

During 1929 four heavy iron cannon and a pile of alien stones were found lying in shallow water on the eastern fringe of the reef forming Amanu atoll, one of the easternmost islands of the Tuamotu Archipelago. Robert Langdon, in his book *The Lost Caravel,* put forward a well reasoned theory that these cannon may have come from the *San Lesmes.* (See p.25.) If indeed this was her fate, the *San Lesmes* was one of the first of a long line of sailing ships which, in spite of the most careful navigation, was to come to grief on the treacherous reefs of the Pacific.

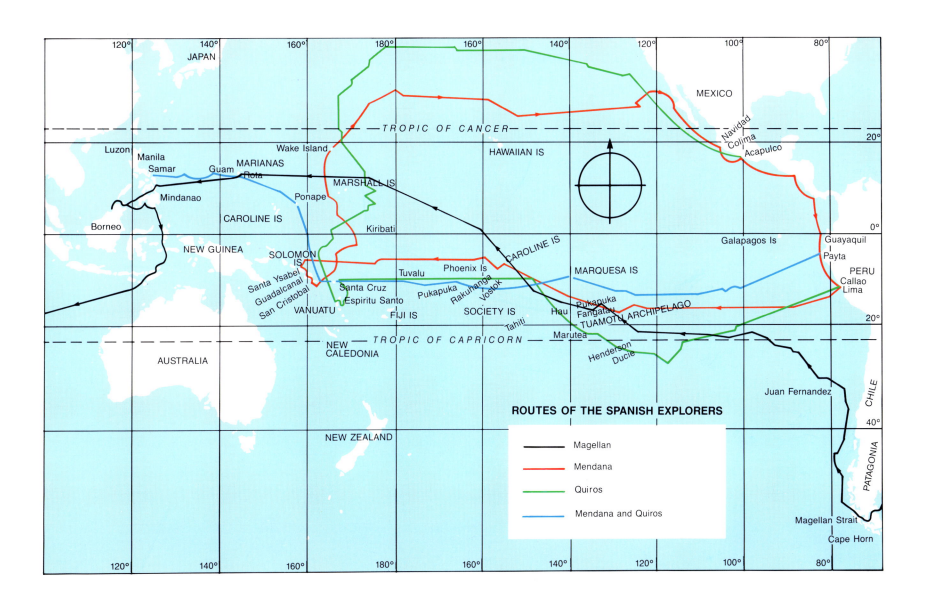

ROUTES OF THE SPANISH EXPLORERS

— Magellan

— Mendana

— Quiros

— Mendana and Quiros

27

The small crew of the *San Lucas* had adventures in plenty during their subsequent wanderings through the Philippines. They overcame attacks by the Filipinos, recovered and forgave four men who had deserted with the ship's only boat, repaired the ship, raised her topsides and left messages for the rest of the expedition. At one stage, when the *San Lucas* passed between Zebu and Bohol, Legaspi was only a few miles away, anchored on the southwest coast of Bohol.

The diminutive size of the *San Lucas* is demonstrated when she ran on to a shoal. Two men were able to pole her head round with the spritsail yard. From south to north they traversed the Philippines, passing out through the San Bernadino Strait and northwards up the Pacific coast of Luzon. Easter eve, 21 April, found her north of the islands with the open sea before her. There had been no sign of Legaspi's ships and to return among the islands was to invite massacre by the natives. Lope Martin, who must have been no mean navigator and seaman, despite his piratical tendencies, wanted to sail to the northeast to try for a fair wind to Mexico. The crew was reluctant, for nobody had succeeded in sailing west and the *San Lucas* seemed hardly the ship in which to try. However, Arellano supported Martin and stood firm on a decision to sail northeast. They struck out on Easter Day. Martin, from his charts, knew that they would pass near to 'Pago' or Japan. In 31°N they sailed close to a rock towering out of the sea (one of the volcanic plugs south of Japan), and at 40°N they turned east but were forced further north by southerlies which caused some anxiety as China was thought to lie in those latitudes. After several overcast days a latitude was observed which, by their charts, placed them in the middle of China.

The weather turned colder and although it was June, snow fell and the lamp oil froze. Strange sealife was seen. Rats chewed through a water barrel and scurvy began to weaken the crew. Sail canvas ran out and the fair-weather bonnets were sacrificed to replace and repair the working sails. As there was

no sail twine, fishing line was made to serve. They were in one of the stormiest parts of the world – north of the north Pacific high where depression after depression sweeps from Japan to Alaska, creating high winds and seas. The huge swell spawned in these regions runs southeastwards for thousands of miles and can be still high south of 30°N. It is the westerlies on the southern side of those depressions that Martin rightly surmised he would find in the north and which drove the *San Lucas* eastwards and finally southeastwards until they raised land which Martin recognised as part of lower California. This was on 18 July 1565. They had completed the first west-to-east crossing of the Pacific, sailing 16,000 miles since leaving Mexico.

The remainder of the fleet, calling at Guam en route, reached the Philippines and founded a settlement at Zebu. On 8 October 1565 Urdaneta brought the *San Pedro* safely back into Acapulco, following a similar track to the *San Lucas* and making a landfall on the offshore islands near Los Angeles. Charges brought against Arellano and Martin failed but history has branded them both as conspirators and deserters. Credit for achieving the first crossing was officially given to Urdaneta, though he seemed to have reaped little reward for it.

Arellano returned to Spain, but Martin was appointed pilot of the *San Jeronimo*, a small galleon hurriedly equipped to take soldiers to the aid of Legaspi. Martin had no intention of reaching Zebu, where he knew Legaspi would string him up, and once again started to employ his talents at plotting a mutiny.

The *San Jeronimo* sailed on 1 May 1566. On her way across the ocean Martin and his co-conspirators took over the ship, murdered the captain, and made for Guam. However, before they reached the island, they nearly lost the ship at Ujelang, the most western of the Marshall Islands. Sailing at night without a proper lookout, they ran down on the eastern reef. By a miracle and Martin's undoubted

ability, they ran through a narrow pass into the lagoon. It was Martin's intention apparently to maroon those still loyal to the murdered captain, but the tables were turned by the duplicity of one of Martin's henchmen; it was Martin who was marooned, along with 26 others, mutineers and loyalists. They were never heard of again.

The remainder of the *San Jeronimo*'s voyage to the Philippines was beset by internal strife and adverse weather. Five times she was driven back towards the Marianas by the powerful southwest monsoon. Driven to the leeward of Guam by the northeast trades, they could neither gain the Philippines nor Guam. On 1 October she made the San Bernadino Strait – down to one barrel of water for 136 people, and her rigging and spars in a desperate state. On 15 October 1566 she arrived at Zebu after a voyage which for murder, mayhem, hardship and adventure has few rivals. At Zebu threats and attacks by the Portuguese and the Filipinos, and the inability of the island to support the growing numbers of Spanish, obliged Legaspi to move the young colony first to Panay and finally to Manila, which was occupied in May 1571.

The Spanish had established a firm foothold in the Philippines; trade was started with the Chinese and the stage was set for the opening of a fabulous trade between Manila and Acapulco.

Now that a Spanish colony had been settled in the Philippines and sailing routes discovered across the Pacific, more interest began to be shown in what the vast ocean may hold away from the usual tracks. Pedro Sarmiento, a mathematician and astronomer, became convinced through his studies of Inca traditions that a large continent lay in the South Pacific about 600 leagues from Peru, stretching from off Tierra del Fuego to within 15 degrees of the equator. Other stories also abounded, particularly one that placed fabulous Ophir in the Pacific. (It was from Ophir that the gold of King Solomon came.)

Sarmiento's lobbying for a voyage of discovery to his 'Great Southern Continent' was successful, and the first of many searches for what became known as *Terra Australis* or 'Beach' was organised. It seems that the orders for the expedition were: to discover the islands of Ophir, and Sarmiento's continent, convert the heathen, form a settlement and send back for reinforcements.

Alvare Mendana's first voyage (1567-9)

Sarmiento was not to lead the venture. He was given command of *Los Reyes*, but overall command of the expedition was placed with the 25-year-old nephew of the Governor of Peru, Alvare Mendana. He was neither a skilled seamen nor a strong leader, yet he possessed qualities of humanity and wisdom, and while standing firm when necessary, generally accepted the advice of his pilots. The chief pilot, Hernan Gallego, provided the knowledge, skill and determination which was to get the ships home to Peru. Sarmiento was jealous of Mendana's promotion over him.

The two ships were manned by a company of 150, nearly half of whom were soldiers, 4 Franciscan friars and several slaves. The ships, built for the west coast of South America, would have been constructed with light scantlings and probably carried a press of sail on light spars and rigging. In addition, they were only provisioned sufficiently to sail about 2000 miles, the distance offshore of Sarmiento's continent. The voyage they were to make is all the more remarkable on account of these handicaps.

On 19 November 1567 the two ships put out from Callao. They steered WSW for 26 days until they reached 15°3'S. No land was sighted, so on Gallego's advice they bore away northwest passing between the Marquesas and Tuamotus, sighting probably one of the northernmost of the Ellice Islands and later nearly running on to a reef athwart their course.

Eighty days after leaving Callao, to the utter relief of Gallego, who was suffering the mutinous muttering and griping of the company, high land was seen to the south at a distance of 45 miles. Two days later, on 7 February 1568, they closed the land and nearly lost the ships among the outlying reefs. At ten in the morning they were in immediate danger of being driven on to the coral but a wind shift and Gallego's skill carried them clear and into a wide bay, named by them *Bahia de la Estrella*. At the moment of greatest danger while the ships were navigating among the reefs, a star had appeared over the main truck, hence the Bay of the Star. (Possibly the star was the planet Venus, although I would have thought that the pilots would have been aware that Venus can be seen in daylight fairly clearly, particularly in the tropics. However, one has to know where to look and in the turmoil and near panic of running on a reef, it strikes me as unlikely that the faint luminosity of the planet would have been noticed. But I will concede that a small break in an overcast sky can sometimes pinpoint and highlight Venus in daylight.)

Once at anchor, endeavours were made to reprovision the ships which were desperately short of supplies. The natives who had come out to them beyond the reefs were at first friendly but reluctant to supply the Spanish and emissaries sent ashore had little success. Mendana was forced to send a party under the command of Sarmiento on a mission to take food by force if necessary but to leave trade goods in return as payment. Sarmiento was also to climb the mountains to find what lay beyond. It was Mendana's desire to treat the natives humanely and fairly but on that mission Sarmiento was forced to defend himself against repeated attacks by the locals and failed to scale the ranges. That was the first of several clashes in the unpredictable relations with the natives which were to plague them until the end of their stay. A later attempt on the ranges revealed they were not on a continent as they had hoped, but on a large island.

Mendana's two ships were unsuitable for inshore work among reefs where their lack of manoeuvrability and probably pathetic windward performance would soon run them ashore. To explore the coast and adjacent lands a five-ton vessel was built from local timber and some materials which were carried in the ships. Started almost immediately after their arrival, she took 54 days to complete; at her launching she was named *Santiago*. Extensive exploration was carried out around the islands in her. As a result of these expeditions the *Los Reyes* and the *Todos Santos* were moved first to Guadalcanal and then to San Cristobal, where the ships were careened and overhauled as circumstances would permit. They still leaked and little could be done to replace worn and rotten spars and rigging. Provisions continued to be scarce and the constant conflict with the natives was getting everyone down.

A council was called and in spite of Sarmiento's opposition, a decision was made to return to Peru. The route was a vexed question. Mendana wanted to attempt a southern route, thereby perhaps chancing on Sarmiento's continent. The pilots proposed making for Mexico by the recently proved northern route and then on to Peru. The friars plumbed for New Guinea and then the Philippines but they were overruled and a compromise was made. They were to steer southeast for 700 leagues. The pilots had reservations about this; rightly so, as it would involve sailing into the teeth of the southeast trades for 2000 miles. Mendana thought the prevailing wind would change with the equinox.

They sailed from San Cristobal on 11 August 1568 and after taking seven days to clear the land they lay off to the northeast, making to the southeast when the wind permitted. The *Santiago*, which was being towed, had to be cut loose in the heavy seas and abandoned. The pilots finally lost patience with Mendana's attempts to get southwards and made a formal protest, at which Mendana let them have their way, and course was shaped for California. They were about 9°S at this stage and just west of the Gilberts. So far out were they in their estimation of longitude that they expected to raise California within days. Landings were made in the Marshall Islands and at Wake Island.

On 16 October 1568 the ships became separated and shortly after they were beset by a violent storm. The *Los Reyes* was not a vessel in which to weather a hurricane; Gallego once complained that in a slight sea 'she would pitch everybody overboard',

and by this time she would have been nearly falling apart. At the onset of the storm she was thrown on her beam ends and filled – probably only keeping afloat by virtue of her timbers and the empty casks inside her. The mainmast was cut away and she was righted. To get her off the wind, an attempt was made to set the foresail, but it quickly blew out.

By utilising a blanket and a piece of canvas, sufficient sail was made to get her head round and away they went to the south, scudding before the wind and sea. By the time the storm had subsided the boat had been lost, along with the 'stern cabin'. (I suspect the latter would be the quarter gallery, unless the poop or 'roundhouse' as it was called in those days, went by the board.)

The months that followed were a nightmare of thirst, starvation and disease. Mendana for once asserted his authority in the face of a near mutiny, the purpose of which was to turn west for the Philippines – a course which would have led to almost certain disaster at that time. The sight of a clean pine log lifted their spirits and a week later, on 19 December, they raised the coast of lower California.

At Colima they surprisingly met up with the *Todos Santos* which had suffered the same pounding and privations as the *Los Reyes*, her boat and a mast lost in the October storm of the previous year. On 11 September 1569 the ships finally returned to Callao.

Mendana's voyage failed in its aims. It did not find Ophir or the 'Great Southern Continent', but the islands which Mendana discovered and knew part of as the Western Islands or *Las Islas del Poniente* became known as the Isles of Solomon. It was to be two centuries before they were rediscovered, and around the waterfronts of the world many tales were woven of the gold that was to be found there.

The brigantine *Santiago*

From the eighteenth century onwards it has become customary to designate sailing craft by the rigs they carry: schooner, barque, ketch, brig and so on. This was not always the way and applying these later meanings to earlier craft can lead to a deal of confusion.

The *Santiago*, as Mendana's expedition named their newly built ship, was termed a brigantine. Whatever that meant to her builders, she would have been similar to small fishing and coastal craft used by the Spanish. Clues to their appearance can be gained by examining the incidental craft in old illustrations. I have represented a hull very like a small caravel. By my calculations, her tonnage would give her a length of 25 to 30 ft (8 to 10 m) and a beam of 8 ft (2.5 m). She would possibly draw about 1 metre –

the size of a small modern keelboat. She was undecked and would certainly have been fitted with sweeps.

For various reasons I have shown her with two masts as is a modern brigantine. On the fore is set a small squaresail and on the main a respectable-sized lateen. This rig would have given *Santiago* a fair turn of speed and satisfactory windward performance. As the halliards were hitched to the yards and entire sail changes could be made quickly and easily, I suspect that a smaller lateen would be carried which would provide an extremely versatile rig. For

The *Los Reyes, Todos Santos* and the brigantine *Santiago* in the Solomons. On the larger ships the sails have been unbent and work is going on about the rigs. The *Santiago* was built in the islands for inshore exploration.

The brigantine *Santiago*—three different rigs

instance, to improve her performance to windward, the small lateen could be set on the foremast. The large lateen would rapidly become unmanageable in a freshening wind. It would be a simple matter to replace the sail with the smaller lateen and thus have a snug rig for a moderate blow.

Altogether, the *Santiago* I have described would be a handy little vessel, as the original proved herself to be about the Solomon Islands.

Mendana's second voyage (1595-6)

During the last quarter of the sixteenth century the Spanish expansion into the Pacific began to slow down. The vulnerability and problems of maintaining bases in new lands became too much for the nation's resources. It was feared that word of new discoveries would leak to Spain's enemies, particularly after Drake's incursion of the Pacific in 1587.

Mendana, however, pursued his dream of settling the Solomons and, in 1574, while in Spain, obtained sanction for his plan. In Peru he was to equip ships and embark 500 men, wives and domestic animals. On establishing a colony, he was to take the title of marquis. His arrival in Panama in 1577 was greeted with hostility by his compatriots, who threw him into jail. He reached Peru, but it was to be April 1595 before his expedition sailed.

It was a disaster. Disorder and lax discipline prevailed from the start. Provisions were scanty, and the soldiers, a murderous gang, were epitomised by the statement of one who declared it was his 'diligence to kill, because he liked to kill'. The mess was exacerbated by a violent and mutinous camp-master and Mendana's shrewish and selfish wife, Dona Ysabel. When the remains of the expedition were limping to Manila, she used scarce water to wash her clothes and refused to share her private stores, recommending that two of the supplicants

be hanged as an example. With her sailed her two brothers, who gave her support after Mendana's death.

As chief pilot sailed a Portuguese, Pedro Fernandez de Quiros, whose skill and character leavened the brutality and incompetence of the others. It was his ability which got the starving survivors to the Philippines.

The fleet consisted of four ships: the *Capitana* or flagship *San Jeronimo*, the *Santa Ysabel*, a frigate *Santa Catalina*, and a galliot *San Felipe*. From Payta they sailed in a general westerly direction, discovering the Marquesas – so named by them after Mendana's friend the Marqués de Mendoza, the Viceroy of Peru. Here the friendly and curious approaches of the natives were rebuffed with gunfire and massacre. Sailing on, they sighted Puka Puka in the Northern Cooks, and Narakita, the most southerly of the Ellice Group. Short of wood, water and food, discontent grew as they sailed westward. The *Santa Ysabel* was proving to be a lame duck; overcrowded, underballasted and a poor sailer, she was a constant worry to Mendana. On 7 September 1595, at night and in fog, they made landfall but dawn showed that the *Santa Ysabel* had vanished. Subsequent searches for her failed to find any trace. The land was an island of the Ndeni Group, which Mendana named Santa Cruz.

Here Mendana lost control over his men and an abortive attempt at settlement ended in murder, famine and disease. Mendana was one of the victims. The decimated expedition described the place as a 'corner of Hell'. It left Santa Cruz in mid November, commanded by Dona Ysabel but led by the honourable and able Quiros. They sailed WSW initially to search for the *Santa Ysabel* and maybe raise San Cristobal, but failed to sight land and turned northwest for the Philippines. The galliot and frigate disappeared, and thirst and starvation severely eroded the crew's ability to handle the decrepit *San Jeronimo*.

Guam was sighted but they had insufficient gear to get a boat away and sailed on. On 12 January

1596 they sighted the Philippines and finally made port in Manila. Sixty people had perished in the *San Jeronimo* since they left Santa Cruz. The galliot turned up in Mindanao but the frigate was never heard of again. The *San Jeronimo* was refitted and sailed to Acapulco where she arrived in 1596. Quiros left her for Peru.

The voyages of Quiros and Torres (1605-7)

Pedro Fernandez de Quiros now dedicated himself to mounting another expedition. Gathering all the information available, he came to the conclusion that Santa Cruz, the Solomons and New Guinea were all close together and were the outlying islands of a southern continent. He returned to Spain and from there undertook a pilgrimage to Rome where he gained the Pope's blessing and impressed the Spanish Ambassador. Armed with letters from Rome, he got permission to equip two ships for the venture. Overcoming the usual opposition in Peru, he managed to fit out three ships. These were: *San Pedro y Paulo*, 60 tons; *San Perico*, 40 tons; *Los Tres Reyes Magos*, a *zabra* or launch. Embarked were 300 sailors and soldiers, six Franciscan friars and four nursing brothers of the Order of St John. At the insistence of its crew, Luís Vaez de Torres was appointed captain of the *San Perico*.

The expedition sailed on 21 December 1605. The character of Quiros, always deeply religious, thereafter seems to have become progressively more fanatical. His sole aim became the conversion of the populations he expected to find, and his proselytising affected the running of the ships. Gaming tables were thrown overboard and cards, dicing, cursing and blasphemy were prohibited. In addition, it was apparent that he became ill at times of crisis.

Sailing WSW from Lima, they sighted Ducie, Henderson and Marutea islands, the Actaeon Group

and Vairaatea, without landing. Short of water, they went ashore on Hao in the Tuamotus, where they bartered with the natives. Still short of water, they navigated through the Tuamotus, turned northwest and landed on Caroline Atoll which provided them with fish and coconuts but no water. The men were turning mutinous and Quiros's control was weak and ineffectual. On 1 March 1606 they sighted one of the Northern Cooks. Boats were sent ashore for water, but one was lost with all the jars, and relations with the natives turned violent despite the attempts of Quiros to achieve harmony.

As they rolled on westwards, shipboard relations deteriorated further still. The Chief Pilot, a troublemaker, was arrested and put in the charge of Torres, and an execution block was hung at the yardarm as a warning.

With their provisions restocked, Quiros sailed southeast from Taumako in search of his southern continent, but his decision-making was marred by his idealism. After being hove to for two days he directed his pilots to 'put the ships heads where they like, for God will guide them as may be right'. After wandering southward through the islands, they

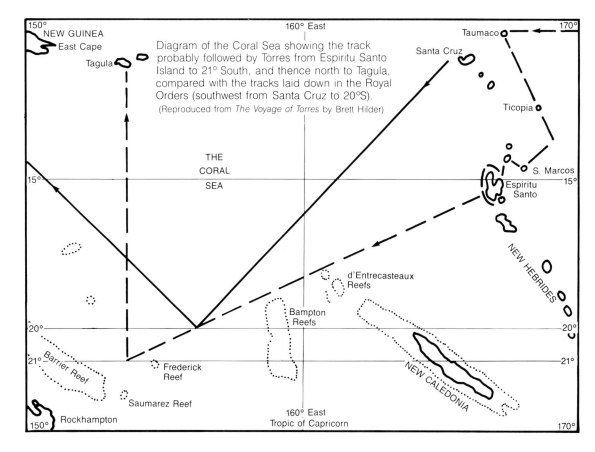

Diagram of the Coral Sea showing the track probably followed by Torres from Espiritu Santo Island to 21° South, and thence north to Tagula, compared with the tracks laid down in the Royal Orders (southwest from Santa Cruz to 20°S).
(Reproduced from *The Voyage of Torres* by Brett Hilder)

sighted what appeared to be an extensive land which was thought might be the continent. What they had actually chanced upon were the high islands of Vanuatu, a pleasant land offering abundant food, fine timbers and safe harbours. Only the natives, naturally anxious for their land, spoilt the Spaniards' stay.

Quiros, with a zeal and futility worthy of Quixote, set in train a series of grand ceremonies creating an Order of Knights of the Holy Ghost, and appointed a Ministry of War and Marine. Ashore, before the assembled company he took possession of

> this bay, named the Bay of St Phillip and St James, and of its port named Vera Cruz, and of the site on which is to be founded the city of New Jerusalem in Latitude 15°20', and of all the lands which I sighted and am going to sight, and of all this region of the south as far as the Pole, which from this time shall be called *Australia del Espiritu Santo*, with all its dependencies and belongings.

Before a sod had been turned, all the administrative officers for the city had been appointed.

Less than a fortnight later Quiros suddenly determined to sail, basing his decision on the hostility of the natives. On 28 May 1606 they set forth, but were forced to return owing to illness caused by the consumption of poisonous fish. Again they sailed, on 8 June.

It was Quiros's idea to sail southeastward to visit the lands to windward. At sea the Peruvian-built ships could make no headway against the strong and rising trade wind. Quiros decided to return to port and winter there. After dark the *San Perico* and the launch managed to get to anchor. The pilot of the *San Pedro*, although within the harbour, found difficulty handling the unwieldy ship at night in the close vicinity of rocks, and stood out into the bay. Unable to beat to windward, they were driven out to sea and far to leeward.

Although Santa Cruz was not a rendezvous, Quiros made for the island, hoping the others would come up with him there. He failed to find Santa Cruz and a council decided to sail to Acapulco, but Quiros overruled their decision in favour of making for the latitude of Guam, where further plans could be made. Miscalculation of their longitude caused them to miss Guam by a wide margin and there followed a four-month weary voyage, northward to latitude 38° and east to America. Fish and rain supplied the necessary sustenance and miraculously, when they let go their anchor off the beach at Navidad in Mexico, only one man had died.

Torres continues the search

Torres, in command of the *San Perico*, believed Quiros had deserted but searched the coast for wreckage. He then waited 15 days before opening sealed orders from the Viceroy of Peru. These directed him to sail to 20°S in search of land. If no land was found, he was to make for Manila, wait there four months and then sail to Spain by way of the Moluccas and the Cape.

Torres, a determined and capable commander, sailed southwest until he was only 190 miles off the coast of Australia at 21°S. Given good weather, he would probably have gone further, but instead he turned north. Unknown to him, he had narrowly missed the Frederick and Saumarez reefs. Nine days after turning north, he made a landfall on Tagula Island, east of New Guinea. Wind and sea prevented him from weathering the easternmost point of the island and they were forced to turn west.

Tagula is linked to New Guinea by a chain of reefs along which Torres coasted, searching for a passage which he failed to find. There followed a two-month rock-hopping passage through the reefs and islands south of New Guinea, a region which is difficult enough to navigate with modern charts and vessels.

All the details of this voyage come from Prado, a noble-born military engineer and surveyor who had been appointed to succeed Quiros in the event of his death. Torres, retaining his command, wrote nothing, but it was his skill and seamanship which brought the ships safely through the strait named after him.

They made Ternate and finally Manila, arriving in the bay on 22 May 1607. Torres vanished from history, and his strait, although known to the Spanish, and perhaps the Portuguese, remained an enigma to the Dutch for many years.

Quiros, back in Spain, continued to enthusiastically lobby for a further voyage. He died at Panama in 1614 on a voyage to Lima where he believed he was to assemble his next expedition. In reality the pestered authorities in Spain had instructed the Viceroy of Peru to entertain him and equivocate; it was as well he died.

Spain's great maritime expansion came to a close. For the best part of a century her ships and adventurers had disclosed hitherto unimagined regions of the Earth. The 'Great South Sea' had been crossed and recrossed, only unveiling a fraction of her secrets. No embargos, laws and Papal bulls, however, could prevent ships of other nations entering the Spanish lake.

Two riddles from the sixteenth century

There can be no doubt that historical records of voyages to the Pacific during the era of Portuguese and Spanish expansion are incomplete. Buried in archives must be a wealth of ancient voyage reports which had the veil of secrecy drawn over them by the jealous and ambitious Iberians. The Lisbon earthquake in 1755, in which 30,000 people died, destroyed the city and with it the Casa da India e Mina, the repository of Portugal's entire records of her maritime endeavours in the East. Lacking the historical sources, it is a matter of chance that evidence of some of these lost voyages come to light, and even then, certain proof may be elusive.

Herb Kane, the Hawaiian historian and artist, believes that the Spanish were in the Hawaiian Islands before Cook but left no cultural or biological imprint. In his book *The Secret Discovery of Australia*, Kenneth Gordon McIntyre puts forward a very good case which indicates that the Portuguese sailed and mapped the east coast of Australia as far as Warrnambool, a hundred miles west of Cape Otway. In New Zealand, on the wild west coast near Dargaville, I am reasonably certain that some startling new evidence is about to add another dimension to the country's prehistory. As this book attempts to be an imaginative glance at European ships in the Pacific, the Australian and New Zealand finds should hold our interest for they both concern apparently ancient wrecks.

The Warrnambool wreck (Australia)

In 1836 two sealers, survivors from an overturned boat, were tramping along the Warrnambool coast to a depot 16 miles (26 kilometres) away. Forced by quicksands to divert inland through the sand dunes, they discovered the remains of an ancient wreck and duly reported their find. John Mills, who later became harbourmaster at Port Fairy (or Belfast as it was then known), later visited the wreck several times and described the wood as being red and very hard. Captain John Mason saw it in 1846 –

Riding along the beach from Port Fairy to Warrnambool in the summer of 1846, my attention was attracted to the hull of a vessel embedded high and dry in the hummocks, far above the reach of the tide. It appears to be that of a vessel of about 100 tons burden, and from its bleached and weatherbeaten appearance must have been there many years. The spars and decks were gone and the hull full of drift sand. The timber of which she was built had the appearance of either mahogany or cedar. The fact of the vessel being in that position was well known to whalers in 1841, when the first whaling station was formed in the neighbourhood, and the oldest natives when they were questioned stated that their knowledge of it extended from their earliest recollection.

...her general appearance bespoke a very slight acquaintance of the builder with marine architecture, and resembled more the outlines of our local lighters, though of greater dimensions.

In 1860 a Mrs Manifold, riding along the beach, examined the stern, which was all that was then showing. She noted that 'the sides, or bulwarks, [were] after the fashion of a panelled door, with mouldings stout and strong'.

Altogether there are records of 27 people having seen the wreck before it disappeared in 1890. A recent search with instruments has given an indication of what might be the wreck buried deep under the sandhills and some decomposed timber has been brought up. Until such time as the wreck may be unearthed, McIntyre properly relies on the proof of a Portuguese voyage to this area being an ancient chart known as 'The Dauphin Map', and other historical records.

The ship, it seems, may have been one of three caravels under the command of Cristovao de Mendonca, a capable and influential Portuguese captain who, in perhaps 1521, was instructed to 'Search the Isles of Gold' for Magellan, who the Portuguese thought may have been coasting along a southern continent stretching from Patagonia to India Meridional, as they named the part of Australia they knew. Mendonca, it appears, sailed from the East Indies eastward through the Torres Strait and mapped the entire east coast of Australia. For some reason, perhaps due to the loss of one or two of his three ships, he was forced to turn back at Warrnambool.

The Dargaville wreck (New Zealand)

In January 1981, Noel Hilliam, now director of New Zealand's Northern Wairoa Museum, was flying his home-built light aircraft in search of a fisherman drowned along the beaches of Northland's west coast near Dargaville. During the last square pattern search in the north he saw something under water, outside the break of the seas, that looked very much like a wreck. Three days later Hilliam and a friend made a dive on the position and found that what he had seen from the air was a ship, and from her appearance a very old one indeed. Realising that his

find could be significant, he notified the New Zealand authorities for permission to start an examination. Unfortunately it was to be 18 months before this was granted; too late, for within nine months of the first sighting, the wreck had vanished beneath the shifting sands of the Tasman shore.

From two dives that were carried out, some idea of the nature of the relic can be assessed, although her position in the disturbed water beyond the breakers made proper measurements difficult. She was a vessel of about 80 ft (24 m). She lay with her bow towards the shore and the hull was inclining downwards so that her deck aft was under the sand, but with the outline clearly visible. Concretions which had accumulated on fixtures made clear identification difficult, but a solidly decked beakhead was clear, set at a level which would indicate that it extended from a gun-deck below the upper deck. The upper deck was still planked, although all fittings and bulwarks had been wiped off. The stemhead could have given a valuable clue to her period but it was unfortunately encased in a mass of concretion from which what may have been the stump of a bowsprit protruded. A hole, about a metre aft of the forward part of the upper deck, may have been the location of the foremast partners, and a hatch was apparent further aft. If the foremast was stepped so far forward it would tell us that this was a very early ship, probably sixteenth or early seventeenth century. If the detail of the relation of the bowsprit to the stemhead could have been ascertained, a much more positive dating might have been possible. Noel Hilliam is fairly positive it was either a caravel or an early galleon, and I am inclined to agree with him. Until the changing currents of the Tasman once more sweep the wreck clear of sand, we can only wait in anticipation. Hilliam flies over the site regularly, waiting for the first sign of its reappearance, when, with a team of divers ready on a few hours' notice, a more comprehensive survey will be made in the time that wind, sea and sand might allow.

The 400—500-year-old Tamil bell and early Portuguese or Spanish helmet part, both uncovered in New Zealand and now deposited with the country's National Museum.
(National Museum, Wellington)

The Northern Wairoa region, in which Dargaville is situated, holds further mysteries waiting to be unravelled. The Maori tribes have legends of a ship which had lost its rudder and came ashore long ago; legends of ginger-haired, fair-skinned, blue-eyed people; an altar found, but now lost, in the Wairoa forest. Remains of stone walls, not of Maori construction, can be seen in the same forest. It was the practice of the Spanish, when wintering over on their voyages, to build such drystone walls, supported by poles, with storehouses and quarters within them.

Noel Hilliam showed me a worm-eaten hunk of timber, clearly from a structure such as a ship. The reddish hardwood has been identified as a species of *Lagerstroemia*, a timber which is found from Southern India to the Philippines and favoured by the Spanish and Portuguese for their ships. Square trenail holes in another piece add to the evidence, for whereas other nations used round holes and trenails, the Spanish used square section fastenings. Tracing clues from Maori folklore, the outline of a boat, 8 metres down under a paddock far up the Northern Wairoa River, has been found by means of subsurface interface radar, and arrangements are being made to investigate this further.

In addition to all this, what appears to be part of a Spanish or Portuguese helmet from about 1580 was dredged from the bottom of Wellington

Harbour at the beginning of this century, and in Whangarei, not far from Dargaville, an old Tamil bell was found by the Rev. William Colenso. An inscription on the bell has been translated as 'the bell of Mukaiyathan's own ship'. Other translations of the name have been given, but each agree that it is a ship's bell having an age estimated at 400 to 500 years, possibly from India or Java. Could this bell possibly have been carried from the East in a Spanish or Portuguese ship? Both helmet and bell are in the care of the National Museum, Wellington.

The following is an extract from Robert Langdon's *The Lost Caravel*.

...Julien Crozet, a companion of the French explorer Marion du Fresne, who was in New Zealand waters in 1772. Crozet said the complexion of many Bay of Island Maoris resembled that of the people of southern Europe and that some had red hair. 'There were some who were as white as our sailors', he added, 'and we often saw on our ships a tall, young man, 5 ft 11 in. high, who by his colour and features might have easily passed for a European.'

One feels for the sailors of long ago, lost on the other side of the Earth with little hope that they would ever be found. What were their relations with the warlike Maori people? Who were they? Sadly, we may never know.

THE MANILA GALLEONS

Today we can perceive our Earth as a whole, a globe turning in space; we can locate the land masses and oceans and measure distance to a minute fraction of a degree. In our conception the planet is reduced in time and distance to the dimensions of a rather large backyard. It is difficult to imagine the awesome vastness which confronted the traveller of the past with his limited concept of the world. Journeys by sea were measured in months, and the risks were so great that no insurance company today would issue cover.

With courage incited by the wealth of the Orient, the Spanish sailed their ships 8000 miles across the north Pacific, establishing a national shipping line which endured for 300 years. Silver, produced in abundance from the mines such as at Potosi in Alta Peru, provided the article of trade that was needed to barter with the wealthy Chinese. At Acapulco the ingots and coin were loaded into the holds of the westbound galleons, where it acted as ballast. On average, at least 3 million pesos in registered silver was carried, plus an additional million above the official *permiso* for the profit of the captain, crew and passengers. A single galleon might carry out of Acapulco more silver than the entire treasure fleet which sailed from Vera Cruz to Spain. It has been estimated that as much as one third of all the silver mined in Spanish America was shipped to the East in the Manila galleons.

Westbound, the galleons slipped down to pick up the northeast trades and sailed in generally fair weather to Guam before passing through the San Bernadino Strait to Manila. It was the eastbound voyage which tested both ships and men. Apart from the punishment suffered from the weather, the

sheer length of the voyage was a danger in itself. Six months at sea in a crowded, insanitary and usually overladen ship took its toll of passengers and crew. In a galleon's hold and cluttering the decks would be carefully wrapped bales containing a

wealth of exquisite Chinese craftsmanship. Silks, carved ivory, furniture, gold chalices, combs, fans, jade ornaments, porcelain and sandlewood were among the diverse wares exchanged for the silver. Most of these articles found their way to Spain but as the American colonies prospered, less was transhipped and many fine houses in Mexico City were furnished almost entirely with magnificent Chinese products. For generations the galleons which transported these treasures were avidly hunted by pirates, buccaneers, privateers and the admirals and commodores of hostile nations.

The drain of silver to China and the lack of return to the homeland caused the Spanish authorities to impose restrictions on the trade. One was to limit the size of the ships, initially, in 1593, to 300 tons and later, in 1720, to 560 tons. However, these were ignored, as were most restrictive regulations pertaining to the galleons.

By the beginning of the seventeenth century, 1000-ton vessels were being used and not much later behemoths of 2000 tons were built. In 1616 Juan de Silva led a fleet against the Dutch which consisted of eight ships ranging from 2000 down to 700 tons.

Some original sources

Few illustrations or details of the Manila galleons have come to light, and such pictorial records which are available are so inaccurately drawn that they should be treated with caution. On p.38 the early eighteenth-century engraving, numbered to show the elements of the rig, illustrates the topmasts stepped aft of the lower masts, which is possible but unlikely, but it also represents the yards crossed

behind the mast. However, by interpolation, descriptions and the study of common European methods, some idea can be gained as to how the ships might have looked.

Once a practice had been found to work, it was held on to grimly. The Spaniards were not going to risk their entire wealth to the reasonings of innovators, no matter how sound the innovations may have proved in other waters. Sailing qualities and speed took second place to size and strength, resulting in horrendously protracted voyages and consequent mortality, as well as multiplying the grey hairs of the pilots who had to work the lumbering ships through the reef- and rock-strewn passages of the Embocadero, as the San Bernadino Strait between Luzon and Samar was known.

It is possible that some of the earlier, very large ships may have been built in the fashion of carracks. References to their high fore- and aftercastles and the occasional portrayal of a ship as a *nao* may

Parts of a ship. The key (in Spanish) has been omitted.
(Detail from an early eighteenth century engraving in the Naval Museum, Madrid)

(*Right*) A Manila galleon of the seventeenth century loading at Cavite near Manila. The towering aftercastle is based on the drawings of Wenzel Hollar (1607-77). Hollar's illustrations depict Dutch East Indiamen with some degree of accuracy and as the design of European ships only seemed to vary in detail, I believe the painting to show a fair representation of a Manila galleon. The device on the stern appears on the flags of the seventeenth- and eighteenth-century galleons.

The ship is at anchor with a flotilla of small craft around her, including an ocean-going junk bringing silks and a wealth of Chinese craftsmanship in the way of furniture and ornaments. Normally goods arriving from China would be taken to Manila and carefully packed before loading into the galleon; perhaps the junk is a late arrival.

indicate this. In Spanish 'nao' appeared to be the generic term for a ship, but it seemed to become more specifically applied to carracks, whereas galleons and caravels were referred to as *galéon* and *caravela* respectively. It is known that the Portuguese built and used large carracks in the East Indies. Some of the early galleons were built with high forecastles of perhaps two or three decks with the beakhead protruding at maindeck level. Examples appear in the Portuguese *Flor de la Mar* and in the construction of the English *Ark Royal* and *Henri Grâce à Dieu*, though the latter seems to be an intermediate stage between carrack and galleon. The forecastle of a carrack would result in a drier ship but would detract from her sailing qualities. A high forecastle on a galleon would serve little purpose except as a fighting platform.

The advantage of the galleon was her ability to lie ahull, that is, under bare poles the aftercastle provided the windage necessary to keep the ship lying with the wind and sea just off the bow. With sea room, a galleon would lie very comfortably, as Alan Villiers found with the *Mayflower* replica. It is likely that the Manila ships reduced the size of the forecastle to the conventional single deck of the early seventeenth century, but retained the high sweeping aftercastle long after these had been reduced in other ships. Thomas Carlyle referred to the heavy and ornate coach in which Louis XVI and Marie Antoinette attempted to escape from France as an 'Acapulco ship'. Basically, if belatedly, the Manila ships followed the trends set in other European vessels, particularly the East Indiamen. The rig may have been varied in small detail but this too appears to have been similar to other ships of the period.

The availability of first-class shipbuilding timber in the East made it worthwhile for the Malinenos to build their own ships. Some were built outside the Philippines in, among other places, Siam and Japan, but most keels were laid in the Philippine Islands, and a regulation of 1679 prohibited

A *nao* sketched from a representation in the *Enciclopedia Pela Imagem*. Notice that the forecastle is more applicable to a galleon.

Drawing thought to be of the English *Ark Royal*, built in 1545
(British Museum, London)

The *Flor de la Mar* was Portuguese but taken over by the Spanish in the sixteenth century
(Detail from 'Roteiro de Malaca', Academy of Sciences, Lisbon)

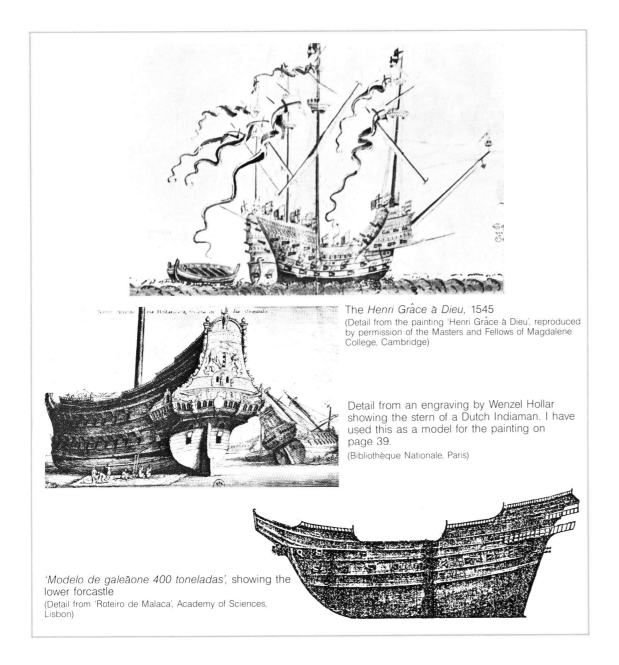

The *Henri Grâce à Dieu*, 1545
(Detail from the painting 'Henri Grâce à Dieu', reproduced by permission of the Masters and Fellows of Magdalene College, Cambridge)

Detail from an engraving by Wenzel Hollar showing the stern of a Dutch Indiaman. I have used this as a model for the painting on page 39.
(Bibliothèque Nationale, Paris)

'*Modelo de galeãone 400 toneladas*', showing the lower forcastle
(Detail from 'Roteiro de Malaca', Academy of Sciences, Lisbon)

construction outside the islands. The cotton sailcloth was woven in the Mexican province of Ilocos and the cordage was laid up from Manila hemp.

Some ships were incredibly strong. The frames were often built of teak and the heavy sheathing of lanang, which was resistant to cannon shot, small balls embedding themselves in the wood and those of heavier calibre rebounding without serious damage. Both Woodes Rogers and Anson remarked on the apparent imperviousness of the hulls to gunfire. The *Begona* withstood the best part of two days of battering, and the 2000-ton *Sanctisima Trinidad* had over 1000 rounds blasted at her; none penetrated her sides. She was sailed to England and arrived with shot still embedded in her sheathing. The defensive practice of the Manila galleons was simply to lie to, batten down and sit out an attack until the attacker would run out of ammunition and give up. Not that the galleons could not hand out punishment if they were well fought.

Well built the galleons may have been, but their maintenance lacked foresight and care. At the end of each voyage the ships were laid up, their running rigging rove off and spars sent down, but no dockyard crew was employed to carry out routine maintenance or repair damage from her last voyage. The effect of a tropical climate on wooden ships and manila standing rigging can be imagined. When the time came to put the ship back into commission, work was often carried out very poorly and at great expense. This, combined with culpable overloading, made some ships so unseaworthy that if they were not lost, they had to put back to Manila, to the distress of the Malinenos, whose solvency depended on a successful voyage.

Between 1600 and 1604 six ships were lost. In 1600 the *Santa Margarita* ran aground in the Marianas. Most of the 260 passengers and crew were massacred by the islanders, and the ship was plundered. Only five of her complement survived.

The same year the *Santo Tomas* was wrecked on the east coast of Luzon, and the *San Geronimo* piled up in the same place the following year. In 1603 the huge *San Antonio*, carrying the richest cargo to that date and hundreds of influential passengers, left Manila and vanished, and later the *Nuestra Senora de los Remedios* was lost with all hands. The same year the *Magdalena* capsized as she was casting off in full view of the farewelling crowds.

Eastbound the ships were generally loaded at Cavite, ten miles from Manila. It was here that the ships were laid up and repaired under the guns of the fort and sheltered from the typhoons which seasonally sweep the bay.

The incentive which lured the Spanish to reside in Manila was the opportunity to acquire space in a galleon. The hold of the ship was carefully measured and divided into parts which corresponded to a *fardo*, a bale consisting of four packages or *piezas*. Each pieza averaged 2 ft 6 in. x 2 ft x 10 in. (76 x 61 x 25.5 cm) and was allotted on the basis of a *boleta* or ticket. The boletas were either granted to or purchased by the citizens of Manila and became an article of trade in themselves, wealthier merchants purchasing more than their share from non-traders. The system became, in the words of Archbishop Rojo, 'a labyrinth of entanglements, complaints and vileness'.

Strict laws were promulgated to ensure that a galleon was not overloaded. However, as everyone from cleric to seaman had a right to space, the restrictions were futile. The sole reason that any officer or seaman would face the rigours of an eastbound voyage was his opportunity to trade. If he survived, his health could quite likely be ruined for life, therefore trading had to be worthwhile. Up to 1734 seamen were not officially entitled to space; not that this prevented them from trading. After 1734 each was legally entitled to carry a chest, which, when packed by expert Chinese, far exceeded the 60 pesos the contents were supposed to be worth. They also used the space in their own personal chests so that, according to the eighteenth-century official, Viana, sea chests littered the decks to the great peril of the ship on the longest and most arduous voyage in the world.

The bales which made up the cargo were very carefully packed, usually by Chinese, to get the maximum advantage of the space, to protect them from vermin and salt water, and to discourage officials in Mexico from opening them to assess duty. In spite of the laws and supervision restricting cargo to the hold, graft and greed ensured that every available space on the ship was utilised. Cabins, passageways, storerooms, magazines and decks were stacked with bales and chests so that gear and essential stores were inaccessible or displaced. Sometimes rafts piled with watertight bales were towed astern. When the sea rose too high, these were brought on board. The hundreds of people in the ship had little space for themselves and working the vessel must have been a nightmare. No wonder so many strong, if slow, ships found themselves in trouble making out through the islands and in the stormy north Pacific.

Provisions for the eastbound voyage were initially profuse, consisting mainly of biscuit, salted fish and meat. However, as the voyage, lasting perhaps six months, progressed, the food deteriorated miserably. Gemelli Careri, a traveller in 1697, wrote:

The Ship swarms with little Vermine the Spaniards call *Gorgojos*, bred in the Biskit so swift that they in a short time not only run over Cabbins, beds and the very dishes the Men eat on, but insensibly fasten upon the Body. There are several other sorts of Vermin of Sundry Colours, that suck the Blood. Abundance of Flies fall into the Dishes of Broth, in which there also swim Worms of several sorts. I had a good share in these Misfortunes; for the Boatswain, with whom I had agreed for my Diet, as he had Fowls at his Table the first Days, so when we were out at Sea he made me fast after the Armenian manner, having Banish'd from his Table all Wine, Oyl and Vinegar; dressing his Fish with fair Water and Salt. Upon Flesh Days he gave me *Tassajos Frites* that is, Steaks of Beef, or Buffalo, dry'd in the Sun, or Wind, which are so hard that it is impossible to Eat them without first they are well beaten. At Dinner another piece of that same sticky Flesh was boil'd without any other sauce but its own hardness, and fair Water. At last he deprived me of the Satisfaction of gnawing a good Biskit, because he would spend no more of his own, but laid the King's Allowance on the Table; in every Mouthful whereof there went down abundance of Maggots, and *Gorgojos* chew'd and bruis'd. On Fish Days the common Diet was old rank Fish boil'd in fair Water and Salt; at noon we had *Mongos*, something like Kidney Beans, in which there were so many Maggots, that they swam at the top of the Broth, and the quantity was so great, that besides the Loathing they caus'd, I doubted the dinner was Fish or Flesh. This bitter Fare was sweetened after Dinner with a little Water and Sugar; yet the Allowance was but a small Coco Shell full, which rather increas'd than quench'd drought.

Water was until the mid eighteenth century carried in earthenware jars which were stowed wherever possible, many being hung in the rigging. Large cisterns were built into some ships, and water was also carried in large sealed bamboo pipes measuring 6 ft (2 m) by about 9 in. (22 cm). On the voyage rain could be expected while running east in the thirties and forties and this was collected by hanging mats from a jackstay stretched along the bulwarks. The water from the mats drained into bamboo gutters and thence into jars or cisterns. The collection, storage and dispensing of water was in charge of a water constable, a seaman appointed to that duty.

Manning the galleons was never easy, for few wished to make a career of the hazardous undertaking and, having made their fortune on one or two voyages, the mariners retired while they still had good health.

The position of commander, known as 'General of the Sea', was one which, throughout most of the period, was granted by the Governor to any he

Por Goltes mas procelofos
efta Nave con tu vuelo
con vaior arefto y zelo
haze galan de Neptuno

ELOGIO

Del General D. Geronymo Montero, Piloto
mayor de la Carrera de Philipinas; ál Almirante
D. Joseph Gonzalez Cabrera Bueno,
Piloto mayor de dicha Carrera, y
Autor de efte Libro.

CON experiencia, y no audacia, | del Arte de Navegar.
Coy Bueno, nos das à ver, | pues das preceptos al Mar,
que es mucho vueftro entender, | yà fus dudas las deshazes,
pues con repoflo, y con paufa | no fiendo menefter Claffes
a los Nauticos descaula | con tu modo de enfeñar.
para poder engolfarfe; | No eftes trifte, alegre fi.
y pues que nos fatisfaces: | que yà efpirò tu tareà;
aclarando tantas Reglas | y pues fue buena tu idea,
yà no precifan Efcuelas | y tu difcurfo fubtil,
à quien tu Libro alcanzafe. | todos fe, que han de decir
Al fon de vna dulze Lira | teneis ingenio divino,
cante pues en tu àlabanza | por que affeguras deftino
a voz mas fuave en bonanza. | de el mas procelofo Mar,
en ècos acordes diga, | y en Affumpto fingular
que yà cesò la fatiga | à todos àbres camino.

A

Part of an eulogy to a Manila galleon pilot
(Reproduced from original material in the Naval Museum, Madrid)

HOMAGE

By General D. Geronymo Montero, Main Pilot of the Philippines Route; in honour of D. Joseph Gonzalez Cabrera Bueno, Main pilot of above mentioned route, and the author of this book.

(Translated by Roy Boland)

With care and experience, and not with undue
    boldness
Oh Good Master, you let us know
that your knowledge is deep,
for with measured care
you give us sailors good reason
to go out to sea;
and since you so open our eyes
by illuminating so many rules
no need is there for Academies and Schools
for those whom your Book may reach.
Thus may to the sound of a sweet Lyre
let the mellowest voice in praise
of you and your good fortune sing,
and may in harmonious sound announce
that the weariness has come to an end
of the Art of Navigation;
for you resolve the doubts
of Maritime precepts,
may you never grow silent
of your teaching ways.
Do not be sad, but happy
that your task is done;
and since your idea was good,
and your exposition subtle,
let all the world tell you
that your genius is divine,
for you ensure that we may reach
    our destination
even when sailing upon the most
    tempestuous seas,
and to all of us you show the way
in a Singular Science.

Translation of the eulogy

wished to reward. It was a coveted post, for one successful voyage would provide enough for the appointee to live in comfort throughout the rest of his life. The muster of other officers consisted of two mates, three or four pilots, two boatswains and their mates, two constables and two surgeons. Also carried were one or two further officers whose concern was financial and related to cargo.

The ranks of the officers were swelled by patronage of the Governor and Viceroys, and posts were often filled by inexperienced youths who knew nothing of the work. The chronic lack of experienced men extended to the position of pilot, few of whom remained long on the run. The whole navigation of the voyage depended on these men and although they were honoured and wealthy, a lonely and frustrating task it must have been. The risk to pilots was not only the hazards of the sea. The pilot of the *Nuestra Senora de la Vida* ran her on a reef about 90 miles out of Manila. The infuriated passengers hanged him on the spot.

A few pilots did stay in the service; one such was Geronimo de Montero, who sailed the galleons for 14 years until his ship, the *Nostra Signora de Cabadonga*, was taken by Anson in 1742. It was he who wrote this eulogy to Cabrera Bueno's book which updated the original work of Urdaneta.

Manila galleon routes

The sailing of the galleons depended on fitting their voyages to the weather patterns of the north Pacific. The main part of the voyage westbound utilised the steady northeast trades between 10 and 14 degrees north, and eastbound the westerlies and variables prevailing between 30 and 40 degrees north. On the coast of the American continent, mainly northerly-quarter winds assisted the ships from the north to Acapulco and from Acapulco south to the trades.

It was the weather systems of the Philippines which determined the most suitable time to sail.

Around the end of September or in early October the northeast monsoon begins and blows strongly, with rain and squalls from the north to northeast until early December. This is the worst season for navigating out of the Embocadero. From mid December to the spring equinox, the winds are from the east to southeast with much heavy weather. Between the end of the northeast monsoon and the beginning of the southwest monsoon the winds vary from north through east to south, with occasional squally weather and calms. By June, but sometimes in May, the southwest monsoon is well established, blowing southwest to west.

The westbound galleon, ballasted with silver, and carrying soldiers for the Manila garrison and aspiring passengers, had a comparatively easy voyage, dropping down to pick up the trade winds and then enjoying weeks of halcyon sailing to either Guam or Saipan where garrisons had been established in the late seventeenth century. From the Ladrones (now the Marianas) to the Philippines was a comparatively short sail, but it was on this leg that difficulties could be encountered. Ideally a galleon would reach the Embocadero well before the onset of the southwest monsoon. To ensure this, the galleon tried to sail from Acapulco as early as possible. In 1633 a law stated the galleons should sail by the end of December. This was patently impossible as the ships usually arrived from Manila in either December or January, so it was common for a galleon to depart from Acapulco in February or March. Any difficulties a ship ran into on the westbound voyage, apart from those caused by a pilot's straight-out incompetence, were most likely because of a delayed sailing from Acapulco. Once the southwest monsoon had set in, the stiff, squally winds blowing across the straits made them extremely dangerous for the cranky and unweatherly galleons. In such conditions the pilot would have to put into an anchorage to wait on a fair wind, the further delay increasing the likelihood of being struck by a typhoon.

The total time for a westward passage was in the region of three months. However, late sailings and the consequent delays after the Ladrones could stretch the voyage considerably, as in the case of the *Sanctisima Trinidad*, which in 1756 took five months and six days. Other delays could be caused by enemies lying in wait about the Embocadero. If this was the case, the galleon was warned by fire signals from onshore and the ship would perhaps be re-routed to Manila.

It was the eastbound voyage which tested the endurance of the ships, crews and passengers. This voyage, lasting perhaps six months, was one of the longest and hardest undertaken in sailing ships. The ideal time to sail was at the onset of the southwest monsoon, when the winds were favourable for clearing the islands and sailing north. Although the galleons sailed at any time between May and late September, June was the ideal month. However, holdups in getting her cargo often delayed a ship's sailing, increasing the chance of having to weather a typhoon and finding herself in serious trouble. If not lost entirely, the galleon could suffer damage, enforcing a return or *arribadas* to Manila.

Typhoons, or *baguiosas* as they are locally known, are the tropical revolving storms of the north Pacific. These storms begin to occur in July and reach their maximum frequency in Mindanao in December. They are akin to the hurricanes of the West Indies where the old adage applies:

June, too soon,
July, stand by,
August, look out you must,
September, remember,
October, all over.

Even sailing in June, the galleons, once in the Pacific, were almost inevitably struck by severe storms which, if not full-blown typhoons, were the tail-ends of storms sweeping northwestward out of the Pacific, or the gales prevalent north of Luzon.

Once a ship had completed loading at Cavite, she was taken as close as possible to the walled city of Manila where the galleon was delivered to a seven-gun salute to her commander and the papers and Royal Ensign handed to her officers. The effigy of the Virgin Mary was carried in procession along the city walls before being installed in the ship and in the churches masses were offered up for a safe voyage. With the Archbishop's blessing, the ship got under way for the difficult passage of the Embocadero to the open sea. More than 30 galleons were lost navigating through the islands. Gemelli Careri gives his experience:

As we were upon getting out, there fell such violent storms of Rain, that together with the contrary Current, whilst the Moon was above the Horizon, we could not, tho' the Wind blew hard for us, advance one Step, but rather lost Ground, so that we are all Night in great Danger, I was astonish'd and Trembled to see the Sea have a Motion like Water boiling over a hot Fire, understanding that several Ships, notwithstanding the help of their Rudder had been by the Violence of the Current whirl'd about, and at last Wreck'd. Friday 10th, the Tide turning for us, we got out of the Straight before Noon.

Calms, contrary winds and currents delayed the galleons, which either had to lie to or anchor, so that the passage could take weeks. Gemelli Careri's galleon took 43 days. Once clear of the strait, course was set to the northeast, driven by the southwest monsoon. Cabrera Bueno lays down the sailing directions as follows:

E by NE about fifty leagues; then ENE in the general direction of the Ladrones; through Los Volcanes or the higher Ladrones NE by E to thirty-one degrees latitude and longitude twenty- eight and a half east of Manila; ENE to thirty-six or seven degrees in longitude forty; thence to the region of Cape

Mendocino; SE to thirty-five degrees latitude without sighting land; SE to the landfall at the island of Cenizas in thirty degrees, or at the island of Cedros a degree and a half lower at the entrance to Sebastian Vizcaino Bay.

This course takes the galleons close to, but usually out of sight of, Japan. Spanish relations with the Japanese were mercurial to say the least, and galleons forced by stress of weather to find refuge in Japan faced an unpredictable reception. The large and richly laden *San Felipe* in 1596 lost her rudder after a succession of storms and put into Hirado in distress. She was deliberately wrecked by the Japanese, her cargo taken ashore, never to be recovered, and the Spaniards interned.

In 1602 after the loss of her mainmast, the *Espiritu Santo* also put into Hirado, and initially it appeared that the Spanish would suffer the same fate as those on the *San Felipe*. Her commander, Lope de Ulloa, was made of stern stuff and refused to be bullied

into putting the cargo and sails ashore, and allowed no shore leave after 20 men had landed and been promptly imprisoned by the Japanese. The situation grew more and more threatening until Ulloa decided to make a break for the open sea. One morning before dawn he had the Japanese guard thrown over the side, slipped his cable and, with only the foresail and spritsail set, sailed towards the entrance. Here a rattan boom had been stretched and a fleet of small craft lay in wait. A negro slave was offered his freedom if he would cut the cable. Clearing the channel with gunfire, Ulloa drove his ship against the boom. The slave was lowered over the bow armed with a machete and with some exertion managed to cut the cable. Keeping a running fire against the small craft and the Japanese on the surrounding hills, the Spanish worked the ship out to sea. Once well clear, a jury rig was set up and the *Espiritu Santo* made for Manila.

Subsequently guarantees were given by the Japanese that no further ships would be molested

and thereafter, although their situation was tense, ships which were either wrecked or forced on the Japanese coast were aided rather than pillaged. The *San Francisco* in 1609 was wrecked on the coast. Her commander, Rodrigo de Vivero, was given use of a ship built by Will Adams, a colourful Englishman employed by the Japanese to build ships in the European style. Will Adams wrote of this ship: '...which theay found so good theay never returned agayn, butt sent so much monny ass shee wass wourth, and afterwards wass imployed in the voyages from Nova Spaynia to the Philippines.'

Somewhere between 31 and 44 degrees north, but usually in the mid thirties, a galleon would fall in with favourable westerlies and, assisted by the Japan or Kuro Siwo current she would turn east for California. The winds here are part of the weather system dominated by the north Pacific high. It is along the northern side of this permanent but fluctuating region of high pressure that the easting is made good. The parallel at which the westerlies are found can vary through up to 10° of latitude. (On the *Bounty* replica we expected to have to rise to nearly 40° and got our woollies out but found the winds at 29°50'; a lucky break for us.)

The old sailors had no weather fax printouts or other reports, which was probably better for their nerves, for the tight, concentric isobars illustrating the massive depressions sweeping from Japan to Canada would make any sailing-ship master pensive. On the southern limits of these depressions, strong but favourable winds are found, but well into the systems winds above force eight are likely—fine for the later windjammers, but hard on less robust ships when near-hurricane-force winds pile the already huge northwesterly swells into mighty seas.

The galleons avoided the thick of these storms and once on their southern edge, could reasonably depend on the ship reaching California safely. For her people, however, it was a different tale. More dangerous on this part of the voyage was the

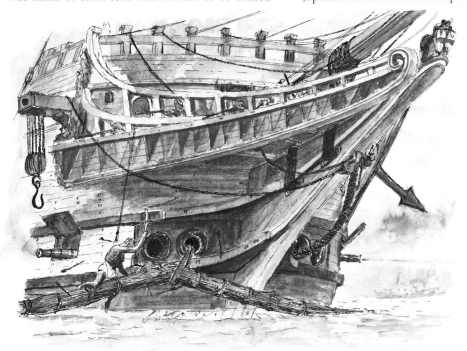

A Negro slave from *Espiritu Santo* cuts the boom placed by the Japanese at the Hirado harbour entrance

insidious and lethal progress of disease, mainly scurvy. In this respect, one of the more disastrous voyages was that of the *Sanctisima Trinidad* in 1755. Of the 435 people who sailed in her, only 27 were able to stand when she reached Acapulco – 82 had died and 200 had been put ashore sick at Cape San Lucas.

The most horrific voyage was probably that of the *San Jose* which sailed from Manila in June 1657. Nine months later she was sighted near Acapulco, closehauled under shortened sail. She was signalled, but there was no response, so she was pursued and a boarding-party sent to her. On board there was silence. Scattered about the decks were the emaciated corpses of her crew and passengers. All had died of starvation and scurvy, the last probably within a few days' sail of succour.

The tedium and discomfort of the passage was relieved by games and pastimes. Although gambling was forbidden it was by no means not enjoyed and many small and not so small fortunes changed hands. Even commanders participated, and some used the pastime to good effect; one acquired 40,000 pesos from his shipmates in the course of one voyage.

Running their easting down, the pilots, relying on dead reckoning for their longitude, were aided by signs or *senãs* hundreds of miles offshore as they approached the Californian coast. The first of the *senãs* was occasion for celebration in a ship. A ceremony very like crossing the line skylarking, with a court or *tribunal de la senãs* was staged by the seamen. Gruesome sentences were handed out to officers and passengers. These were commuted on

the payment of fines in the way of money or delicacies such as sweetmeats. In Gemelli Careri's ship the pilot was accused of quarrelling with the sun and the chaplain of being the 'guide of death' because whenever he went below to minister to someone, the next day the latter would be thrown overboard. The sailors were not exactly gentle and apparently sometimes got out of hand:

. . .he who did not pay immediately or give good Security, was laid on with a Rope's End, and at the least sign given by the President Tarpaulin. I was told a Passenger was once kill'd aboard a Galleon by Keelhaling him; for no Words or Authority can check or persuade a whole Ship's Crew.

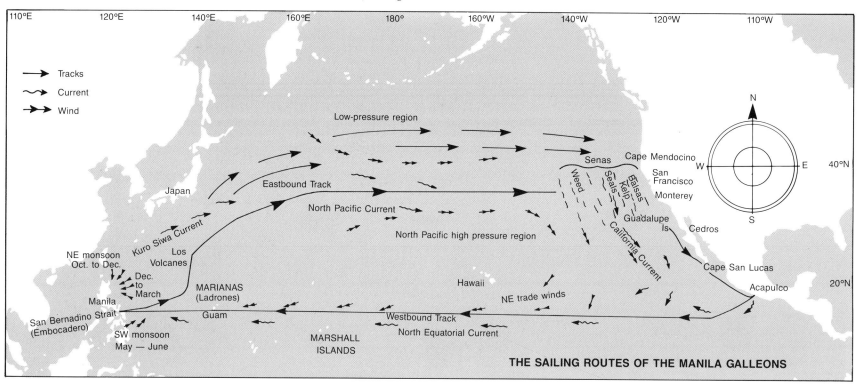

THE SAILING ROUTES OF THE MANILA GALLEONS

After sighting the *senās* the galleons could either stand inshore for a landfall or bear away for lower California. The latter was the common practice in the later years. Earlier the ships usually stood inshore, making a landfall in the vicinity of Cape Mendocino. Course was then laid southeastward past Point Reyes, The Farallones, Point Pines and Conception. A cautious distance was kept off the land to avoid being embayed on a lee shore on the rugged coast north of Point Conception, a region often shrouded in fog and subject to strong winds. Often, on rounding Conception, the galleon would sail through the Santa Barbara channel to lower California.

Suggestions to provide a way-stop at Cape San Lucas were made early in the seventeenth century, but it was well into the eighteenth century before the galleons could find refuge on the Californian coast. The threat of the Russians moving down from the north and the possibility of French and English incursions inspired settlements at San Francisco, Monterey and San Diego, any of which could serve for the galleons. In 1773 commanders were instructed to call at Monterey, and a fine of 4000 pesos for failure to comply was imposed. However, most captains would not brook any delay and stood on down the coast.

The waters about Cape San Lucas provided the galleons with a final hazard on their long voyage. It was off this cape that any pirate, privateer or enemy was likely to patrol, knowing that the galleon would not pass too far off. Cavendish, Woodes Rogers and Anson, among others, waited here. Only two galleons were lost off San Lucas; the *Santa Anna* to Cavendish in 1587 and the *Nostra Senora de la Incarnacion Disenganio* to Woodes Rogers in 1709. In fact, only four galleons were lost to enemies at sea and all of these went to the English.

The relief and joy of the crew and passengers on their arrival at Acapulco can be imagined. The news would spread quickly to Mexico City where bells would be rung out and prayers of thanksgiving said in the churches. Frantic preparations would be made to set off for Acapulco; the town only came alive at the galleon fair.

From the end of the eighteenth century competition with other ships ended the monopoly of the Philippine trade. The Napoleonic Wars and rebellion in Mexico hastened the demise of the failing enterprise. In 1815, bearing the illustrious name *Magellan*, the last galleon put out from Acapulco for Manila.

The story of the Manila ships has, I think been unfairly neglected in our history books. An epic trade maintained for two and a half centuries across the little known and vast north Pacific deserves a place in the annals of human endeavour. Inspired by greed and maintained by graft it may have been, but the enterprise possessed many noble aspects. The great galleons themselves suffered the contemptuous and derisive comments of seamen, but they sailed and succeeded in spite of losses no greater than was common among many other trades of the time. What these galleons were really like is lost to us. However, we can build up a composite picture from various sources, and distinctive they certainly were. What a grand sight they must have made, scending over the long, blue-grey swells of the north Pacific.

SHIPS OF THE ELIZABETHAN ENGLISH

Francis Drake's *Golden Hinde* was a small warship of her period, designed to be fast, handy and carry 18 guns. Whereas my interpretations of the Spanish ships are based on informed guesswork, much more reliable sources are available for late sixteenth and early seventeenth century English ships. Two well researched and carefully constructed full-size replicas of ships of the period have been built and it would be difficult to contradict or fault the conclusions arrived at in their reconstruction.

The first of these, the *Mayflower II*, launched at Brixham, Devon, in 1956, is the nearest approach possible to an early seventeenth-century merchant ship of 180 tons. The original *Mayflower* was probably built during the very first years of the 1600s and would have differed little from ships built 20 or 30 years earlier. The other is a replica of the *Golden Hinde*, launched in April 1973 near Appledore, also in Devon.

Early shipping design

The design of these replicas leaned heavily on master shipwright Matthew Baker's *Fragments of English Shipwrightry* which for the first time set down the 'Reulles of proportyons' used in their construction. Most people who have glanced at anything on early shipping will be familiar with the drawing of a fish superimposed on the underwater hull of a ship, drawn by Baker to illustrate the theory that a good ship should have a 'cod's head and a mackerel's tail'.

Although it is frequently stated that English ships were on the whole faster and better sailers than their

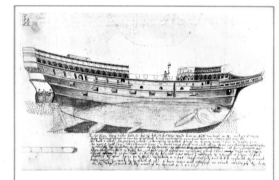

Matthew Baker's drawing of a fish superimposed on the underwater hull of a ship to illustrate that a good design should have 'a cod's head and a mackerel's tail'.
(Reproduced from *Fragments of English Shipwrightry* by Matthew Baker in the Pepys Library; courtesy of the Master and Fellows, Magdalene College, Cambridge.)

counterparts abroad, their success at sea and against their enemies can be attributed to superior seamanship and gunnery rather than any innovation of design in the vessels themselves. Most English ships were modelled on the design of the Mediterranean, Spanish and French galleons, and any improvements in design were initiated by the French and Dutch rather than the conservative English.

The *Golden Hinde* is described as being of 'the French pattern' and built along Venetian lines. She may have been built in England or possibly a prize taken on a privateering voyage. In building the replica, her size was partly arrived at by the known size of the berth at Deptford where she was preserved for almost a century after her voyage. The

replica is a vessel of about 100 tons and had the following dimensions:

Length of keel	60 ft (18.3 m)
Length of waterline	75 ft (22.88 m)
Length overall	102 ft (31.11 m)
Mean draught	9 ft (2.75 m)
Breadth to outside of planking	20 ft (6.1 m)
Foremast	46 ft (14.03 m)
Fore topmast	25 ft (7.62 m)
Mainmast	59 ft (18 m)
Main topmast	29 ft (8.85 m)
Mizzen mast	36 ft 6 in. (11.13 m)
Sail area	4150 sq ft (385.5 m²)

Lofting the lines

All curves, including the stem, were constructed from the true arcs of circles linked tangentially either to other arcs or to straight lines. The only tools the shipwright used for describing his lines were the compass and straight edge. The shape of the transverse section at the point of maximum beam was draughted as opposite:

This completes the half section at the point of maximum beam. For the rest of the frames, it seems that once the rising and narrowing lines of the floor and the maximum breadth were determined, the remaining transverse sections were constructed by suitable variations of lines and arcs. Fairing as it is done today was not invented.

The location of the maximum section on the keel was forward of the midpoint and rules were given for its location. Other methods of draughting are described using four arcs, and national variations affected the shape of the section. The rising line

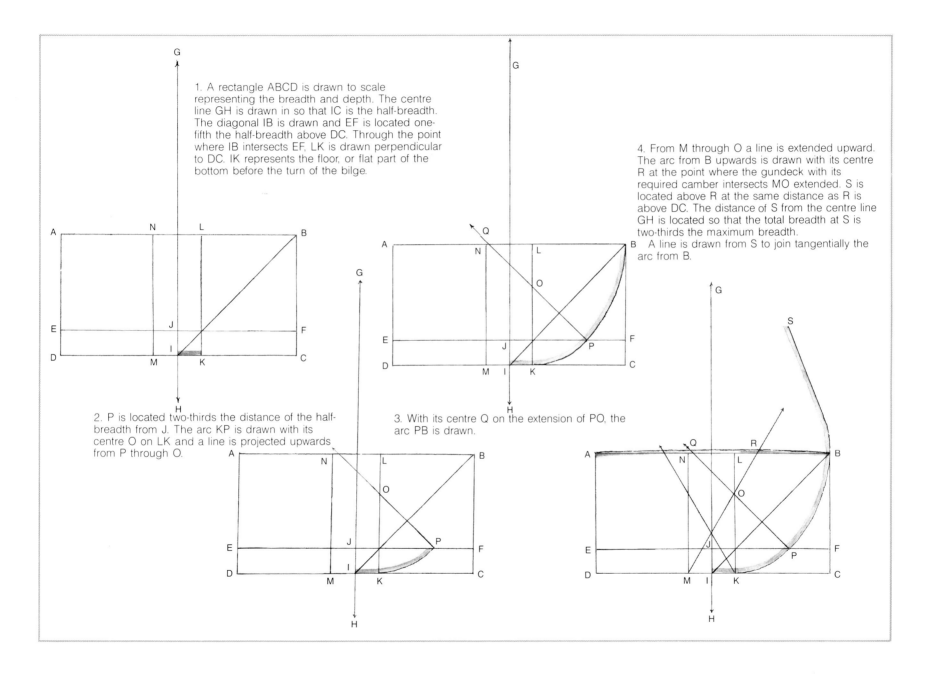

1. A rectangle ABCD is drawn to scale representing the breadth and depth. The centre line GH is drawn in so that IC is the half-breadth. The diagonal IB is drawn and EF is located one-fifth the half-breadth above DC. Through the point where IB intersects EF, LK is drawn perpendicular to DC. IK represents the floor, or flat part of the bottom before the turn of the bilge.

2. P is located two-thirds the distance of the half-breadth from J. The arc KP is drawn with its centre O on LK and a line is projected upwards from P through O.

3. With its centre Q on the extension of PO, the arc PB is drawn.

4. From M through O a line is extended upward. The arc from B upwards is drawn with its centre R at the point where the gundeck with its required camber intersects MO extended. S is located above R at the same distance as R is above DC. The distance of S from the centre line GH is located so that the total breadth at S is two-thirds the maximum breadth.
  A line is drawn from S to join tangentially the arc from B.

49

describing the point of maximum breadth at each section, rose steeply, especially forward, creating quite fine underwater lines. Later ships, so as to carry the weight of armament and prevent hogging, had bluffer bows and the line of maximum breadth lowered to near the load waterline.

The measurement of tonnage

In researching these early ships I found that tonnages were most often given. Very rarely would another measurement be supplied, so it was with some relief that I found a key which would determine the approximate dimensions of a ship from its tonnage. The tonnage usually referred to *tons burden*, which was based on the number of *tuns* of wine a ship would carry. A tun was a large cask holding usually 252 wine gallons. A wine gallon is now the standard US gallon of 231 cu. in. It is apparent that by measuring in tons, or tuns, the result is a capacity measure rather than one of weight. To arrive at the deadweight of a ship, it was common practice to add one third on to the tonnage.

Matthew Baker provides a clear statement of the rule of thumb and used a merchant ship of his time as a model:

By the proportion of breadth, depth and length of any ship to judge what burden she may be of in merchant's goods... The *Ascension* of London being in breadth 24 ft [7.32 m], depth 12 ft [3.66 m] from that breadth to the hold, and by the keel 54 ft [16.4 m] in length doth carry in burden of merchants's goods (in pipes of oil or Bordeaux wine) 160 tons...

By finding the product of the length of keel, breadth and depth and dividing by 100, Baker provides a formula for finding the vessel's tonnage. In the case of the *Ascension*, the factor is 97 to arrive at 160 tons. If 100 is used, the tonnage results in a figure of 155½ tons, a discrepancy of 4½ tons.

In the state of the art relating to finding the volumes of irregular curved spaces (at that time), the result is pretty close. The basic formula can be expressed:

$$\frac{K \times B \times D}{100} = \text{tons burden}$$

For the proportions between length, breadth and depth, Baker states:

Proportions for shippinge

The bredth is arbitarie, ye depth must never be more then ½ ye bredth, nor less then ⅓, The length never less then double ye bredth nor more then treble...

Another useful guide is given by William Borough, Comptroller of the Navy from 1589 to 1598, who listed the following rather more precise proportions:

1. The shortest, broadest and deepest order—To have the length by the keel double the breadth amidships and the depth in hold half that breadth. This order is used in some merchant ships for most profit.
2. The mean and best proportion for shipping for merchandise likewise very serviceable for all purposes. Length of keel two or two and a quarter that of beam. Depth of hold eleven-twentyfourths that of beam.
3. The largest order for galleons or ships for the wars made for the most advantage of sailing. Length of keel three times the beam. Depth of hold two-fifths of beam.

Using this information and knowing the type of vessel I was dealing with, whether merchantman or fighting ship, I found that I could arrive at sensible dimensions for the ships I have painted. I also found that the formulae could be used for ships of later periods, but not so accurately, for these vessels possessed fuller lines.

Using Borough's three conditions and given the tonnage, the breadth can be arrived at by the following:

1. $B = \sqrt[3]{100 \times T}$

2. $B = \sqrt[3]{\dfrac{100 \times T}{1.031}}$

3. $B = \sqrt[3]{\dfrac{100 \times T}{1.2}}$

Once the breadth has been found, it is a simple matter to arrive at the length of keel and depth using the proportions in Borough's three conditions.

An appreciation of the points of measurement for length of keel, breadth and depth is necessary:

Length of keel is the length of the straight timber laid along the blocks at building.

Breadth was measured ideally at the inside of the planking at the widest part of the hull. However, once a ship was in service, the points of measurement could become inaccessible and it became usual to measure to the outside of the hull, thus increasing the breadth but not the usable space—a loss to a charterer paying on tonnage. It was also common practice to apply extra layers of planking to the outside of the hull to improve stability and strength. This was termed *furring* or *girding* and the English had more ships modified in this manner than any other nation.

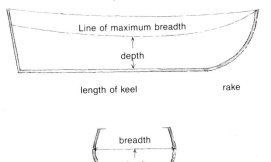

Depth was measured from the height of the maximum moulded breadth to the top of the keel, but this measurement also was taken outside to the bottom of the keel, once again increasing the tonnage but short-changing the capacity. It would be thought that the depth of hold would have been taken from under a continuous deck but ships of this period had their decks arranged as convenient in the bow, waist and stern and had no tradition of a continuous deck.

Note: Much of the foregoing technical information is based on that set out in *The Voyage of the Mayflower II* by Warwick Charlton. In a note at the end of Chapter 5, 'The design for the *Mayflower*', this author states that the summary is based on two articles by Bill Baker, first published in the January and October 1954 issues of American *Neptune*. The other source I have used in this chapter is the magazine *The Golden Hinde*, published in 1973 by Jarrold and Sons Ltd, Norwich.

Francis Drake (1597-8)

'. . .the maine Ocean by right is the Lord's due, and by nature left free for all men to deal withall, as very sufficient for all men's use, and large enough for all man's industry.' So claimed John Drake, the nephew of Francis. These words, with reservations, are valid today, despite overfishing, whaling, nuclear testing and other rapacious activities. The sixteenth century

Drake's little 100-ton warship, the *Golden Hinde,* off the Pacific northwest coast of America. There is some doubt as to how far north Drake made his landfall as the weather conditions do not tally with early summer at the latitude of 48°N which was recorded. Part of Drake's instructions may have been to look for a strait, described as the 'Codfish Strait', which was believed to lead to the North Atlantic.

A replica of the *Golden Hinde*, on which this painting is largely based, was launched in England in 1973. Here she is represented making inshore for an anchorage. A boat is out ahead to guide her in.

Drake subsequently sailed down the coast to near San Francisco, where he claimed the land for England and named it 'New Albion'.

Spanish thought otherwise, but with their enormous empire and limited human resources, they could do little to thwart the invasions into their seas of ships belonging to other, more vigorous, nations. During the late sixteenth century the English, in a burst of exuberant enterprise, dared to trespass into the Spanish 'Great South Sea' in a series of brief forays which were not to be repeated for over 100 years. Drake blazed the trail in 1578, to be followed by Cavendish in 1587 and the unsuccessful Sir Richard Hawkins in 1593.

So much has been written about Sir Francis Drake that it is not necessary to go into details of his voyage; it is really the ships of the Elizabethans which are the concern here. There are two features of Drake's circumnavigation, however, which are intriguing, for they contain the elements of mystery.

Drake sailed from Plymouth on 13 December 1577 with five ships: *Pelican* (100 ton), *Marigold* (30 ton), *Elizabeth* (80 ton), and two victuallers. For good reasons, a veil of secrecy was cast over Drake's actual instructions from Elizabeth I. On 6 September 1578 the ships *Pelican*, *Elizabeth* and *Marigold* passed Cape Deseado and entered the Pacific. Three days later began the greatest trial of the whole voyage. The wind backed to the northeast and blew in storm-force squalls from the land. Little or no sail could be carried and the ships were driven WSW into the Southern Ocean. The *Marigold* was lost, probably foundering in the heavy seas. She may have been the wreck which Cavendish saw later at Port Famine and judged to be the *John Thomas*. The name of the captain of the *Marigold* was John Thomas and it is probable that his name was painted on the stern.

The *Pelican* and *Elizabeth* drove until the end of September when, in latitude 57°S, the wind came fair. Seven days later they were off the coast a degree north of the straits. Here *Pelican* tried to anchor in 40 fathoms but dragged and weighed again after an hour. On the morning of 8 September the *Elizabeth* had vanished; she had run back into the strait and

finally returned to England. Drake named the bay where they became separated 'The Severing of Friends'. Once again the *Pelican* was driven south until on 13 October, at midnight, they got in with the coast. The next day, Nunō da Silva, the Portuguese pilot Drake had earlier captured in the Atlantic, noted they 'came to anchor in 54½ degrees, three leagues from the land in 50 fathoms'.

Conditions must have been desperate to have attempted to anchor in such a depth so far offshore. Working up the coast, they anchored twice more until the twenty-third. They managed to get a little water, but lost a pinnace with seven men, one of whom survived and returned to civilisation. On the twenty-third the cable parted and Drake was forced to stand off the grim and threatening coast.

The wind fell Northwest, whereapon they sailed Westsouthwest. . .and with this foule weather they ranne till they were under seven and fiftie degrees, where they entered into a haven of an Island, and ankered about the length of a shot of a great piece from the land, at twentie fathome deepe, where they stayed three or foure dayes.

Felix Riesenberg, in his book *Cape Horn* (1941), rightly points out that this course, even allowing for leeway, would take them nowhere near land. Apart from the Diego Ramirez Islands at 56½°S, there is no land in 57°S latitude anywhere near the Horn and Drake's latitudes, apart from on his most northerly trip, are usually accurate. Historians and writers appear to have ignored the logistics, and it is generally understood that Drake anchored under an island near the Cape. In that case he would have seen land far off, if there was anywhere he could have anchored – which would have been unlikely. The descriptions of the island, named Elizabeth Island, bear no relation to anything near the Horn. At Elizabeth Island they found a safe sheltered anchorage and collected 'herbes of great virtue'

while they waited for a fair wind for the north. Riesenberg proposes, with good reason, that this island has since vanished. Allowing for the set of the Cape Horn current, of which Drake would have bene unaware, the *Pelican*'s course made good would have been nearer south than southwest, which would have placed them over the Burnham Bank.

In 1885, while running before a gale, Captain W.D. Burnham of the American ship *Patroclus* was approaching Cape Horn in latitude 56°36'S when the wind and sea went down. He noticed that the sea was highly discoloured, whereupon he hove to and took soundings, getting each time 60 to 70 fathoms, black sand and small rocks. He then ran south for 30 miles before leaving the thick yellow water behind. The finding was partly confirmed by an English ship bound from San Francisco to Liverpool, the master of which reported discoloured water in the area. When Riesenberg propounded his theory the presence of the bank was indicated on charts but not confirmed by later surveys. However, it remains on contemporary charts and is described thus in the South American Pilot, Vol II: 'Patroclus Bank (56°35'S 74°20'W) was reported in 1885 to rise from the deep; it has a least known depth of 122 m (67 fms) with a bottom of black sand and rock.' Given the geological instability of the region, it is not unlikely that the Burnham (or Patroclus) Bank is the sunken remains of Drake's Elizabeth Island.

It should be pointed out that Sir Francis Chichester, in his book *Along the Clipper Way*, was convinced that Drake had anchored in the lee of one of the Diego Ramirez Islands which lie 60 miles southwest by west of the Horn. One of the islands has an anchorage of 16 fathoms close to the eastward, and their latitude of 56½° does not conflict with da Silva's 'under seven and fiftie degrees. . . '.

Drake, once back on the coast, renamed the *Pelican* *Golden Hinde* after the crest of Sir Christopher Hatton, a major stockholder in the enterprise.

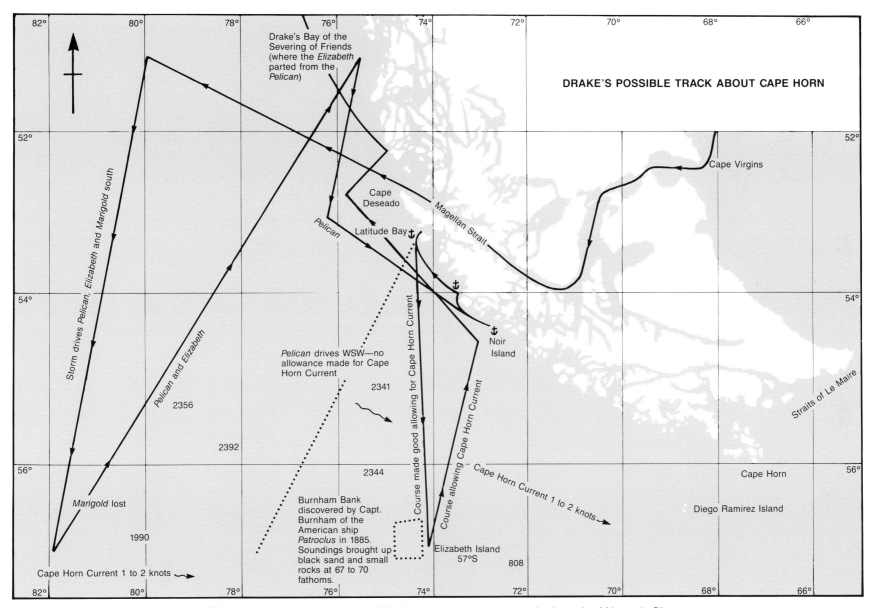

DRAKE'S POSSIBLE TRACK ABOUT CAPE HORN

Drake's Bay of the Severing of Friends (where the *Elizabeth* parted from the *Pelican*)

Cape Virgins

Storm drives *Pelican, Elizabeth and Marigold* south

Pelican and Elizabeth

2356

2392

Marigold lost

1990

Cape Horn Current 1 to 2 knots →

Cape Deseado

Pelican

Latitude Bay ⚓

Magellan Strait

⚓

Noir Island

Pelican drives WSW—no allowance made for Cape Horn Current

2341

2344

Course made good allowing for Cape Horn Current

Course allowing Cape Horn Current

Cape Horn Current 1 to 2 knots →

Burnham Bank discovered by Capt. Burnham of the American ship *Patroclus* in 1885. Soundings brought up black sand and small rocks at 67 to 70 fathoms.

Elizabeth Island 57°S

808

Straits of Le Maire

Cape Horn

Diego Ramirez Island

Drake's courses from Magellan Strait to Elizabeth Island as suggested by Felix Riesenberg and based on the journals of Nuño da Silva

Sailing north, Drake carried out his series of raids on the coast, culminating in the capture of the Plate galleon, *Nuestra Señora de la Concepcion*, nicknamed irreverently the 'Cacafuego'. Further north he captured a ship laden with silk and porcelain from a Manila galleon, and on 13 April 1579 he boldly sailed into the small Mexican seaport of Guatalco. He sacked the town, provisioned the *Golden Hinde* and released the pilot da Silva, from whom a deal of interesting commentary is available on Drake's voyage.

After the *Golden Hinde* left Guatalco the second enigma concerning the voyage began. Drake had three possible routes home to England. He could return by Magellan Strait or around Cape Horn, for he then suspected that the Atlantic and the Pacific joined in the south. He could sail west to the Philippines or the Moluccas and get home by way of the Cape of Good Hope, or he could explore northward to find the Strait of Ainian, the 'Northwest Passage' on which the English had so fervently set their hearts.

When he left Guatalco Drake had prepared the *Golden Hinde* for sea, struck his guns below and readied her for a long passage. His statements and conversations were contradictory, as though casting a smokescreen over his intentions. He had available to him all the pilotage information known at that time and would have been aware of the best sailing routes, either to the west or northwestward up the coast. With his ability as a seaman and a ship as handy as the *Golden Hinde*, although laden deep as she was, Drake would have had no difficulty working out into the northeast trades, even with the southwest winds that frequently prevail from April. According to da Silva, Drake had often confided that he was under orders to return by 'Codfish Strait – . . .which he had come hither to discover, and that failing to find an exit through it he was bound to return by way of China'. Drake had also shown da Silva a chart and indicated that he must seek the strait at about 66°N.

What Drake actually did was to stand out to the west for about 1500 miles and then turned northwest, not coming up with the coast again until well into westerlies far to the north. *Ocean Passages of the World* have definite advice to sailing-ship masters sailing from anywhere between Panama and the lower Californian coast. They are to stand offshore to the northeast trades then, holding the starboard tack, make sufficient offing to allow one to work in with the westerlies and northwesterly winds in higher latitudes. This is precisely what Drake did and what any modern-day shipmaster would do.

The question remains as to where he regained the North American coast. It was early summer. Had he come into the land at about 48°N, which generally seems to be assumed, that places his landfall at just south of Vancouver Island; a little late for the reported accounts of sleet and frost. He may well have had bad weather; rain and fog, but not snow.

One wonders if perhaps he went much further north in search of the strait, maybe higher than 60°? His run down the coast would be made fast and easy before the strong northwesterlies. Maybe in the miserable conditions that can prevail on that coast, he was unable to get a latitude, or if he did, he kept it under his hat. What happened to Sir Francis Drake's record of the voyage? He must have submitted a report to Queen Elizabeth I. Did she destroy it or bury it so deep in secrecy that it has never come to light?

Thomas Cavendish (1586-8)

When Thomas Cavendish sailed in Drake's wake in 1586, England was at war with Spain and, in contrast to Drake, his course up the Pacific west coast left a trail of burned towns and shattered ships. Three

small ships, fitted out and provisioned at Cavendish's own expense, wreaked damage to Spanish property and morale out of all proportion to their size.

Using the second proportions of Borough (page 50), the following dimensions for these ships can be arrived at:

Desire (140 tons)

Breadth	23 ft 8 in. (7.22 m)
Length of keel	53 ft 7 in. (16.34 m)
Length on deck	77 ft 3 in. (23.56 m)
Depth	10 ft 9 in. (3.28 m)

Content (60 tons)

Breadth	18 ft (5.49 m)
Length of keel	40 ft 6 in. (12.35 m)
Length on deck	58 ft 6 in. (17.84 m)
Depth	8 ft 3 in. (2.52 m)

Hugh Gallant (bark) (40 tons)

Breadth	15 ft 9 in. (4.8 m)
Length of keel	35 ft 4 in. (10.78 m)
Length on deck	51 ft 1 in. (15.57 m)
Depth	7 ft 3 in. (2.21 m)

The rig of the two larger vessels would have been the conventional three-masted rig of the time; that of the *Hugh Gallant* is anyone's guess. The appellation 'bark' means little as at this time the word did not designate rig.

On 6 January 1587, Cavendish's ships entered the Strait of Magellan. Here in this strait they came upon the tragic remnants of the Spanish fort of Ciudad del Rey Felipe. Drake had managed a comparatively easy passage of the strait, but it was a passage the Spanish had failed time and time again to make, until in 1580 Don Pedro Sarmiento passed through comparatively easily from west to east. His success and enthusiastic reports on the nature of the strait inspired the Spanish to send out an expedition the following year. An armada of 23 ships and 3500 men and women sailed to found forts and settlements in the Magellan Strait to bar the passage of the English. Foul weather south of the Plate three times forced the expedition back and the fleet was progressively dissipated. Sarmiento put out once again from Rio in 1583. In the strait, shipwreck and desertion left Sarmiento with a small pinnace, 430 men and women ashore and provisions for only eight months. He founded a strong fort named Rey Felipe and another at Nombre de Jesus. With winter coming on, Sarmiento decided to combine his forces at Rey Felipe and sailed to Nombre de Jesus. There a storm forced him out to sea and in spite of his efforts he was driven back to Brazil, where he failed in repeated attempts to get relief to the forts.

Lieutenant Viedma, the commander of the fort at Nombre de Jesus, marched his men and women overland to Rey Felipe but found the fort was too small to contain the combined forces. Two hundred men were sent out to live as best they could off the countryside.

When Cavendish came upon Rey Felipe he found it deserted. The inhabitants had been forced out of the little town:

> At last they died like so many dogs, in their houses, in great numbers; and the stench of the putrifying carcasses infecting those that survived, they were forced to quit the town with one consent, and go rambling upon the sea coasts living upon leaves and roots and sea herbs, or what animals they at any time happily caught.

A few, 22 men and 2 women, survived out of the 400 men and 30 women who had landed. These, according to Tomas Hernando, whom Cavendish captured, were attempting to walk out to the north.

In 1588 Thomas Cavendish returned to England from his voyage round the world. In the hold of the 140-ton *Desire* was a wealth of gold and merchandise from the captured Manila galleon *Santa Anna*.

After arriving at the port of Plymouth, Cavendish made a grand progress up the Thames. Thousands turned out to watch as the *Desire* worked upriver, her crew decked out in splendid silk, her tops wrapped in cloth of gold and her sails made of damask.

Cavendish renamed Rey Felipe 'Port Famine', the name it retains today.

The capture of the *Santa Anna*

Cavendish entered the Pacific on 24 February 1587 and started on his depredations along the coast to the north. His final insult to the Spanish was the capture, off Cape San Lucas, of the Manila galleon *Santa Anna*, bound from the Philippines. The galleon carried an immensely rich cargo and put up a bold fight:

Now as we were ready on the ship's side to enter her, being not past fifty or sixty men at the uttermost in our ship, we perceived that the Captaine of the said ship had made fights [strongpoints] fore and after, and lay'd their sails close on their poope, their midships, with their forecastle, and having not one man to be seene, [as they] stood close under their fights with lances, javelins, rapiers and targets [shields], and an innumerable sort of great stones, which they threw overboard upon our heads and into our ship so fast, and being so many of them that they put us off the shippe again, with the loss of two of our men which were slaine, and with the hurting four or five [others].

But, for all this, we new trimmed our sailes, and fitted every man his furniture, and gave them a fresh encounter with our great ordnance and also with our small shot, raking them through and through, to the killing and maiming of many of their men. Their Captaine still, like a valiant man with his company, stood very stoutly unto his close fights, not yielding as yet. Our General, encouraging his men afresh with the whole noise of trumpets, gave them the third encounter with our great ordnance and all our small shot, raking them through in divers places, and spoiling many of their men.

It was the cannon fire which finally forced the commander of the galleon to strike. Cavendish took her into Porto Segura, just east of San Lucas. He put ashore all the Spaniards with stores for their sustenance and selected as much of the cargo as he could take, including 122,000 dollars worth of gold (well over a million dollars today). Before he put to sea, he had the galleon set on fire and watched her until she seemed to be a total loss.

At sea the *Content* became separated from the *Desire* and was never seen again. It is possible that the separation was deliberate, for prior to sailing, Cavendish had had to put down a mutiny led mainly by those in the *Content*. The cause was the usual squabble over the division of the spoils. It is possible that the *Content* was wrecked on Hawaii.

Among the Spanish left at Segura was Sebastian Vizcaino, later to become a famous navigator and explorer. The storm which perhaps separated the English ships drove the burning *Santa Anna* ashore. Vizcaino led a party to the wreck and succeeded in putting out the fire. The hull, below water, was found to be still sound and by dint of hard work and ingenuity they managed to plank up the topsides sufficiently for the survivors to cross the Gulf of California to Mexico.

It is to Vizcaino we owe so many of the place names on the California coast, including the islands off Los Angeles. It was at White's Landing, Santa Catalina, that we found an anchorage for the *Bounty* replica and it was here that we were told Vizcaino anchored. It would be quite likely, as all these islands possess precious little in the way of safe anchorages. The Straits of Juan de Fuca are named after his fellow pilot, who claimed they were the entrance to the Straits of Anian.

Cavendish crossed the Pacific, called at Guam and sailed through the Philippines, to the consternation of the Spanish. He went through the Portuguese East Indies, round the Cape and arrived in Plymouth on 9 September 1588. Shortly afterwards, Cavendish sailed the *Desire* up the Thames, his crew decked out in satin and silk, his tops wrapped in cloth of gold and what appeared to be sails made of damask. One authority has it that the sails were not damask but Philippine seagrass, but I am inclined to believe, considering the temper of the times and of Cavendish, that it would have been not out of character for him to have run up a suit of sails for the occasion; there were plentiful bolts of silk under his hatches.

THE DUTCH ENTER THE PACIFIC

Within a few decades of their declaration of independence in 1581, the Dutch had virtually supplanted the Portuguese in the East, contained the Spanish in the Philippines and driven the embryonic English East India Company to the coasts of India.

The success of the Dutch can be attributed to their single-minded desire to trade. Whereas the Iberians, along with their trading activities, set out to conquer and convert, the Dutch had no interest in the acquisition of souls. They fought successfully for their sea routes and trading posts and were utterly ruthless with their competitors. They didn't slay the goose by proselytising and pirating their markets and consequently gained trust and preferences from the oriental traders.

For as long as they could, the Portuguese had barred the Cape route and the Spanish guarded the way of Magellan, but both monopolies were soon broken. The Dutch East India Company was founded in 1602, and in 1609 the Spanish were forced to a treaty, under the terms of which there should be no interference with Dutch commerce in the East, but resistance to their activities continued along the sea routes. About the turn of the seventeenth century the Dutch sent out two expeditions through Magellan Strait. That of Simon de Cordes ended with his ships scattered, but succeeded in reaching the Moluccas with one ship. Oliver Van Noort's expedition was more successful, for he was the first Dutchman to sail around the world, but little came of the enterprise.

Setting out in 1614, Joris Spilbergen, a Dutch admiral, fought his way around the world by way of Magellan, but about this time the Dutch were

experimenting with a new route across the Indian Ocean, pioneered by Commander Hendrik Brouwer. He was the first to run his easting down from the Cape before turning north 4000 miles out, halving the passage time of the Portuguese route. Brouwer's initiative soon led to landfalls on the west coast of Australia.

By 1615 the Dutch star was truly ascending. Home and foreign trade was booming, her ports were crowded with ships and the shareholders of the Dutch East India Company were counting their dividends but keeping their fingers crossed that the

good fortune would continue. To ensure their monopoly in the East, they restricted the use of the Cape and Magellan routes to company ships, enforcing the ban with their own warships. This provided the spur which was to lead to the discovery of that other great cape, Cape Horn.

The le Maires and Willem Schouten (1615-16)

Isaac le Maire was a Dutch merchant who had long been at odds with the monopoly held by the Dutch East India Company. In the year 1610, under a charter granted by the States General he founded the Compagne Australe with permission to trade in Tartary, China, Japan, 'Terra Australis' and the South Sea islands. However as the Dutch East India Company had complete control and sole use of the Cape of Good Hope and the Strait of Magellan, the success of the Compagne Australe was dependent on the discovery of a new sea route into the Pacific – a route which le Maire was convinced existed south of the Magellan Strait. Le Maire's belief was shared by Willem Cornelisz Schouten, an accomplished navigator who had already sailed three times to the East Indies, and between them a plan was evolved to send two ships in search of the new passage. The project was underwritten by le Maire and Schouten and subscribed to by many citizens of the port of Hoorn. Complete secrecy was maintained as to their goal as careful and very thorough preparations for the voyage went ahead.

Two ships were chosen: the *Eendracht*, 360 tons, mounting 19 cannon and 12 swivel guns, with a crew of 65, was to be captained by Willem Schouten; a smaller ship, the *Hoorn*, 110 tons, mounting 8 cannon and four swivels, and manned by a crew of 22, had Jan Schouten, brother of Willem, as captain. Isaac le Maire's son, Jacob, was appointed overall commander of the voyage. Aware of the need for good boats, the *Eendracht* carried a large sailing pinnace, a smaller, oared pinnace, a launch and small workboat. The *Hoorn* carried two small boats.

The two ships left Texel on 14 June 1615. On their way down the Channel they anchored in The Downs to seek an English gunner, and put into Plymouth to find a carpenter – a commendation for English seafaring tradesmen.

Calling only at Cape Verde, the ships made an uneventful voyage to Port Desire apart from an unusual incident in the *Hoorn*. Rolling down the trades in 4°S, four months out, a tremendous shock jarred her timbers during a morning washdown. Sail was taken in and the pumps manned. Nothing showed in the well and soundings taken around the ship showed no bottom. Alongside, the water turned red 'as if a fountain of blood were gushing up from the Keel'. Later, while careening in Port Desire, they found a narwhale tusk had pierced three layers of planking, protruding over a foot into the ship. It had broken off at the snout.

By the time the ships had reached Port Desire they were foul. They were beached, and in breaming, or burning off, the growth, the *Hoorn* caught fire. Efforts to quench the flames were fruitless as the tide was too far out to bring water to the ship in sufficient quantity. Anything which was salvageable was brought aboard the *Eendracht*. After a month of revictualling and preparation, they set out for the south. On 20 January 1616 they estimated they were about 60 miles south of the entrance to the Strait and three days later found themselves within soundings. At sunset land was visible to the west and WSW. After an anxious and watchful night, they found land still lay in the west, but during the forenoon high and rugged land

appeared in the east with open water ahead to the south. They named the land they discovered to the east Staten Landt in honour of the States General.

The ships passed through the passage we know now as the Strait of le Maire on 25 January. The following night they were standing to the southeast on the starboard tack and were beginning to meet the long Cape Horn greybeards by which 'we judged and held for certaine that we had great deepe water to leeward from us, nothing doubting but that it was the great South sea, whereat we were exceeding glad, to thinke that wee had discovered a way, which untill that time, was unknowne to men . . . .'

For three days they fought their way south and westwards against contrary winds – the weather very cold, with haile, and raine' – until on the twenty-ninth a favourable northeasterly breeze carried them in sight of 'a sharpe point, which wee called Cape Horne'. The final proof of their discovery came on 12 February when they sighted the western entrance to the Strait of Magellan and so returned to known and charted waters.

The party called at Juan Fernandez, then took a fairly southerly track across the Pacific, passing through the Tuamotus and discovering several minor islands before they left the Pacific. At the beginning of April Jan Schouten died 'after he had

The 360-ton Dutch *Eendracht* ('Unity') under the command of Captain Willem Schouten off Cape Horn. With the aim of circumventing the Cape of Good Hope route to the East Indies, controlled by the powerful Dutch East India Company, Isaac le Maire and a number of citizens of the Hoorn, in Holland, underwrote a voyage to find a westerly sea route. Two ships, the *Eendracht* and the *Hoorn* left the Texel in June 1615. At Port Desire the *Hoorn* caught fire while the marine growth was being burned from her bottom, and the *Eendracht* continued to complete the voyage alone. They rounded the Cape at 8 pm on 29 January 1616, naming it after their home town of Hoorn.

been lyen sicke a moneth', probably as a result of the hardships encountered on the route to Cape Horn.

After trading their way through the East Indies, the party arrived at the Dutch East India Company port of Bantam, only to be told by John Peter von Koeuen, the Company's President, that 'they must leave their shippe and goods there and deliver it up into his hands'. Koeuen refused to believe that a new passage had been discovered. Schouten and le Maire and several of the crew were given passage home in Spilbergen's ship *Amsterdam*, but Jacob le Maire never reached Holland – he died on board, supposedly of a broken heart. After two years of litigation, old Isaac le Maire was compensated for his ship and cargo by the Dutch East India Company, who were ordered to pay costs and interest from the date of seizure. The validity of Schouten and le Maire's discovery of the Cape Horn passage was at last officially recognised.

Abel Janszoon Tasman

During the first half of the seventeenth century Dutch commerce under the management of the powerful Dutch East India Company increased year by year. Naturally some of their resources were directed at extending their knowledge of the East and investigating alternative routes to and from Europe.

Antony van Diemen, appointed Governor General at Batavia in 1636, was particularly active in encouraging and providing for expeditions to investigate Eendrachtsland, as the west Australian coast was known, and eastwards to Japan and beyond. Matthijs Quast's voyage in 1639 took him over 600 miles east of Japan searching for the legendary islands of gold and silver reported by the Spanish. Quast lost 41 of his complement of 90, and was forced to return without sighting any land. In

command of the expedition's second ship was Abel Janszoon Tasman, who had come out before the mast to Batavia in 1633 and had risen swiftly to command in the company's service.

In 1642 an able pilot of the company, Frans Jacobszoon Visscher, produced a *Memoir Concerning the Discovery of the Southland* which was favourably received in Holland and Batavia. The memoir contained proposals which encompassed almost the whole Southern Hemisphere and which anticipated the southern sailing routes of the nineteenth century.

One of Visscher's proposals formed the basis for Tasman's instructions; in essence, it was that an expedition should be sent to Mauritius from where they would sail south to 52° or 54°S latitude. Sailing east in this latitude, should no land be found, they were to turn north on the longitude of the Solomons, or possibly continue 800 miles further than the longitude of the Solomons, to investigate the likelihood of a shorter route to Chile. From the Solomons he was to return to Batavia by way of the north coast of New Guinea.

On 14 August 1642 the *Heemskerck* and *Zeehaen*, under the command of Tasman, sailed from Batavia. From Mauritius he sailed to 49°4'S, but cold forced him north and he steered east in the lower forties, discovering Tasmania, which he named 'Antony Van Diemen's Landt', and New Zealand which he named 'Staten Landt', mistaking it for the western end of the 'Southern Continent' that Schouten believed he had discovered. He anchored in a bay in the north of the South Island where he lost four men when the Maoris unexpectedly attacked the cock-boat. Tasman gave up any attempt to communicate with the native people and after naming the place Murderer's Bay, weighed anchor. The name has since been changed to Golden Bay and is the site of the town of Nelson.

After having some difficulty in beating out of the western approaches of Cook Strait, which he thought was a bay, Tasman sailed up the west coast of the North Island, visited the Three Kings Islands,

then bore away northeast to the Tonga Group where he found a peaceable people and was able to reprovision his ships. From the Tongas he sailed north around the Fiji Islands, then north again to about the latitude of the Solomons. At this stage he could have run west and rediscovered the Solomons, but the weather in that season, when the monsoon and southeast trades meet, was foul, wet and miserable, with strong, variable northerly winds. Had they found themselves on the southern coast of New Guinea at this season, they might have been on a lee shore with the prospect of a protracted beat northwards. The weather, dark and overcast, prevented sights for many days and they were uncertain of their longitude. Discretion prevailed and they worked to the north, making a generally WNW course which took them north of the Solomons. After sighting and naming Ontong Java, they made a landfall on New Ireland. Working round the islands to the north coast of New Guinea, they coasted westward, looking for a possible passage south which would take them to Cape Keerweer on the York Peninsula.

Part of Tasman's instructions was to examine the coast between Keerweer and Eendrachtsland. No passage was found and he took his ships home to Batavia, arriving on 14 June 1643.

I have deliberately skimmed over the course of this quite outstanding voyage, for it was remarkable in the sheer competency with which it was carried out. If I was asked to choose with which of the early commanders I would prefer to sail and if I was worried about my skin, my choice would be Tasman. The only nasty event of the whole voyage was the loss of the four men in New Zealand and this was unprovoked and can cast no slur on that able and competent commander. The journal for Tasman's whole voyage can be read in a couple of hours, but if it is excitement the reader is seeking, he or she will be disappointed. Situations such as lee shores, dragging anchors, foul weather and broken spars are written off as all in a day's work;

A Dutch fluyt. Developed in Holland at the end of the sixteenth century, the fluyt was characterised by a round, apple-cheeked bow and stern, a steep tumblehome and narrow decks and poop. Fluyts were longer in proportion to their beam than other ships, easy to manage, sea-kindly and good carriers. With minor modifications, this design sailed the seas for nearly two centuries. Anson's *Anna Pink* and Cook's *Endeavour* were developments from the original fluyt.

they happen, are dealt with and that is all. Probably the most dangerous situation was in the Fijis when they found themselves embayed. Tasman describes the traumatic experience in his usual economical way:

Item the 6th. In the morning we saw land, to wit three small islets, on all sides surrounded by shoals and reefs; we tacked about to the south, and saw a large reef to the westward, stretching as far as the south, which we sincerely regretted; this land is fully 8 or 9 miles in length; straight ahead there were also breakers, which we were unable to pass. Seeing that we could clear neither the reef straight ahead, nor another which lay to the north of us, we observed to leeward a small space about two ship's lengths wide, where there were no breakers; for this we made, since there was no other way of escape; we passed between the rocks in four fathom, though not without great anxiety; all about here there are reefs and 18 or 19 islands, but the shoals which abound here are very dangerous, render[ing] it impossible for ships to pass between them.

Decisions by ship's council

It was the practice of most European ships in those early years of maritime expansion to resolve problems of strategy and organisation by council. The commander would call together all the senior officers of his squadron for their views and either act on the general consensus of opinion or, as Drake was wont to do, say 'Thank you very much, gentlemen' and go his own way. The Dutch, in particular, were meticulous in calling and following the resolutions of their councils, which seemed to have contained the best elements of democracy. In Tasman's ships, the hoisting of a white flag was the order to meet on board the flagship and all present would submit their views in writing. These council records were carefully kept and handed to the authorities at the end of the voyage. In Tasman's ships the views of the council almost always coincided with those of the commander – not for sycophantic reasons but because each officer had all the facts and experience necessary to make a sound judgment. Sometimes the ship's councils decided on matters of discipline (see opposite).

When Tasman's ships were north of the Fijis a decision had to be made on what course they should pursue. The weather was continuously bad, with strong, squally north to northeast winds, and their position was in doubt. It was impossible to call together the councils from both ships because of the adverse weather, so the decision was made by the *Heemskerck*'s council to make as much northing as possible in the conditions. The written submissions of the officers were unanimous and Tasman, in what must have been careful regard to any inquiry as to why he did not search for the Solomons, recorded each submission in his journal.

The *Heemskerck* and the fluyt *Zeehaen* sailing out of Storm Bay, Tasmania, and passing the Organ Pipes at Cape Raoul on the southern tip of the Tasman Peninsula.

The *Heemskerck* was a Dutch war yacht of 120 lasts, equivalent to about 240 English tons. Yachts were small, lightly built, fast ships, the term *yacht* meaning 'a swift craft' or 'hunter'. A whole range of small ships and boats were referred to as yachts, the most well known being the single-masted *staten yacht*, which was equipped with lee boards and originally rigged with a spritsail, staysail and jib. Later the spritsail was replaced by a gaff mainsail. These craft were the prototypes of the modern yacht.

Part of the success and apparent ease with which Tasman made his voyage can be attributed to the well matched sailing qualities of his ships. Neither ships were new nor, at the start of the voyage, in very good condition, but repairs were carried out at Mauritius and subsequently they had very little difficulty keeping company with each other, which speaks well of the sailing qualities of the fluyt.

Seeing that on the 27th instant at night, we have found that some persons, even officers, do not properly stand their ordained watches, the which in many cases might cause hurt and peril to our ships and crews, in order to prevent such inconveniences and perils for the future, the plenary council of the ships Heemskercq and Zeehaen has this day resolved and ordered that whoever shall, after now, be found sleeping or neglecting to keep a proper look-out, shall for the first offence be flogged by the partners of his watch; for the second offence, besides being flogged, he shall forfeit a month's pay; for the third offence he shall be deprived of six month's pay, and for the fourth offence he shall be deprived of his office and forfeit his pay, or if the offender should be a sailor, be forced to serve without pay.

According to the same articles, all persons on board, none excepted, are strictly forbidden to use or carry about their persons any live matches, candle or other lights, of any sort; unless such matches, candles etc. shall be wanted in the discharge of office or for the requirements of the ship's service, and be used with the knowledge of the ship's officers; all this on pain of being put in irons for eight days in succession, and of forfeiting a month's pay over and above this.

Likewise, after the watches have been set, no one shall be permitted to make any noise whatever, but each person shall keep watch over such places as have been assigned to his care by the Commander, the skipper, the steersmen or the quartermasters; all this on pain of summary punishment.

The men on watch shall, whether by day or night, not allow any one to come on board, except with the consent of the commander, the skipper, or the supercargo, on pain of corporal punishment.

Given on board the Heemskercq, at anchor in Latitude 20°15', average Longitude 206° 19', south of the line equinoctial. This 30th day of January, A.D. 1643. (Signed) ABEL JANSZ. TASMAN

BUCCANEERS AND PRIVATEERS

Henry Morgan's attack and pillage of Panama in 1671 awakened the avarice of the bold and lively buccaneers of the Caribbean to the possibilities of easy loot in the Pacific. The 'bretheren' as they were known, were faced with a formidable barrier, for at that time only two suitable means of access to the vulnerable wealth of the Pacific west coast of the Americas were possible; the overland route pioneered and alerted by Morgan and the long haul around Cape Horn or through the Magellan Strait. The amphibious fighting skills of the buccaneers, when well led, were capable of either approach. However, to once again attack Panama by going south about required too many ships and too great a demand on the democratic organisation of the crews, so in 1680 a confederation of buccaneers, including William Dampier, ventured across the Isthmus. Their action marked the inception of a new generation of freebooters who, by inadvertently opening the door to the Pacific a little wider, paved the way for legitimate commerce, expanded science's

concerns and provided some notable literary inspiration.

These 366 freebooters, led by Captains Sawkins, Sharpe, Harris, Coxon and Cooke, descended on the Bay of Panama in a fleet of 35 pirogues. While Bartholomew Sharpe disported himself with a cask of wine and a Spanish lady on Pearl Island, the others in their canoes fell upon the Spanish shipping in the bay. A fierce fight near the island of Perico

ended with the defeat of the Spanish and the capture of three galleons; two they burned and the third, the Spanish Admiral's ship *Most Blessed Trinity*, they kept. With this ship the buccaneers terrorised the coast for a year. Richard Sawkins was killed and the leadership taken over by the religious and ruthless John Watling, under whom they were soundly defeated when they attempted to take the town of Arica.

At the Ile de la Plata, on 16 April 1681, the band split up. Sharpe remained in command of the *Trinity* and 43 disaffected buccaneers, accompanied by William Dampier and John Cooke, set out in canoes to return to the Caribbean.

Sharpe, in the *Trinity*, continued to harass the shipping on the coast with some success. The *San Pedro*, taken shortly after Dampier's departure, held 4000 pieces-of-eight, silver bars and some gold, and they removed several chests of pieces-of-eight, wine and brandy out of the *San Rosario*. Ironically, they let the *San Rosario* go with silver to the value of £210,000 sterling, the equivalent today of several million dollars. They had mistaken the unrefined bars for tin and took one only, to make bullets. The remains of the bar, about one third, was exchanged for the price of a drink in the West Indies and later was sold in Bristol for £75. Sharpe had fallen head over heels for 'the beautifullest creature', a Spanish lady in the *San Rosario* and at her entreaties the smitten captain let the ship go with the fortune in her hold.

The *Trinity*, still under Sharpe's command, was sailed back to the West Indies where the buccaneers split up. Sharpe was later tried for piracy in England but was acquitted, claiming that the *San Rosario* had fired on him first.

The capture of the *Trinity*

William Dampier (1681-6)

Without doubt William Dampier has left us with, the most interesting and informative travel record of his time. His accounts tell us of the marauding tactics of the buccaneers with whom he sailed and marched, extensive detail on plants and, in particular, fruits, also fish and animals, descriptions of towns, peoples and customs, useful meteorological, geographical and navigational information, with suggestions for improving the latter. But in all this and more, rarely does he expound on the ships in which he sailed. Hardly ever does he even mention the vessel's name, merely stating, for instance, 'Our fleet consisted of ten sail: first Captain Davis 36 guns, 156 men, most English, Captain Swan 16 guns, 140 men, all English . . .' and so on. Occasionally hints can be gathered, as when he tells of riding out a typhoon and 'at Eleven a-Clock we furl'd our Mainsail, and ballasted our Mizen'. The latter expression had me scratching my head after envisioning weights hung on the foot of the lateen mizzen, until, reading further, one comes to '. . .we set our Mizen again . . .'. Obviously the mizzen yard had been lowered to the deck to decrease windage and top-weight, standard practice when lying-to or scudding under bare poles.

After Dampier and Captain John Cooke, along with the rest of the estranged members of Captain Sharpe's company, left the *Trinity* at the Isle of Plate in April 1681, they managed, with numerous adventures, to get back into the Caribbean. Dampier spent some time with the English and French buccaneers until April 1683, when he sailed again for the Pacific. His little ship, named the *Revenge* and under the command of Captain Cooke, was small for her task, carrying only eight guns and 70 men in all. However, this was soon put to rights when off Sierra Leone they pirated a Danish ship of 40 guns, renamed her *Batchelor's Delight* and somehow disposed of *Revenge*. Not a hint of this appears in Dampier's account, and no doubt he felt some guilt over the affair, but then he was reticent on many details affecting his friends and their involvement in highly illegal activities.

After rounding the Horn they met up with Captain John Eaton in the *Nicholas* and were informed that another captain, Charles Swan in the *Cygnet*, was on the coast attempting lawful trade. All Captain Swan succeeded in doing was getting shot at and alerting the whole region to a new wave of English marauders. Cooke and Eaton teamed up and planned their cruise but, frustrated by Swan's inopportunism, decided to retire to the Galapagos until the dust settled. In a later raid in Honduras, Cooke died and was succeeded by Captain Edward Davis, a mild illiterate but skilful companion of Sharpe on his earlier voyage. Some fruitless raids on the coast ensued and after a few months of hand-to-mouth subsistence, the *Nicholas* and the *Batchelor's Delight* parted in September 1684.

Meanwhile Captain Swan had utterly failed in his honest endeavours and his disenchanted crew, spurred on by meeting a band of well heeled buccaneers under Captain Peter Harris, elected to 'go on the account' whether Swan liked it or not. In order to retain command of his ship, Swan joined them. A large number of French and English buccaneers were flooding overland to the west coast

Captain Swan's *Cygnet* careening at Mindanao. The cladding, or protective planking, is being stripped off, much to a local worthy's surprise, for he had thought that the teeming shipworm in the river to which he had directed the *Cygnet*'s captain would soon destroy the ship. He had never seen a ship with its hull protected by tar and hair covered with a layer of light plank. A Dutch ship had previously had the bottom eaten out of her in the same river and the local ruler had acquired her guns.

and a united attempt on the Lima fleet, in which the *Cygnet* took part, failed due partly to the withdrawal or mismanagement of the French contingent.

Later Dampier transferred from the *Batchelor's Delight* to the *Cygnet* as he understood Swan was to cruise up the Mexican coast to California and then to the East Indies. This cruise was singularly unsuccessful, for there was no seaborne trade from which to extract prizes. The coast held few ports and provisions were hard to come by because the towns lay a long way inland. They also missed a Manila galleon owing to the necessity for taking time off patrol to supply the ship.

On 19 February 1686 a disastrous raid on Santa Pecaque in Mexico decided them to leave the coast and sail for Guam, short of provisions. The fair trade winds brought them across successfully, although there were murmurings among the crew about eating Swan and the officers. From Guam they sailed to the Philippines. On arrival at Mindanao they were welcomed by the Filipinos and the local ruler, entitled the 'General', invited them to lay up their ships in a river until the rainy season and the chance of typhoons were past. However, Dampier suspected that the General's motives were not exactly altruistic:

About the middle of *November* we began to work on our Ship's Bottom, which we found to be very much eaten with the Worm: For this is a horrid place for Worms. We did not know this till after we had been in the River a Month; and then we found our Canoas Bottoms eaten like Honeycombe; our Bark, which was a single Bottom, was eaten thro'; so that she could not swim. But our Ship was sheathed, and the Worm came no further than the Hair between the sheathing Plank, and the main Plank. We did not mistrust the General's Knavery 'till now: for when he came down to our Ship, and found us ripping off the sheathing Plank, and saw the firm Bottom underneath, he shook his Head, and seemed to be discontented; saying, he never did see a Ship with two Bottoms before. We were told that in this place, where we now lay, a *Dutch Ship* was eaten up in 2 Months time, and the General had her Guns; and it is probable he did expect to have had ours: Which I do believe was the main Reason that made him so forward in assisting us to get our Ship into the River, for when we came out again we had no Assistance from him.

At an island off Mindanao they put in to careen and took advantage of the tall timber growing there.

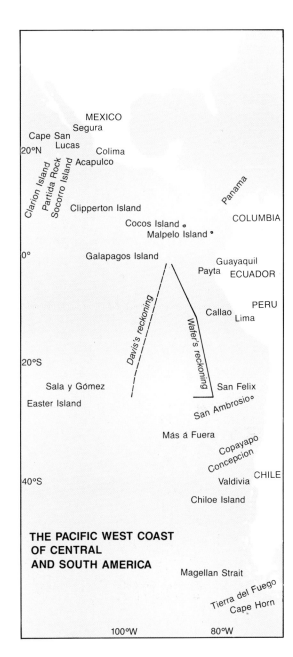

...here they made a new Boltsprit, which we did not set here also, our old one being very faulty. They made a new Fore-yard too, and a Fore-top-mast: And our Pumps being faulty, and not serviceable, they did cut a Tree to make a Pump. They first squared it, then sawed it in the middle, and then hollowed out each side exactly. The two hollow sides were made big enough to contain a Pump-box in the midst of them both, when they were joined together; and it required their utmost skill to close them exactly to the making a tight Cylinder for the Pump-box' being unaccustomed to such Work. We learnt this way of Pump-making from the *Spaniards;* who make their Pumps that they use in their Ships in the *South-Seas* after this manner; I am confident that there are no better Hand-pumps in the World than they have.

There is no doubt that their ability to use natural resources, their skills and ingenuity, were essential elements in the enterprises these people undertook. Provided the hull of the ship maintained its integrity, there seemed little they could not repair or replace, given the materials.

In the Philippines, Captain Swan appeared to go to pieces and was left ashore with other crew. The *Cygnet* sailed off under the command of Captain Reed, Dampier still aboard. They hoped to capture some prizes among the islands and off the China coast, but were disappointed. Weary and homesick, they made for the Indian Ocean, keeping south to avoid the Dutch and the English. It was this part

of the voyage that first brought Dampier to northern Australia.

Davis land

After Dampier left the *Batchelor's Delight* in 1685, Captain Edward Davis continued to cruise off the coast with mixed success until 1687, when he determined to wind up and sail for the Atlantic. Either on a passage to Cape Horn or to Juan Fernandez (their destination uncertain), they sighted land. Dampier writes of what Davis later told him:

...he went, after several Traverses, to the *Gallapagoes*, and that standing thence Southward for Wind, to bring him about Terra del Fuego, in the Lat. of 27°South, about 500 Leagues from Copayapo, on the Coast of *Chili*, he saw a small sandy Island just by him; and that they saw to the Westward of it a long Tract of pretty high Land, tending away to the North West out of sight. This might probably be the Coast of *Terra Australis Incognita.* [The last sentence is Dampier's.]

Possibly Davis's longitude was in error, for there is no land of that description in that position, although there are islands that might answer, both inshore and further out in approximately the same latitude. However, the later search for 'Davis Land' did lead to the discovery of Easter Island by Roggeveen 35 years afterwards. You will have noticed that in Dampier's report of what Davis said, they were standing southward for a wind to bring them about Tierra del Fuego. This makes sense, as by standing in for the coast to round the Horn, they would be battling headwinds and currents. A southerly course would indeed take them 1500 miles off, and near Easter Island.

There is a puzzle, however. Lionel Wafer, the surgeon on *Batchelor's Delight*, tells a slightly different story. He said that they were bound from the

Galapagos to Juan Fernandez, and from a position about 150 leagues off the coast in 12°S, they steered S by E ½ E, until in 27°S they saw 'a small, low, sandy island and heard a great noise like that of the sea beating upon the shore right ahead of the ship'. The next day they saw, far away, 'a range of high land, which we took to be islands'. Now S by E ½ E is about 167°–true. Lay that off from Wafer's point of departure and you will not go near Easter Island; nor will you approach anywhere like 1500 miles offshore, but you will be roughly on course for the Fernandez Group, and you will pass near two small islands, San Felix and San Ambrosio, about 500 miles offshore.

Davis's story is secondhand but, given that he was heading for the Horn, rings true. Wafer's story also makes sense *if* they were heading for Juan Fernandez and *if* he got his distance offshore wrong. His account is first hand, but he was not the captain. Which is correct? Whatever was seen, the reports of Davis's sighting gave weight to the proponents of a 'Great South Land' until that chimera was finally laid to rest by Wallis, Cook and Bougainville.

Spanish vessels on the Pacific west coast

The prey of the buccaneers in the South Seas was the Spanish coastal shipping which consisted of a wide variety of craft from canoes to galleons. Most of the ships were built on the American west coast, a practice started with the first Spanish settlements, and the type of craft followed the style of the period, although there were some specialised craft such as the indigenous *balsas* and vessels designed to commute up and down the coast.

An interesting craft, the *balsa* was a very large sailing raft which handled remarkably well, being controlled by a battery of *guaras* or centreboards which could be arranged in a variety of positions,

so she could be trimmed to maintain almost any heading relative to the wind. These craft were sailing on the coast before the Spanish arrived.

The main trade was from Panama south; trade to Mexico was scant and at periods was banned completely as it interfered and competed with trade from Spain. South of Panama the winds, mainly light southerlies, meant a long tedious beat down the coast against the prevailing current. The 1200 miles between Panama and Callao could take two-and-a-half months tacking offshore at night and inshore during the day. The ships employed to regularly make this run were built low and carried a rig enabling them to make to windward well. In the early days this was probably a combination of lateen and square-sail, and a lot of it. These vessels, to reduce windage, lacked the high superstructures of many other ships of the time. They must have been specialist craft, like the scow is to North America and New Zealand, and the Thames barge is to southeast England.

Along with the local balsas, and probably outnumbering them, was a host of craft ranging from galleys to galleons. Trying to puzzle out what these country craft of the Spanish Pacific coast were like is not easy. While lurking near Panama, the *Bacthelor's Delight* was nearly destroyed by a fireship and the incident resulted in this comment by Dampier:

The Spaniards of Panama could not have fitted out their Fire-ship without this Capt. Bond's assistance; for it is strange to say how grosly ignorant the *Spaniards* in the *West-Indies*, but especially in the *South-Seas*, are of Sea-Affairs. They build indeed good Ships, but this is a small Matter: For any Ship of a good bottom will serve for these Seas on the South Coast. They rig their Ships but untowardly, have no Guns, but in 3 or 4 of the King's Ships, and are meanly furnished with War-like Provisions, and much at loss for making any Fireships or other less useful Machines. Nay, they have not the sense to have their Guns run within the sides upon their

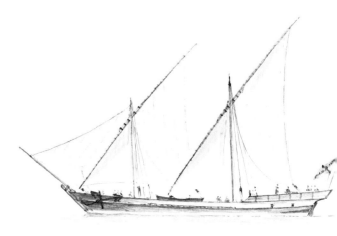

In the late sixteenth and seventeenth century the coasting craft which had to ply regularly between Panama and Peru may have appeared very like an Arabian craft. The Spanish ships and seamen acquired much of the traditions and technology of the Moors and may well have applied it to their craft in the Pacific, where their windward performance would be to advantage. These special ships were reported as having a low freeboard, no superstructure and having their maximum beam well forward. Unfortunately there seems to be no record of their rig. I have included a jib which would have been set flying and was common among smaller European craft.

discharge, but have Platforms without for the Men to stand on to charge them; so that when we come near we can fetch them down with small shot out of our Boats. A main reason of this is, that the Native *Spaniards* are too proud to be Seamen, but use the *Indians* for all those Offices: One Spaniard, it may be, going in the Ship to command it, and himself of little more knowledge than those poor ignorant Creatures: nor can they gain much Experience, seldom going far off to Sea, but coasting along the shores.

The rigs seem to have been large and light, and little attempt was made to follow the solid and tried rigging practices of Northern Europe.

The Natives of Old *Spain* are accounted but ordinary Mariners, but here they are much worse; all the Prizes we took being rather cobled than fitted out for the Sea: So that had they such Weather as we often meet with in the *European Seas* in Winter, they could scarce ever reach a Port again, as they are fitted, but they sail here hundreds of Leagues.

One can imagine the rig that Captain Woodes Rogers is describing here. Probably it was very like in technique, if not in plan, the rig one might find on an average dhow. (My apologies to any Arab seamen who may read this; your rigs are, or were, shaky due to lack of resources, not sloth.) Running and standing rigging would have been hitched, bent and spliced any old how, the standing rigging untarred and badly set up at that; the sails would have been light, fair-weather stuff. These rigs brought forth derisive comments from the salty European seamen over the whole period, but it should be remembered that the ships served their purpose. If the coast was as stormy and dangerous as northern Europe's, then they would have built their craft to suit. The difficulties arose when these ships were used for purposes other than that for which they were prepared. Many of the early Spanish navigators complained that they handled badly under little sail and opened their seams when close-hauled on a bowline in moderate weather.

In Europe by the mid seventeenth century very seaworthy ships were being built and every detail of hull and rig had a solid and established method of construction and assembly. Standing rigging was laid up differently from running rigging, each splice and collar was wormed, parcelled, served and tarred and some entire shrouds treated likewise. Every type of seizing, knot and splice had its purpose, and the complete rig had become a marvellously strong and powerful machine, fit to stand the worst wind and sea could do. European ships used flax canvas and bent on new when expecting the worst, such as during winter in the North Atlantic, the Horn or the seas around Japan. A European ship could be recognised easily in the South Seas by her compact rig and dull ochre and grey, often patched, sails.

The hulls of the west coast ships would be built to the usual Spanish practice, but less strongly. The native woods generally lasted well but as already mentioned, the ships worked badly. Quiros says of the *San Jeronimo* that she was only kept afloat by the timber from which she was constructed. This was rot-resistant hardwood from Guayaquil, called *guatchapeli*. Gallego in Mendana's *Los Reyes* said she was good in smooth waters but with a little sea 'would pitch everybody overboard; and for these seas and gulfs she was fit only to drown us all'. Underballasting seems to have been another fault common to these ships. Drake narrowly escaped some Spanish warships which could easily match him in speed but, being underballasted, they had to give up the chase as they could not carry sail when the wind got up.

The larger ships were mostly built in the style of galleons. Woodes Rogers describes one of his prizes: '…she was call'd the *Ascension*, built Galeon-fashion, very high with Galleries, burden between 4 and 500 Tun.' Dampier says of Sharpe's *Trinity*: '[they cut off her tall] Round House Coach and all the high carved woodwork belonging to the stern of the ship…when we took her from the Spaniards she was as high as any Third Rate Ship in England.'

The Plate galleons would have been the largest on the coast, the equivalent to, but generally smaller and less sturdy than, the Manila galleons.

Dampier's second voyage to the Pacific (1703-6)

After he returned to England and published the account of his voyage around the world, Dampier, who was no more than a buccaneer and able seaman, was given command by the Admiralty of the *Roebuck*, in which he was to make an exploratory voyage to New Holland. Dampier sailed in 1699, but his ability to command did not measure up to his skill as a writer and he had chronic problems with his crew due to his irresolute and excitable temperament. On the return voyage from the Australian coast, where little was accomplished, the *Roebuck* sank of Ascension Island. Dampier and his crew survived to return to England in 1700.

Accounts of his voyages continued to win Dampier acclaim and as Britain was then at war with Spain and France, he managed to get backing for a privateering venture into the South Seas. In 1703 he left Kinsale, Ireland, with two ships, the *St George*, 26 guns and 120 men, and the *Cinque Ports*, a 90-ton 'galley' mounting 16 guns with a crew of 63, commanded by Captain Charles Pickering. The initial aim of the enterprise was to waylay a fleet

A Plate ship (early to mid seventeenth century)

of galleons which was due to leave Buenos Aires. These they missed, so they wandered on in the general direction of Cape Horn, with Dampier uncertain what to do.

The two ships became separated near the Falklands, but came up with each other again at Juan Fernandez. While refreshing themselves there, a ship was sighted and they enthusiastically put to sea in chase. She turned out to be a well-armed French vessel which fought them off. Dampier, indecisive as ever, did not return to the attack and set off back to the island where they had left five men, all of the *Cinque Port*'s spare sails, spare anchors and a quantity of stores. They found the island blockaded by two 36-gun French ships, whereupon Dampier appeared to have lost his nerve. Instead of making some effort to recover their men and equipment, he persuaded Thomas Stradling, who had taken over command on Pickering's death, to abandon any attempt and sail for the Peruvian coast.

On that coast, apart from a couple of prizes, little was achieved. A raid on Santa Maria was beaten off and the crews became progressively more disaffected with Stradling's leadership. After taking a prize laden with stores which included 32 tons of marmalade and a good supply of brandy – a godsend, as by this time the freebooters were starving – they put into an island in the Bay of Panama. Here Stradling and Dampier quarrelled violently and the ships and crews split up. Stradling sailed to Juan Fernandez where Alexander Selkirk, the master, opted to leave the ships and take his chances on the island. He detested Stradling and was not prepared to risk his life any further in the unseaworthy *Cinque Ports*. He was right, for not long after the *Cinque Ports* went down off the South American coast and only Stradling and seven seamen survived, to be captured by the Spanish.

In the *St George* Dampier lurked off the Central American coast, capturing some small prizes as the ship gradually fell apart around them. Dampier's mate, Clipperton, had had enough and, with 21 seamen, deserted in one of the small prizes, leaving Dampier to set out on a cruise for the Manila galleons with his sick ship and depleted crew. Off Colima they raised one of the galleons, but instead of pressing home an attack swiftly, before the galleon's guns could be got out of her hold, they stood off and argued over tactics. When Dampier did finally run in for the attack, he nearly got the rotten old *St George* blown out of the water by the Spaniard's 24-pounders. The disgusted and infuriated crew demanded to go home, but Dampier persuaded them to hang on for a further six weeks.

On 6 January 1705 William Funnell, the mate, threw in his hand and compelled Dampier to let him take over a small 70-ton barque they had captured. Leaving Dampier on 1 February, Funnell, with 35 men, few provisions and no boats, sailed his small, worm-eaten, two-masted ship 8000 miles to the Dutch East Indies where they were cruelly mistreated by the Dutch. Funnell got back to England in 1706.

Meanwhile Dampier did his best to keep the *St George* afloat. The shot holes inflicted in her encounter with the Manila galleon had to be filled with a compound of charcoal and tallow, for her timber was so decayed nails could not be used, and the rig was worn out. However, sullen and dispirited as the crew was, they continued on the coast. They took a small ship, into which they transferred and sailed to the Indies where the vessel was confiscated by the Dutch. Dampier got back to England broke – but still able to write a good account of his voyage. His reputation as a commander was shattered, but nobody questioned his ability as a sailor and he was admired for his enterprise. He was presented to the Queen, to whom he gave his account first hand, but his financial difficulties were not improved and he looked for further employment where his seafaring abilities could be put to good use.

Woodes Rogers (1708-9)

In the latter part of 1708 two small Bristol privateers were ploughing southward down the Atlantic bound for Cape Horn and the Pacific under the command of a Bristol entrepreneur, Captain Woodes Rogers. This young commander was to lead one of the most successful raids by the British on the long-suffering Spanish in the South Seas. It was a voyage even more remarkable for its minimal loss of life and the humanity shown to the Spanish victims.

The two ships, named *Duke* and *Dutchess*, were small vessels, probably similar to a sixth-rate frigate, having no gundeck but a quarterdeck and fo'c's'le. The *Duke* was the largest, being about 320 tons and 30 guns, the *Dutchess* was about 260 tons and 26 guns. The largest of this armament were only 6-pounders, very light for ship-to-ship engagements with well armed opposition.

On board was a carefully selected and large complement of officers, including the ageing William Dampier, who was engaged as pilot for the Pacific. The people were not so talented.

Our Complement of Sailors in both Ships was 333, of which above one Third were of Foreigners from most Nations; several of her Majesty's Subjects on board were Tinkers, Taylors, Haymakers, Pedlers, Fidlers, etc. one Negro, and about ten Boys. With this mix'd gang we hop'd to be well mann'd, as soon as they had learnt the Use of Arms, and got their Sea-Legs, which we doubted not soon to teach 'em, and bring them to Discipline.

I estimate the length on deck of the *Duke* to be roughly 105 ft (32 m), with a beam of about 31 ft (9.5 m), and the *Dutchess* about 95 ft (29 m) and 29 ft (8.8 m) respectively. The total complement for the *Duke* was 183 and for the *Dutchess* 151, and this, together with the enormous quantity of stores necessary for such an extended voyage, must have made the ships extremely uncomfortable.

Their passage down the Atlantic was marked only by a near mutiny, quickly quashed, and the capture of a small prize off the Canaries. Stops for refreshment were made at St Vincent in the Cape Verdes and at Grande in Brazil. The New Year they celebrated south of Cape Horn with bumpers of punch for all hands, dished out from the quarterdeck. On south they went, driven by hard gales to 61½ °S. The *Dutchess* was badly pooped, her stern windows stove, and the officers nearly drowned in their quarters. Scurvy began to afflict the crews and the first death was on 7 January 1709. By the end of January, when they were approaching Juan Fernandez, two men on the *Duke* and five on the *Dutchess* had died.

Boats sent on 31 January to Cumberland Bay to reconnoitre returned '. . .with a Man cloth'd in Goat Skins, who looked wilder than the first Owners of them'. This was Alexander Selkirk, left by Captain Stradling of the *Cinque Ports* four years and four months before. Dampier, having sailed with Stradling on that voyage, remembered Selkirk and recommended him to Rogers, who promptly made him mate on the *Duke* and later master of the biggest prize. (Daniel Defoe, on reading of Dampier's voyages, later used Alexander Selkirk as his model for *Robinson Crusoe*.)

After wooding, watering and repairing the ships and recovering the crews, they set sail for Juan Fernandez on 14 February. By then the ill-disciplined and inexperienced men were tuned up and hardened to the tasks ahead of them. Gambling and swearing were forbidden and strict discipline imposed on the crews.

In the subsequent cruise up the coast several prizes were netted; one, a French-built ship named the *Havre de Grace* and almost as large as the *Dutchess*, was added to the squadron and renamed the *Marquiss*. In capturing this ship, Woodes Rogers's brother was killed. A successful attack on Guayaquil was undertaken, after which the ships made for the Galapagos with some very sick men. The looting of graves at Guayaquil had infected those who had been ashore, and by the middle of June, 15 had died and 70 were unfit for work.

Alexander Selkirk comes out to the *Duke*

In the Galapagos the third mate of the *Dutchess*, Simon Hately, in command of a captured bark, became separated from the rest and after some hardships landed on the coast near the equator where worse trials were endured in the hands of the Spanish. Hately was finally freed, but the harsh treatment had probably ruined his mental balance and we run across him again under another captain.

From the Galapagos the ships sailed to Gorgona and then on to Cape San Lucas to cruise for the Manila galleons. On 1 November the *Duke*, *Dutchess*, *Marquiss* and a small prize, the *Jesus, Maria y Jose*, sighted the Cape and took up their stations. The *Duke* patrolled 60 miles offshore, the *Marquiss*, which was having some difficulty keeping the sea, inshore, with the *Dutchess* in between. The *Jesus, Maria y Jose* was to act as a despatch vessel. By 14 December hopes were beginning to fade along with the privateers' provisions. The *Marquiss* was sent into Port Segura to refit while the rest were to remain on patrol for another eight days.

The allotted time slipped away and the horizon remained empty. At a meeting on the *Dutchess* it was decided that, in order to make Guam with their depleted supplies, the patrol should end. The ships began to work their way inshore to prepare for the voyage. Next day, while making for the port, a sail was seen far away in the west. At first it was thought to be the *Marquiss*. Calms prevented them from coming up with the strange vessel, but by evening she was positively identified as a Manila galleon. The pinnaces dogged her all night while the *Duke* and *Dutchess* prepared for action. Before eight in the morning those in the *Duke* were disturbed at prayer by the 'chase' opening fire, and by eight the *Duke* was fully engaged.

For three hours the two ships thundered away at each other until the superior rate of fire of the *Duke* obliged her opponent to strike. At this moment the *Dutchess*, which had been struggling to make to windward in light airs so as to join the fray, managed to get within range and opened fire, which

was unanswered. On the *Duke* only two men were wounded, one of whom was Rogers.

I was shot thro' the Left Cheek, the Bullet struck away great part of my upper Jaw, and several of my Teeth, part of which dropt down upon the Deck, where I fell . . . I was forced to write what I would say, to prevent Loss of Blood, and because of the Pain I suffered by speaking.

The prize was the *Nostra Senora de la Incarnacion Disenganio*, a frigate-built ship, about 450 tons, carrying 20 guns and 20 *patereroes* or swivel guns. On board were 193 men, of whom 9 were killed, 10 wounded and a number badly burned. She was a very rich prize, but clearly not the usual class of Manila galleon. By questioning the prisoners it was discovered that another ship – new, tall and lofty, of 900 tons burden, had sailed with them, but they had been parted three months prior to capture. As this ship was a better sailer, they judged she would have already made Acapulco. This was good news and it was resolved to lay in wait for her for eight days, leaving the *Duke* in port, much against the wounded Rogers' wishes and judgment. He was of the opinion that this galleon, the *Begona* would be a tough opponent, particularly as it was learned that 150 of her crew were English or Irish, one-time pirates with all their wealth on board.

Rogers considered that a united assault and immediate boarding, while the *Begona* was unprepared, stood the best chance of success. Within hours of the *Dutchess* and *Marquiss* arriving on station, on Christmas afternoon, watchers from ashore sighted a third ship. Rogers immediately secured his prisoners on the *Jesus, Maria y Jose* and weighed, wounds notwithstanding. That Christmas night the *Dutchess* kept up an intermittent running engagement with the chase. The next morning the *Marquiss* also went into action while the *Duke* battled the light headwind

to come up. It was midnight before she gained the company of the other ships.

The *Dutchess* had her foremast disabled and the ring of an anchor shot away, and the *Marquiss* had nearly expended all her powder and shot. The rest of the night was spent replenishing the *Marquiss* and planning their next assault and the remaining hours of the engagement are described by Woodes Rogers:

In the morning as soon as 'twas Day, the Wind veering at once, put our Ship about, and the Chase fired first upon the *Dutchess*, who by means of the Wind's veering was nearest the Enemy; she return'd it smartly: we stood as near as possible, firing as our Guns came to bear; but the *Dutchess* being by this time thwart the *Spaniards* Hawse, and firing very fast, those Shot that miss'd the Enemy flew from the *Dutchess* over us, and betwixt our Masts, so that we ran the risque of receiving more Damage from them than from the Enemy, if we had lain on her Quarters and cross her Stern, as I design'd, while the Enemy lay driving. This forced us to lie along side, close aboard her, where we kept firing round Shot, and did not load with any Bar or Partridge, because the Ship's Sides were too thick to receive any Damage by it, and no Men appearing in sight, it would only have been a Clog to the Force of our Round Shot. We kept close aboard her, and drove as she did as near as possible. The Enemy kept to their close Quarters, so that we did not fire our Small Arms till we saw a Man appear, or a Port open; then we fired as quick as possible. Thus we continued for 4 Glasses, about which time we received a Shot in the Main Mast, which much disabled it; soon after that the *Dutchess* and we firing together, we came both close under the Enemy and had like to have been all aboard her, so that we could make little use of our Guns. Then we fell a-stern in our Birth along side, where the Enemy threw a Fire-ball out of one of her Tops, which lighting upon our Quarter-deck, blew up a Chest of Arms and Cartouch Boxes[1] all loaded, and several Cartridges of Powder in the Steerage by which means Mr. *Vanbrugh*, our Agent, and a Dutchman, were very much burnt; it might have done more Damage, had it not been quench'd as soon as possible. After we got clear of each other, the

Dutchess stood in for the Shore where she lay braced to, mending her Rigging, ec. The *Marquiss* fired several Shot, but to little purpose, her Guns being small. We were close aboard several times afterwards, till at last we receiv'd a second Shot in the Main Mast not far from the other, which rent it miserably, and the Mast settl'd to it, so that we were afraid it would drop by the board, and having our Rigging shatter'd very much, we sheer'd off, and brought to, making a Signal to our Consorts to consult what to do; in the interim we got ordinary Fishes[2] for a port[3] to the Main mast, and fasten'd it as well as we could to secure it at present. Capt. *Courtney* and Capt. *Cooke* came aboard with other Officers, where we consider'd the Condition the 3 Ships were in, their Masts and Rigging being much damnified in a Place where we could get no Recruit, that if we engag'd her again, we could propose to do no more than what we had already done, which was evident did her no great Hurt, because we could perceive few of our Shot enter'd her Sides to any purpose, and our Small Arms avail'd less, there being not a Man to be seen above-board; that the least thing in the World would bring our Main-mast, and likewise the *Dutchess* Fore-mast by the board, either of which by its Fall might carry away another Mast, and then we should lie a Battery for the Enemy, having nothing to command our Ships with, so that by his heavy Guns he might either sink or take us: That if we went to board her, we should run a greater hazard in losing a great many Men with little Hopes of Success, they having above treble the Number aboard to oppose us, and there being now in all our 3 Ships not above 120 good Men fit for boarding, and those but weak, having been very short of Provisions a long time; besides we had the Disadvantage of a Netting-deck[4] to enter upon, and a Ship every other way well provided; so that if we had boarded her, and been forc'd off, or left any of our Men behind, the Enemy by that means might have known our Strength, and then gone into the Harbour and took possession of the Prize in spight of all we could do to prevent it: Besides, our Ammunition was very short, having only enough to engage a few Glasses longer. All this being seriously consider'd, and knowing the Difficulty we should have to get Masts, and the Time and Provisions we must spend before we could get 'em fitted, 'twas resolved to forbear attempting her further, since our battering her signify'd little, and we had not Strength enough to board her:

Therefore we agreed to keep her company till Night, then to lose her, and make the best of our way into the Harbour to secure the Prize we had already took. We engag'd first and last about six or seven Hours, during all which time we had aboard the *Duke* but eleven Men wounded, 3 of whom were scorch'd with Gun-powder. I was again unfortunately wounded in the Left Foot with a Splinter just before we blew up on the Quarter-deck, so that I could not stand, but lay on my Back in a great deal of Misery, part of my Heel-bone being struck out, and all under my Ankle cut above half thro', which bled very much, and weaken'd me, before it could be dressed and stopt. The *Dutchess* had about 20 Men killed and wounded, 3 of the latter and one of the former were my Men. The *Marquiss* had none kill'd or wounded, but 2 scorch'd with Powder. The Enemy's was a brave lofty new Ship, the Admiral of *Manila,* and this the first Voyage she had made; she was call'd the *Bigonia,* of about 900 Tuns, and could carry 60 Guns, about 40 of which were mounted, with as many Patereroes, all Brass; her Complement of Men on board, as we were inform'd, was above 450, besides Passengers. They added, that 150 of the Men on board this great Ship were *Europeans,* several of whom had been formerly Pirates, and having now got all their Wealth aboard, were resolved to defend it to the last. The Gunner, who had a good Post in *Manila,* was an expert Man, and had provided the Ship extraordinary well for Defence which made them fight so desperately; they had filled up all between the Guns with Bales to secure the Men. She kept a *Spanish* Flag at her Main-top mast Head all the time she fought us; we shatter'd her Sails and Rigging very much, shot her Mizon-yard, kill'd two Men out of her Tops, which was all the Damage we could see we did 'em; tho' we could not place less than 500 Shot (6 Pounders) in her Hull. These large Ships are built at *Manila* with excellent Timber, that will not splinter; they have very thick sides, much stronger than we build in *Europe.*

---

1. Boxes containing cartridges for muskets.
2. Two long pieces of hard wood, convex on one side and concave on the other, bound opposite to each other to strengthen the masts.
3. Evidently a misprint for support.
4. A netting extending fore and aft to prevent an enemy from boarding.

Woodes Rogers subsequently sailed the *Duke, Dutchess* and *Disenganio* (renamed *Batchelor*) back to England via Guam, the East Indies, round the Cape of Good Hope to Holland and finally, after some disputes with the Dutch East India Company, back to England.

Note: The names of the ships *Dutchess, Bigonia* and *Marquiss* are as written in Woodes Rogers's journal. The correct Spanish name for the Manila galleon is *Begona.*

Clipperton and Shelvocke (1718-22)

In the year 1718 a company calling itself 'The Gentlemen Adventurers' fitted out two ships to cruise in the South Seas. In overall command and captain of the 24-gun *Speedwell* was Captain George Shelvocke, lately of the Royal Navy, and in command of the other ship the *Success* (36 guns), was Captain John Clipperton, the same man who had left Dampier in the Pacific in 1704.

A three-month wait for a fair wind preceded their departure from Plymouth, during which time overall command was taken from Shelvocke and given to Clipperton. That got the enterprise off on the wrong foot from the start. For the men of the *Success,* worse was to come, for not long after they set sail on 13 February 1719 the ships became separated in a gale. In itself this was a serious setback, but for those in the *Success* it was infinitely worse – for the *Speedwell* had in her hold the entire stock of liquor for the two ships. Although he suspected Shelvocke had deliberately made off on his own account, Clipperton dutifully made the rendezvous at the Canaries, the Cape Verdes and Juan Fernandez without coming up the *Speedwell.* His crew, sick and starving, blamed their infirmities on their enforced abstinence and cursed Shelvocke.

Woodes Rogers in the *Duke* (30 guns) and *Dutchess* (26 guns) attacking the Manila galleon *Begona*, off Cape San Lucas, lower California, in 1709. Having previously captured the smaller galleon, the *Nostra Senora de la Incarnacion Disenganio,* the privateers had learneed of the approach of the 600-ton *Begona*. They kept up their patrol and were rewarded within a few days when the galleon was sighted. A two-day running battle ensued, but Woodes Rogers' little ships could make little impression with their six-pounders on the Philippine-built ship.

The *Begona*'s crew, strengthened by dozens of pirates taking their passage to Mexico with their spoils, fortified the ship with barricades and spread boarding nets. Gunports were only opened to fire. Although it is not referred to in the accompanying account written by Woodes Rogers, it was common practice for the Manila galleons to hoist fused barrels of gunpowder to the bowsprit and yardarms. I believe the intention was to lower them to the rail, light the fuse and swing them into any ship attempting to board. One would have thought the practice highly dangerous to both ships; it certainly inspired caution among the attackers. It was said that the reason the Spanish fought so well here was that one of their pirate passengers was sitting in the magazine with a lighted match, threatening to blow them to Kingdom Come if they surrendered.

The privateers eventually gave up the attack. Woodes Rogers, who had had a ball shot through his jaw while engaged with the *Incarnacion*, was wounded again when his ankle was shot away. In spite of this, he continued to command his ships, lying on the deck and giving orders in writing. Both the *Duke* and *Dutchess* suffered a great deal of damage to their masts and rigging. The ship astern of the *Begona* is the *Havre de Grace*, a prize taken by the privateers, armed and re-named *Marquiss*.

After leaving a message at Juan Fernandez, the *Success* descended on the Spanish coast with results that lived up to her name. So many prizes were taken that Clipperton overreached himself; he had already lost 30 men through sickness and manning the prizes thinned out his strength still further. Finally he lost a 200-ton London-built pink, to which he sent a weak prize crew who were attacked by the passengers hidden below. Clipperton stripped his other prizes of everything and sailed to the Galapagos to careen and water. From the Galapagos he cruised northwards to the Mexican coast and again had some success, marred by interference by Spanish warships from which he had to run. Clipperton and his crew became disheartened and the captain, always fond of a spot, took to the bottle in earnest.

Off the coast of Mexico he gave chase and came up with an English pinnace and a Spanish ship named the *Jesu Maria*. In command was none other than Shelvocke who had lost the *Speedwell* at Juan Fernandez and had only 40 men left. After Clipperton had supplied Shelvocke and his crew with some essentials, they separated, but were to meet again several times. On the last occasion they agreed to a joint attack on a Manila galleon. However, they delayed too long and lost their opportunity. Clipperton then deserted Shelvocke and sailed west.

Nearly two months later the *Success* arrived at Guam. Clipperton, aware that England and Spain were no longer at war, requested provisions and arranged the ransom of a captured Spanish marquis. To a five-gun salute the marquis was sent ashore in company of the agent and two officers. The Governor promptly took the two officers hostage and made demands which included a supply of powder and shot. Clipperton in turn demanded the release of his men, the marquis's ransom and more provisions, and threatened to destroy the town and sink the shipping in port if he was not satisfied. The Spanish, having built a battery on the approaches,

refused, whereupon Clipperton got very drunk, weighed and stood in and finally took up a position between an armed ship and the battery overhead at point-blank range.

At 9 o'clock in the evening Clipperton, drunk and incapable of command, ran the *Success* ashore under the battery. Lt. Cooke, one of his officers, took charge. Already one anchor had been lost and the next afternoon, at 4 o'clock, they managed to lay out a kedge. The cable parted and, having no remaining anchor, they used a lower-deck gun and an old hawser. At five the next morning they got out another gun, with a topmast stay as a cable. By 11 o'clock they had laid out ahead of the ship two more guns attached to the remains of their best bower cable, and, as she was fast aft, shifted their upper- and lower-deck guns and cargo forward and trimmed her by the head. At last, at 6 o'clock that evening, they got her off, but lost the yawl. Up to that time, remarkably, only one man was wounded, but as the pinnace towed the ship clear, a last effort from the Spanish battery brought the total casualties in the action to two killed and six wounded.

All that time – 50 hours – they had been under fire from the fort, unable to elevate their guns sufficiently to answer effectively. They had lost all their anchors and cables, four lower-deck guns and had used 19 barrels of gunpowder. The *Success*'s rigging was shot to pieces and her hull was peppered with shot.

Clipperton got his ship, crazy as she was, to China, where subsequently the crew split up and the ship was condemned. In 1722, a week after arriving back in Ireland to his wife and family, Clipperton died. The owners received only £1840, for the ship carrying their share of the money from China was burned in Brazil. If you look at a chart of the Pacific, 660 miles SSW of Cape Corrientes on the Mexican coast lies a tiny atoll, Clipperton Island – a lonely memorial to the resourceful but thirsty sailor.

Shelvocke's cruise

On the passage to Juan Fernandez, Shelvocke had problems with his crew and the elements. During one of the protracted spells of foul weather after they had traversed the Straits, the *Speedwell* was driven as far as 61°S and it was in this region that Simon Hately, the mate, shot a black albatross which had been following them for days. Samuel Coleridge, reading Shelvocke's account of the morose mate's deed, was inspired to write his *Rime of the Ancient Mariner*.

On the coast at Concepcion the *Speedwell* took several prizes, among them a small barque they named *Mercury* in which Simon Hately later deserted to be subsequently taken again by the Spanish. On the way from Concepcion to Juan Fernandez the plunder was sold 'on account' to the men. It appeared that Shelvocke was losing control and the enterprise was taking on aspects of a straight-out piracy. A further foray to the coast captured Payta and they were nearly blown out of the water by a Spanish warship. Their activities on the coast caused the Spanish to stop all sailing for six months so Shelvocke returned to Juan Fernandez. While the *Speedwell* was at anchor, a gale drove her ashore where she became almost a total loss; the inertia of the demoralised men lost them anything that might have been salvaged. Under the custom of the time, a captain no longer had command once his ship was lost, a flaw in English law that was to trouble many shipwrecked captains, including Captain Cheap of Anson's *Wager*.

The only way to get off the island – where at any moment a Spanish warship might arrive – was to build a boat. After much prevaricating and bickering, work was started under the resourceful charge of the armourer, whose entire supply of steel consisted of five Spanish swords. Within two months a small boat was completed and reasonable progress was made on the larger (a barque) while the crew continued to squabble and split into cliques. They compelled Shelvocke to agree to the 'Jamaica discipline', the agreement traditionally arranged between buccaneers.

On 9 September 1720 the barque was launched – and sank. The rough planking, probably split logs, was caulked and she was relaunched and named *Recovery*. Twenty-four men voted to remain on the island while Shelvocke with 40 men embarked in the *Recovery*.

On October 6 we left Juan Fernandez Island, forty of us crowded into a small boat, lying on top of the bundles of conger-eels, with no means of keeping ourselves clean, so that all our senses were as greatly offended as possible. The only means we had of getting water was by sucking it from the cask, through a gun-barrel. The unsavoury morsels of conger-eel that we daily ate, created incessant quarrels amongst us, as every one was contending for the frying pan, and our only convenience of fire was a tub half filled with dirt, which made our cooking so tedious that we had the continuous noise of frying, from morning until night.

The pumps which they had managed to salvage from the *Speedwell* were kept busy, for the *Recovery* had a freeboard of only 16 in. (40 cm), an open deck, and she leaked atrociously.

On 10 October they came up with a large ship and took it on, armed only with a few muskets, three cutlasses and a small cannon with no carriage, for which they had 'only two shots, a few chain bolts, a clapper from the *Speedwell*'s main bell, and some stones . . .'. Not surprisingly, they were beaten off, despite some desperate and determined attacks – particularly as the prey was an ex-French privateer carrying 40 guns.

Shelvocke finally captured the *Jesu Maria* in Pisco Roads. She was a well known ship and this fact was used to good effect, for they sailed in and took Payta unawares. They cruised on until on 25 January they sighted a sail which turned out to be Clipperton's pinnace.

After Clipperton deserted Shelvocke and sailed for Guam, the *Jesu Maria* continued on the coast and managed on separate occasions to take two ships which had been especially fitted out to capture Shelvocke. One of these, the 300-ton *Sacra Familia*, he exchanged for the *Jesu Maria* and as he had learned that his country and Spain were no longer at war, he resolved to surrender to the Spanish at Panama. All their efforts to give themselves up failed in a hail of gunfire and curses from the Spanish – resulting in the capture of another prize, the second ship that had set out to take Shelvocke!

With the well found and provisioned *Sacra Familia*, Shelvocke sailed first to Port Segura in lower California. Here he prepared the ship, then continued on to China, where he was deserted by his officers and forced to sell the ship to defray exorbitant anchorage fees imposed by the Chinese. Shelvocke, a sick man, arrived back in England in an English East India Company ship in August 1722. In England he was accused of embezzlement and piracy, but managed to escape to the Continent where he lived on the illegal proceeds of his voyage.

GEORGE ANSON'S EXPEDITION

Soon after war was declared between England and Spain in 1739, George Anson, who was later to become First Lord of the Admiralty, was given command of an expedition to the South Seas where he was instructed to 'use his best endeavours to annoy and distress the Spaniards'. Whether Anson's voyage around the world can be considered a success depends on the value one places on life. Out of about 1900 men who sailed from England, four died by enemy action and over 1300 by disease and accident. Only 145 of the original company of the expedition were on the *Centurion* when she sailed home. The punishment meted out by the oceans and disease was so ferocious it is remarkable that even one ship and her valuable spoils returned. That this ship did get back can be attributed to the superb seamanship and dogged courage of Commodore George Anson.

To give a full account of this remarkable voyage is beyond the scope of this book, but the story of the ships, their tribulations and management, epitomises the difficulties, dangers and hardships of distant voyaging up to the mid eighteenth century. Eight ships were prepared, and on 24 September 1740 they cleared the English Channel.

Months of delay were to cost them dearly in a Cape Horn winter. On board, apart from the rather doubtful crews, 470 marines were embarked and their recruitment is remarkable for its callous stupidity. In 1688, when there had been a threat of invasion, invalids from Royal Chelsea Hospital, London, had been liable to be called up for garrison duty in times of emergency. In 1719 the Regiment of Invalids was formed and these men, who were granted a pension, were often forced to serve in more

rigorous activities under threat of withdrawal of their pension. In spite of Commodore Anson's protests, he was supplied with 500 of these Chelsea Pensioners. However, all those ancient soldiers who were sane and could walk, lit out for the hills and only 259 embarked. For these poor souls, their employment was a death sentence. To make up the balance, 211 raw recruits (none of whom was trained even to fire a musket) were rounded up, making a grand total of 470 marines who, if they managed to survive one of the worst passages in the world, were supposed to terrorise the Spanish on the American Pacific coast.

The passage to Madeira dragged on to 40 days, a journey which would often take less than two weeks. At Madeira commands were reshuffled. Here it was learned that a Spanish fleet was barking at their heels, the Spanish having been alerted to Anson's intentions. When, on 3 November, the squadron left Madeira, course was laid for St Catherine's island off the coast of Brazil instead of the Cape Verde Islands where the Spanish may have been lying in wait.

Consistent bad luck did not fail them; the trades were not where they should have been and were fickle when they found them. Scurvy began to make its appearance. A theory that foul air was a cause of this disease was prevalent at this time, but due to the heavily laden condition of the ships, the gundeck ports could not be opened, so ventilators were cut through the deck to clear the fetid miasma trapped below.

From 17 to 19 November the *Industry Pink* was discharged and dismissed at sea, but the *Anna Pink* was retained as the squadron had no room for her stores.

The ships anchored at St Catherine's on 21 December. Eight sick men were put ashore and it was found that *Tryal*'s mainmast was sprung at the upper wolding, her foremast was so rotten it was useless and her main topmast and foreyard were also rotten. No replacement could be found for the foremast, so it was fished in three places. All ships set up preventer shrouds and looked to their standing rigging, ready for the passage south and around the Horn.

Before the expedition got under weigh from St Catherine's, 28 men had died; 96 re-embarked sick. The mosquitos and humidity of the island had taken its toll. Richard Walter, who sailed as chaplain as far as Macao and helped Benjamin Robins to compile a detailed account of the voyage (published under the name of Richard Walter), has made some interesting remarks about the water taken on board at St Catherine's:

> The water, both on the Island and the opposite continent is excellent, and preserves at sea as well as that of the Thames. For after it has been in the cask a day or two it begins to purge itself, and stinks most intolerably, and is soon covered over with a green scum: But this, in a few days subsides to the bottom, and leaves the water as clear as crystal and perfectly sweet.

Three days out from St Catherine's, a storm forced the ships to lie to. Anson was careful to maintain the integrity of the squadron and a series of rendezvous were arranged should separation occur, but in spite of this, in the thick fog which accompanied the wind, the *Pearl* lost touch and when the weather cleared there was no sign of her. In addition the *Tryal* was a sorry sight for she had lost her mainmast 12 ft (3.5 m) below the cap, and to prevent damage to the hull it was necessary to cut the wreckage adrift, thus losing most of her mainmast gear. The *Gloucester* took the *Pearl* in tow and the squadron sailed on for Port St Julian.

Pearl came back into the fold on 17 February 1741. In her absence she was very nearly captured by the Spanish squadron, still pursuing Anson. Her commander had mistaken one of the Spanish ships for the *Gloucester* and another for the *Centurion*, for she was flying a broad red pennant at her main

topmast exactly like Anson's. After a chase, the *Pearl* escaped. Her commander, Dandy Kidd, died before rejoining the rest of the fleet.

On 19 February the squadron anchored at St Julian. Here the commands were once again reorganised, the *Pearl* going to George Murray and the *Wager* to Lieutenant David Cheap. Cheap's first lieutenant, Charles Saunders, took over the *Tryal*. The latter ship's remaining mainmast was made to serve and *Wager* supplied her with a spare main topmast which was stepped and rigged as a foremast. Thus *Tryal* sailed from St Julian with a much reduced rig, but as she was previously somewhat overcanvassed, this did her no harm at all in view of what was to come.

After designating rendezvous at Socorro, Baldivia and Juan Fernandez, the squadron sailed from St Julian, not without mishap as the *Gloucester* was

unable to break out her anchor and lost her best bower. The ships now were rigged down for the Horn, their topgallant masts, spars and rigging sent down, the standing rigging beefed up with preventers, jibbooms rigged in, the sprit topsails of the large ships unrigged and got aboard. Lower-deck ports were carefully sealed and deadlights, which were heavy stormboards, fixed across the vulnerable stern windows. Some of the upper-deck guns were sent into the hold to give extra stability and lessen the danger of them breaking loose on deck. On the way south to the Le Maire Straits, new canvas was bent on aloft.

On 7 March the straits were navigated in fine weather but it was to be 'the last cheerful day that the greatest part of us would ever live to enjoy'. Before all the ships had cleared the straits, the weather broke.

Ships of Anson's expedition

	Tons	Length	Beam	Depth	Guns	Built
Centurion	1005	144 ft 1 in. (43.95 m)	40 ft 1½ in. (12.24 m)	16 ft 5 in. (5.01 m)	60	1732
Gloucester	866	134 ft (40.87 m)	38 ft 8 in. (11.79 m)	15 ft 9 in. (4.8 m)	50	1736
Severn	853	134 ft (40.87 m)	38 ft 6 in. (11.74 m)	15 ft 9 in. (4.8 m)	50	1739 (rebuilt)
Pearl	595	124 ft (37.82 m)	33 ft 2 in. (10.12 m)	14 ft (4.27 m)	40	1726 (rebuilt)
Wager	559	123 ft (37.52 m)	32 ft 2⅜ in. (9.82 m)	14 ft 4 in. (4.37 m)	24	1739 (bought)
Tryal	200	84 ft (25.62 m)	23 ft 6 in (7.16 m)	9 ft 6 in (2.9 m)		1732
Anna Pink (Victualler)	400					
Industry Pink (Victualler)	200					

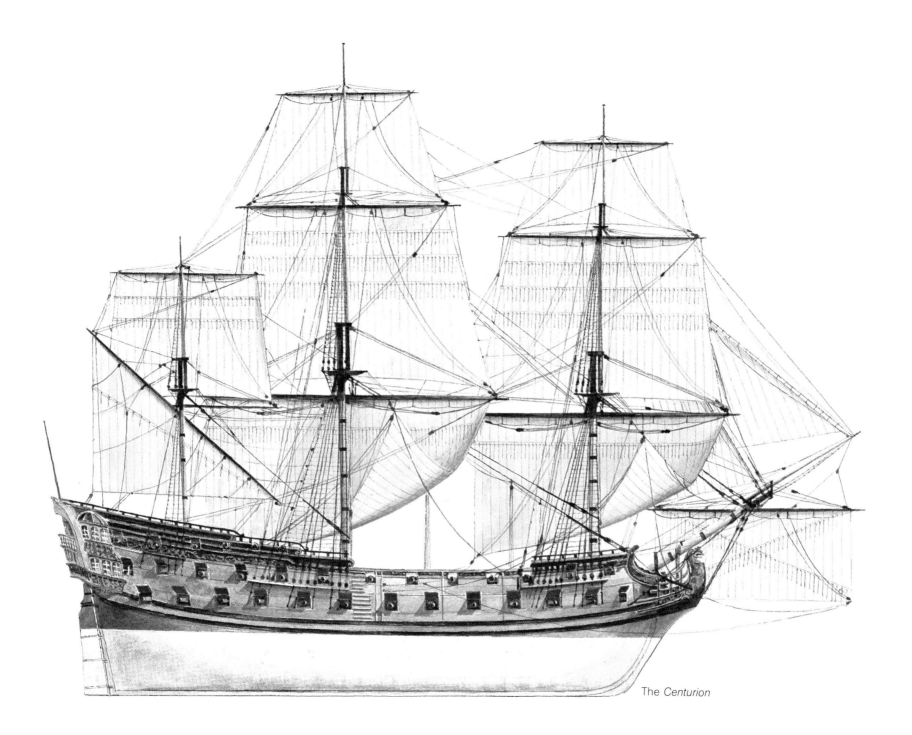

The *Centurion*

Manning the shrouds

Under reefed mainsails the ships were driven eastwards. 'What they had hitherto called storms were inconsiderable gales'. Steep dangerous seas caused violent rolling, killing and injuring men on the *Centurion*. One of her best seamen drowned, another dislocated his neck and a third broke his thigh. A bosun's mate broke his collarbone twice. The storm moderated after four or five days, leaving huge seas which continued to hurl the ships around, but the winds were unpredictable. As soon as a sail was set it would likely as not have to be handed or, as often happened, it would blow to pieces. Snow and sleet squalls froze the rig and the lines became brittle with ice. More gales struck on the eighteenth and the *Centurion* lost her main topsail and broke the strap of one of her main deadeyes. The twenty-third brought an even more violent storm and by this time the *Centurion* was letting in water everywhere; there was not a dry place on board. The main topsail yard sprung and the mainsail blew out, most of it being lost. The squadron, still amazingly intact, was ordered to bring to and the topsail yard was sent down and a new mainsail bent. The next day it blew 'a perfect hurricane'.

To keep company with the others the *Centurion* had to wear ship. As no sail could be set, they were lying to under bare poles. To wear it was necessary to man the fore weather lower shrouds – providing a living sail which enabled the ship's head to pay off. During this evolution, one of Anson's best hands went overboard. He was a good swimmer, but could not reach the ship; nothing could be done except watch him draw astern and vanish into the murk to windward. The chance of rescue for a man overboard from a square-rigger was always slim and in that sort of weather, negligible. Many old sailors claimed they preferred not to be able to swim for this reason.

During this storm, two of the *Centurion*'s mainshrouds and one mizzen shroud broke but were knotted and set up immediately. Fog followed, obliging the ships to fire guns to keep station. On 31 March a gun fired from the *Gloucester* brought attention to her mainyard which had broken at the slings. The *Tryal*'s pumps were malfunctioning and they were scarcely able to keep her free. More moderate weather allowed a team effort to repair *Gloucester*'s mainyard and *Tryal*'s pumps.

On 1 April the weather worsened again and a storm which 'exceedeed all that we had hitherto encountered' broke upon them. At the onset, a sea breaking on *Centurion*'s port quarter stove in the quarter gallery and roared into the ship. A strap of one of the main deadeyes parted, as did also a main and a futtock shroud. All sail was handed and the fore and mainyards lowered to ease the ship and she lay thus for three days.

On 7 April the squadron had to bring to, for the *Wager* had lost her mizzen mast, maintopsail yard and all the weather chain plates had carried away on a roll. The *Wager*'s carpenter was in the *Gloucester* and unable to return. The next day the *Anna Pink* was in distress, having parted the forestay and bowsprit gammoning, endangering the whole rig. The squadron was forced to run while the pink's rig was secured.

By the end of March, thinking they had sufficient offing to the west, the ships began to work north and by 15 April were only a degree south of the western entrance to the Strait of Magellan. Believing they were hundreds of miles offshore, on the morning of the fourteenth, in thick and hazy weather they were horrified when a fortuitous clearance showed land only two miles ahead of the *Anna Pink*. Even more fortunate, the wind allowed them to stand away to the south and west, without the *Severn* and *Pearl*, with whom they had lost all contact.

Fair weather for the Horn favoured them until 24 April, when they once more ran into very heavy weather. The *Centurion* lost touch with the other ships and the next morning, while clewing up the topsails, the clew and buntlines parted and every seam in the fore and main topsails split. The main topsail thrashed so violently that it carried away the top lanthorn and threatened the lower masthead. Some very brave men laid out on the maintopsail yard and cut away the sail close to the reef points while the foretopsail flogged itself to bits and the mainsail blew out of its gaskets. The mainyard was lowered to secure the sail and the fore yard was also brought down. The ship then hove to under her mizzen. To top it all, a main studdingsail boom was lost from the chains.

The weather had moderated sufficiently by 25 April to enable them to sway up the lower yards and carry out makeshift repairs. There was no sign of the other four ships, nor were they to come up with any of them again until Juan Fernandez. The *Severn* and *Pearl* had finally turned back and sailed to Brazil. After the twenty-second, when they had reached below 60°S and gained their westing, Anson started edging northward, continually beset by hard gales until, on the last day of the month, they considered themselves in the Pacific, having got north of the straits. More trials were ahead of them, however; scurvy began to have a disastrous effect on the crew of the *Centurion*. Forty-three men died in April and the toll continued to mount, with nearly double that number dying in May. By mid June, when they reached Juan Fernandez, about 200 men had died and only six foremast hands could be raised in each watch.

The foul weather had not finished with them. Arriving off the island of Socorro on 8 May to await the rest of the squadron, they had great difficulty keeping off the fearsome lee shore in the violent squalls. The necessity of keeping sail on to get to windward in the severe gales where they would have otherwise lay to, caused further damage to sails, masts and rigging. The gales persisted until 22 May when 'all the storms which we had hitherto encountered, seemed to be combined, and to have conspired our destruction'. All the *Centurion*'s sails were blown out, a great deal of standing rigging broken and a mountainous sea struck the ship on her starboard quarter, throwing her down, breaking several shrouds and shifting stores and ballast. With the heavy port list and damaged rig, the *Centurion* was brought little relief by the abatement of the storm, for without sails to steady her, the ship rolled gunwales under, and there was a very real danger of rolling her masts out. Apprehensively watching the island of Chiloe close under their lee, the crew frantically made repairs. A shift of wind relieved their anxiety and they steered off the land. It was then decided to make directly for Juan Fernandez where, sick, worn out, short of water and scarce able to work the ship, the surviving hands brought

their battered and crazy vessel finally to anchor on 11 June.

Soon after they had anchored the *Tryal* arrived and some hands from *Centurion* were sent to assist her to anchor. Scurvy had so affected the *Tryal*'s crew that only Captain Saunders, his lieutenant and three men were able to work the ship. Thirty-four had died. Both ships then set about geting their sick ashore and setting up tents.

A fortnight passed and hopes were almost given up for the rest of the squadron when, on 21 June, a ship under only courses and maintopsail was seen to leeward, her hull below the horizon. Thick hazy weather obscured her and days passed without further sightings. On the twenty-sixth she hove in sight again and assistance was sent out to her as she approached. The *Gloucester*, as she turned out to be, was so short of water that the survivors could well have died of thirst and scarcely any of her complement were capable of duty. With help from the other ships' boats, which also took supplies to her, the *Gloucester* worked within three miles of the anchorage, but in spite of all efforts, the wind and currents prevented her from getting in.

For two weeks the ship got no closer and on 9 July she vanished in the east and did not appear for a week. She was sighted again off the eastern end of the island on the sixteenth but could not get within 12 miles of the anchorage. Captain Mitchell sent distress signals and the *Centurion*'s longboat was dispatched. It was three days before weather permitted the boat to return, when it was reported that *Gloucester*'s men were in a desperate state, short of water and sick. Appearing and disappearing, the distressed ship struggled to make the bay without success until finally, on 23 July, a fair wind brought her to anchor. It had taken the ship 32 days to complete the last few miles to that anchorage.

Attention was then paid to the men and to the ships while a search for the missing vessels was started by the *Tryal*. The *Centurion*'s foremast was badly sprung just above the partners at deck level

and this was fished with two leaves of an anchor stock. Worse was the shortage of spare cordage and canvas. Junk, or unlaid rope and old shrouds were made into cable-laid rope and a spare hawser unlaid and worked into running rigging.

A major worry was put to rest when the *Anna Pink* came to anchor on 16 August, apparently in fine fettle in spite of her late arrival. She had nearly been driven ashore on 18 May near the island of Inchin. Her sheet anchor had been put over but she drove, on and off, until within a mile of the land. Both bowers were then let go but she continued to drive until almost ashore. A small opening in the land was seen, her anchors cut away, and she sailed into a perfect harbour. Here the pink stayed two months, lying to one small anchor while her crew was refreshed. This accounted for their condition on arrival at Juan Fernandez.

Unfortunately *Anna Pink*'s stores were not so healthy, for a large part had rotted due to water damage. Anson wished to discharge the pink but her master considered that his ship was in no fit state to put to sea and asked for a survey. This disclosed that she

. . . had no less than fourteen knees, and twelve beams broken and decayed; that one breast-hook was broken and another rotten; that her waterways were open and decayed; that two standards were broken, as also several clamps, besides others which were rotten; that all her spirketing and timbers were very rotten; and that having ripped off a part of her sheathing, they found her wales and outside planks extremely defective, and her bows and decks were very leaky.

It was a miracle that a ship in that condition was able to complete the voyage to Juan Fernandez. She was bought by Anson and broken up for her iron and equipment, her crew taken into the other ships and her foremast became *Tryal*'s mainmast.

A sail was sighted on 8 September and was first thought to be one of their consorts. However, she turned out to be Spanish. Within a few hours the *Centurion* had got all hands on board, set up her rigging, bent sails and weighed–no mean achievement. Setting up the standing rigging alone is an ordered and generally lengthy business. I have spent days with a gang of riggers just setting up lower rigging, aided by chain hoists. After the bobstays and bowsprit shrouds have been set up, the forestays followed by each fore lower shroud in turn were dealt with, working aft. The lanyards, one by one, would be led to a luff on luff tackle to which a sizable gang would have hauled, while the lanyard was assisted to render through the deadeyes or harts with tallow and a leather maul. A seizing was then clapped on, and in the case of deadeyes, the lanyard was cow-hitched around the upper deadeye and seized again. On *Centurion*'s fore lower mast alone there was the stay, the preventer stay and 14 shrouds. If all standing rigging had to be set up, then 82 stays and shrouds would have had to be tensioned, excluding the topgallant rigging. While this was being undertaken the sails would have been sent up and bent on, making it somewhat difficult to nicely judge the tension. I can only conclude that either the whole rig did not have to be set up or they made some extraordinary compromises.

The *Centurion* lost the Spaniard but came up with another ship which they at first thought was a man-of-war and so cleared for action, dumping cabin screens and cluttering stores. However, she turned out to be a merchantman, the *Nuestra Senora de Monte Carmelo*, their first prize. From her it was learned that the Spanish force pursuing them had failed to round Cape Horn and put back in distress to the Plate and from there had sent warning to the west coast.

On 19 September the *Centurion, Tryal* and *Carmelo* weighed to cruise off Valparaiso, leaving the *Gloucester* to complete her refit, after which she was to proceed to a rendezvous of Payta.

Since leaving England the squadron's mortality had been enormous, the *Centurion* having buried 292, leaving 214. Only 4 out of her 50 pensioners and 11 of the 79 marines survived. In the *Gloucester* only 82 survived out of her original 292; no pensioners, and only two marines were still alive. The *Tryal* came out best, having lost 42, leaving 39. In total, out of 961 men, 626 had perished.

Shortly after leaving Juan Fernandez, the *Tryal* made a prize of a vessel named the *Arranzazu*, a large ship of about 600 tons. Unfortunately the *Tryal* had sprung her mainmast in the chase and her main topmast had gone by the board. The next day, in strong winds, she sprung her foremast, leaving her unable to set any sail at all. For the best part of two days it blew so hard that nothing could be done, but on the twenty-seventh a boat was got across to her to discover that, in addition to the sprung masts, she was leaking so badly that the water was gaining. A decision was made to scuttle her, and the *Arranzazu* was fitted out to take her place and renamed *Tryal's Prize*.

The adventures of the squadron on the Spanish-American coast, the taking of various prizes and the capture of Payta must be left out of this account. The ships and men suffered comparatively little while on the coast, and on 6 May 1742, after a long and fruitless patrol for the Manila galleons, the *Centurion* and the *Gloucester* set out across the Pacific, bound for China.

Steering first southwest from Cape San Lucas, lower California, they hoped to pick up the northeast trades and make a fast passage, but it was seven weeks before the true trade winds set in and scurvy was beginning again to decimate the crews. The *Centurion* had sprung her foremast and shortly after this was fished the *Gloucester* badly sprung her mainmast, which was discovered to be rotten. The mast was cut down to a stump, leaving sufficient to form a step for the topmast to serve as a jury rig. The ships sailed slowly on in light trade winds

until they failed on 26 July and in the ensuing calm the *Gloucester*'s rolling split her forecap. The foretopmast came down on the way, breaking the foreyard at the slings. To add to their problems, the next day a gale blew up and as the *Gloucester* could not make any sail, the *Centurion* took her in tow. It took the combined efforts of both crews ten days to make repairs, and scarcely had they finished when a violent westerly storm forced them to lie to. The *Centurion* sprung a bad leak, necessitating both men and officers to man the pumps continually and, the following day, dawn showed that the *Gloucester*'s foretopmast was down again. While they were viewing this latest calamity, her jury mainmast went overboard. With the deplorable state of the crews, the *Centurion*'s leak and the almost total loss of the *Gloucester*'s rig, the outlook was grim. It was grimmer still when Commodore Anson learned that there was about 7 ft (2 m) of water in the *Gloucester*'s hold and this was rising in spite of continual pumping.

A boat was sent from the *Centurion* to examine the disabled *Gloucester* and returned to report that

she had sprung a leak by the stern post being loose, and working with every roll of the ship, and by two beams amidships being broken in the orlope....that both officers and men had worked twenty-four hours at the pumps without intermission, and were at length so fatigued that they could continue to labour no longer; but had been forced to desist with seven feet of water in the hold, which covered their cask, so that they could neither come at fresh water, nor provision: The ship was besides extremely decayed in every part, for her knees and clamps were all worked quite loose, and her upper works in general were so loose, that

the quarter-deck was ready to drop down: and that her crew was greatly reduced, for there reamained alive on board her no more than twenty-seven men, eighteen boys, and two prisoners, officers included; and that of this whole number, only sixteen men, and eleven boys were capable of keeping the deck, and several of these very infirm.

It was clear that the ship could go no further, and the following two days were spent getting out accessible stores, the sick and, with some difficulty, the prize money. Due to the exhaustion of the crews and the sinking state of the *Gloucester*, all the prize goods and cables and anchors had to be left. During the evening of 15 August the *Gloucester* was set afire. She burnt the whole night as the *Centurion* stood away, watching her burn fiercely and hearing her guns firing as the flames reached them. At six in the morning, from a distance of 12 miles, those in the *Centurion* saw her blow up, sending a towering column of black smoke into the air.

On 26 August the exhausted crew of the *Centurion* raised the three islands of Saypan, Tinian and Aguigan lying approximately 80 miles northeast of Guam. Course was made for Tinian and on the twenty-seventh they came to anchor in idyllic surroundings. The crew were so weak that it took five hours to furl the sails. Only 71 men were capable of any sort of duty and most of these were so incapacitated that they could not undertake any exertion.

Tinian was used as a food supply for Guam where there was a Spanish garrison and when the *Centurion* arrived a small Spanish ship was taken. The natural wealth of the island soon enabled the men to recuperate, but the exposed anchorage was to provide a potentially disastrous situation.

In the expectation of bad weather, the cables were protected against the foul bottom with extra chafing gear, and the fore and main lower yards were lowered to the deck. On 22 September the weather broke and a violent southerly gale blew up. Anson and most of the crew were ashore and the sea was too heavy to get a boat out to the ship. At five in the afternoon, the small bower parted, leaving the ship riding to the best bower. The sea became very confused, with a high steep swell which hurled the longboat against the captain's gallery, smashing the transom and the boat. The boatkeeper was very lucky to escape with only bad bruising. At 11 pm the cable of the best bower parted, upon which the sheet anchor, with the usual two cables bent, was let go, but before it reached the bottom the ship had been driven into deep water. Guns were fired to alert those ashore to their distress as the ship drove out to sea. Barely a quarter of the crew were aboard, the sheet anchor at the end of 200 fathom or more of cable hanging straight down, two other cables over from which the bowers had gone, the ship leaking and taking water through the unsecured ports and hatches, no guns lashed down, the topmasts unrigged and the fore and mainyards lowered. The only sail they could set was the mizzen until the yards were swayed up. An attempt was made to do this soon after being blown out to sea, for there was a grave risk of going ashore on a neighbouring island. When the jeers broke they gave up in despair and let the ship drift.

It was three days before the weather moderated sufficiently to attempt to sway up the yards. The fore yard was got up but the main jeers broke, killing a seaman, and the yard was not got up that day. The next day, 26 September, they undertook the enormous task of getting their sheet anchor. As this was their last remaining anchor, it was imperative that it was recovered and officers and men laboured at the capstans all day until, after 12 hours, the 2½-ton anchor was in sight. Darkness and exhaustion forced them to stop for the night and the next morning the anchor was catted and hung. The same day the mainyard was got up and they were able to make sail. They were in some doubt as to their position until a landfall on Guam showed them they were some 130 miles out in their reckoning. In getting to the east, toward Tinian, they frequently had to bring the ship about which, in their reduced condition, involved all hands, and it was on 11 October, 19 days after being driven offshore, that they came again to anchor at Tinian.

In the absence of the *Centurion*, the anxiety of those ashore can be imagined, and they had to consider her lost. A start had been made to lengthen the little Spanish barque and when *Centurion* returned she had already been cut in two and some of the midship section frames set up. Before departing Tinian for good, the *Centurion* was once again driven offshore but this time got back fairly comfortably in five days, during which time the few who had been left ashore had already started to put the Spanish ship back together again.

The *Centurion* sailed on to Macao where she was refitted and stored, not without some problems with the Chinese authorities, whose deviousness must have completely exasperated the straight-dealing Anson. The exuberant and energetic activities of the sailors in putting out a major fire in Canton finally smoothed the way for Commodore Anson, but before this, one of the goals of the whole voyage was attained; the capture of an eastbound Manila galleon off Cape Espiritu Santo. The *Nostra Signora de Cabadonga* was taken into Macao and proved to be a rich prize so that, in addition to the treasure already taken, the *Centurion* returned to England with almost 400,000 in pieces-of-eight, silver and specie.

On the 15 June 1744 the *Centurion* anchored at Spithead. So ended what must be the most disastrous but most heroic circumnavigation. I have confined this accout to the ships and their story as far as possible, intending to highlight the seamanship and endeavour required to work the vessels of those days on extended voyages. The account is incomplete, for it must be remembered that the ships were but tools and it was the men who sailed them who strove and suffered.

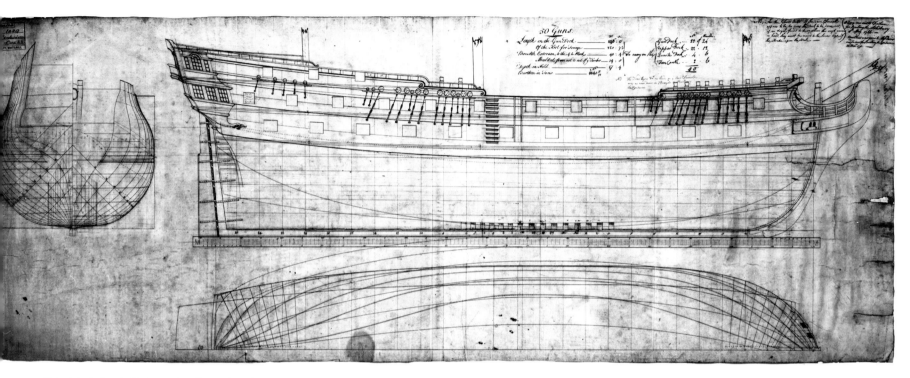

This Admiralty draft shows the *Centurion* after a major refit subsequent to her voyage round the world. Note that, because of the damage they suffered, the channels have been raised from main-deck to upper-deck level in line with French and Spanish practice. Her armament was also reduced to 50 guns. (National Maritime Museum, Greenwich)

Also omitted from my account is the fate of the *Wager*, wrecked on a lonely south-Chilean island. Freed from authority by the wreck, as was the custom, her crew mutinied and sailed one of the boats to Brazil, leaving the surviving officers to struggle northwards to captivity.

THE RUSSIANS IN THE FAR NORTH

During the early years of the eighteenth century, in the reign of Tzar Peter I, Russian authorities became aware of the need for some naval presence in the distant Siberian possessions. Two factors demanded attention. For a number of years northern Europeans had searched in vain for a northeast passage which would provide easier access to Japan and China. The Dutch, French and Germans urged Tzar Peter that an attempt from the east might find this passage and properly chart some of the chimerical islands supposed to exist north of Japan. Russian naval involvement was given greater urgency when, by 1713, Cossack rebellion and attacks by the warlike Koriak and Chukchi tribes had reduced the Russian northeast to anarchy. Inaccessible to Russia's wild Cossack policemen on the shores of the sea of Okhotsk, the peninsula of Kamchatka was in danger of being lost completely, along with the *iasak* or fur tribute which was gathered on almost the sole commercial product of the region.

The only vessels available on those bleak shores were the native *shitiki* or sewn boats and other local river craft. Not one substantial wooden ship existed. Nor could one be built, for there were no shipwrights to build or seamen to man them. Not an anchor, nor any of the other hardware essential to even a small ship, was available. Yet if Russia was to retain control of her east, it was imperative to get a ship afloat on that coast.

There were two possible ways of getting a ship to the eastern seaboard. The sea routes, either by Cape Horn or Good Hope, were feasible, and apart from the last leg north of Japan, both routes had become well travelled. Under Tzar Peter, Russia was improving her Baltic fleet and she could have drawn

The eighteenth-century Russian naval endeavours in the far north Pacific were notable not for their voyages but for the enormous difficulties they had to overcome before they could even put out to sea

on the expertise of the Dutch and English to make the voyage. However, right up to the end of the eighteenth century a pathological fear of the tropics seemed to haunt the Russian seamen. The attitude was nicely expressed by the poet-scientist Mikhail Lomonosov, an ardent supporter in the search for the northeast passage (north of Russia), in his ode *Peter the Great:* '. . .the very ice, which seems so awesome, will offer us a path free of those fierce dangers.'

The alternative was to transport men and material overland on an incredibly long journey of well over

3000 miles (4800 km) and this was the method undertaken. The first 50-strong party assembled and dispatched from Iatusk in July 1714 consisted of carpenters, seamen and specialists; it was led by Iakov Neveitsin and Nikita Triaska. With them went three anchors, about 480 yds (439 m) of sailcloth, tackle, ropes and tools. Timber was to be felled on the coast. At the mouth of the Okhota River the first small ship was launched in April 1716. Named the *Okhota*, she was 51 ft (15.55 m) in length, had a beam of 18 ft (5.49 m) and drew only 3 ft 4 in (1.02 m) laden. She was rigged with a single mast, probably carrying a gaff mainsail, staysail and topsail. To draw so little, her hull must have been

(Below) Mid eighteenth century Russian ships: a hooker (*left*), galliot (*centre*), and brigantine (*right*).

very like that of a scow. In June 1716, under the command of Triaska, *Okhota* made her maiden voyage to Kamchatka.

During the next few years other small craft were launched; none were really more than large boats. The sheer isolation of Okhotsk and the scarcity of men and materials militated against any rapid expansion. It was difficult enough to build, sail and maintain even the small craft in the dismal political and physical climate of those coasts.

In 1721 two graduates of the new naval academy, Fedor Luzhin and Ivan Evreinov, were sent east to ascertain 'whether or not Asia and America are joined by land; and you will go not only north and south, but also east and west, and will place on a map all that you see.' In Okhotsk the two had the *Okhota* repaired and sailed to Kamchatka. From there in June 1721 they sailed southwest and charted some of the islands in the Kurile chain before a storm blew out their sails and forced them to lie ahull for a week.

Driven to leeward on to Paramushir Island, they attempted to anchor using an anvil and a cannon. The cable parted, but they survived and limped back to Okhotsk. The charts the young officers brought back were valuable and a piece of the north Pacific jigsaw fell into place. The relationship of Kamchatka, the Kuriles and Japan had been established.

Ships of the Russians

Most vessels built on the Russian Pacific shores for the fur trade or exploration ranged in length between 40 and 80 ft (12 and 24.5 m). Their shipwrights were often Scandinavians, so these small craft would have been similar to those plying the North Sea and the Baltic. There was a great variety of hulls and rigs, but from records it seems that the most common rigs used by the *promyshlennik*, or hunter-traders, were hookers or galliots. A few larger vessels were

(Below) Mid eighteenth century Russian ships: a hooker (*left*), galliot (*centre*), and brigantine (*right*).

brigantines or brig-rigged. Often sloops are referred to, but this seems to have been a general term, particularly in the British Navy, for a whole range of small craft stepping anything from one to three masts. (Philip Carteret's *Swallow* was classed as a sloop and was ship rigged.) However, single-masted craft were often used by the Russians.

From Okhotsk or Kamchatka the Russians would cruise through the Aleutians to the American mainland, hunting and collecting otter and seal pelts from the indigenous people. One of their small ships would carry up to 60 men for the season and there were enormous losses in the miserable sub-Arctic climate. Before they returned it would be expected that over half would have died of scurvy or other diseases, and shipwreck was more than just common. Between 1801 and 1804 not one vessel succeeded in making the passage from Okhotsk to Sitka or Kodiak. All were wrecked and the supplies for the outposts lost.

Up to the last quarter of the eighteenth century, because of the lack of iron, all these ships were wooden fastened. When nails became available the ships built with them became known as *grozdeniki* or nailers. Most of the ships were so badly built and maintained that they were downright dangerous.

Hookers

These came in a variety of sizes, although most used in the Pacific were small. The rig could be viewed as a ship rig without the foremast, hence the long jibboom necessary for balance. Large hookers carried a mizzen topsail and often had their topmast fidded aft of the lower mast. Both the hooker and the galliot I have shown are based on the drawings of Frederik af Chapman in the last half of the eighteenth century. Later the mizzen may have carried a boom. The gaff sail behind the mainmast was known as the spenser and the top-gallant was sometimes, but not always, set flying – that is, with no brace or lifts as it is in the sketch.

Galliots

Note the deep roach in the topsail to clear the stays, and the lead of the topsail braces to the gaff, then to the mizzen. The mainmast appears very poorly supported above the stays, whereas the lower mast seems to have the additional support of what we would term a running backstay. Galliots were generally smaller than hookers.

Brigantines

As I doubt whether the shipbuilders of Okhotsk would have spent time, effort and money in fancy work, I have shown this without the headrails and jibboom. Working ships in Europe often dispensed with one or the other. Without the beakhead and headrails, the gammoning holding down the bowsprit was passed through a large ringbolt on the stem.

The first Bering expedition (1725-30)

In 1724 Tzar Peter was dying. His passion for the sea was the cause of his fatal illness, which was brought about by attempting to salvage a grounded boat in icy water. Peter, aware of his approaching death, gave the orders that would send the first large expedition overland to build ships in the northeast and to seek out the northern strait.

Appointed to the command was Vitus Bering, a Dane but a captain in the Russian Navy. In his earlier career he had served with the Dutch East India Company in the East. Second in command was Morten Spanberg, a fellow Dane and a good sea officer, but surly, cruel and only semiliterate. Third in order of command was Lieutenant Aleksei Ivanovich Chirikov, a Russian-born naval instructor who has gone down in history as the leading light of the expedition.

In 1714 Triaska's party had assembled their men and materials east of the Urals. Bering's larger expedition was to start from far in the west, in European Russia. In January 1725 Chirikov and 24 men set out in advance with 25 large waggons of provisions and equipment; Bering followed a little later with a similar caravan. The journey by land and river was an epic in itself. Swamps and streams hindered their progress, rapids had to be portaged and obstructive officials dealt with. As they progressed their numbers were increased as men and horses joined the march.

The men, waggons and 600 horses spread over a lot of territory, creating problems with provisioning. After Iakutsk, Bering split the expedition into three groups. He reached Okhotsk in October 1726, but Spanberg and Chirikov ran into trouble. Failing to reach Okhotsk before the onset of winter, they had their boats frozen in the ice of the Gorbeia River, forcing them to march, hauling makeshift sledges, throughout the winter. Provisions ran out and the starving men ate the horses and finally the leather harnesses. The remnants of Spanberg's group reached Okhotsk in April 1727. Many men had died and all the equipment and material dragged with such effort and hardship across the entire breadth of Russia was lost. The expedition had taken 28 months to assemble on the banks of the Okhotsk.

A decked ship had already been started by the time Bering arrived, but it was a long way from being finished. Named the *Fortuna*, she was to transport the expedition to Kamchatka, where a second vessel was to be built. After a winter of frustration and discontent, the *Fortuna* was launched on 8 June 1727 and made two voyages to Bol'sheretsk on the west coast of Kamchatka. From there Bering employed the local Kamchadals to haul everything across the peninsula to Nizhne Kamchatsk on the east coast. Here a cold, miserable winter was spent while work on the new ship progressed.

> Timber we hauled by dog-team. Tar we manufactured from a tree known there as larch . . . For lack of anything to take on the coming voyage, we distilled a liquor from grass, by a process known in that country. Salt we boiled out of sea-water; fish-oil gave us our butter; and instead of meat we took salt fish.

By July 1728 the 60 ft (18 m) vessel, named the *Sviatoi Gavriil* (*Saint Gabriel*) was complete. The *Fortuna*, with the pilot Moshov on board, arrived on 6 June and the expedition put to sea on 14 July. They stood northeast up the coast. On 29 July they crossed the mouth of the River Anadyr and continued rock-hopping along the shore. No doubt the small size of their ship was an advantage, allowing them the additional manoeuvrability of sweeps to keep them out of trouble. St Lawrence Island was discovered and named. The indigenous people, the Chukotski, were questioned as to land in the east, but their replies were of little help. They rounded Cape Chukotskii until they reached 65°30′N with no land in sight. Bering concluded that they had passed the eastern tip of Asia and, with the prospect of winter not far off, consulted Spanberg and Chirikov. Spanberg proposed venturing northwards for three more days while Chirikov was for proving the strait by making for the mouth of the Kolmya River in northern Siberia. Spanberg's suggestion won the day. On 16 August in latitude 67°18′N, 45 miles inside the Arctic Circle, they turned back, passing close to, but not sighting, the fog-enshrouded Alaskan shore.

After wintering back at Nizhne Kamchatsk, Bering set out again the following June, sailing out to sea for 115 miles and turning back to chart the southern Kamchatkan coast. That completed, he sailed on to Bol'shaia and Okhotsk from where he returned to St Petersburg, arriving there on 30 March 1730. He had been away five years, during which less than four months had been spent at sea. Although not absolutely proved, Bering was given the credit for finding the strait which now bears his name.

Bering's great northern expedition (1733-42)

After the death of Tzar Peter the Russian Navy was neglected, but Bering's first expedition aroused sufficient interest for another much larger venture to be organised, with a scope which included aims other than maritime. Bering was given the impossible task of overall command of seven parties with differing goals. The first five parties were concerned with a detailed survey of the northeastern littoral while the sixth and seventh were to make voyages to America and Japan respectively. Any meeting with foreign vessels was to be treated with caution because Russia did not want to get involved in any international incident she was unlikely to be able to deal with from a position of strength.

The expedition left St Petersburg in the spring of 1733. The next seven years were spent in a mare's nest of squabbling, delays and threatened violence, brought about mainly by the uncertain authority of the naval commanders over the local Cossacks, in particular, their commandant, Pisarev, whom Spanberg claimed was a drunkard and a villain, tortured the natives and was known to have kept a harem.

The coastal parties got on with their work with good results, and during 1738-9 Spanberg, Lieutenant William Walton and Ensign A.E. Schelting made the first voyages and contacts with the Japanese. The ships they used were a new 60 ft (18.3 m) hooker, the *Arkangel Mikail*; a double sloop, probably a ketch or a schooner, the *Nadezhda*; and the *Sviatoi Gavriil*. They were civilly received by the Japanese people, although the visits were regarded with suspicion by the authorities.

It was not until June 1740 that the two 80 ft (24.4 m) 14-gun brigs, *Sv Peter* and *Sv Pavel*, were ready for sea. That year was spent establishing a new base on the eastern Kamchatkan seaboard. In the spring of 1741 Bering and Chirikov were ready to sail east.

The two ships sailed at the end of May; the *Sv Peter* under Bering and the *Sv Pavel* commanded by Chirikov. It was their intention to sail southeast to about the 45° parallel in search of the non-existent 'Gama Land' shown on some maps, then, if no land was sighted, to sail north by east to America and then coast northwards to the mid sixties. They kept company to latitude 46°N, then changed course eastwards. In June they became separated in filthy weather and never met up again.

Bering made his landfall at about 58°28′N and then beat up the coast to anchor in the lee of Kayak Island. The highest mountain he could see he named Mt St Elias after the saint whose day it was. They landed on the island and Georg-Wilhelm Steller, the scientist, was allowed ashore and the ship was watered. However, Bering was overcome with anxiety and ordered the return to Petropavlovsk after less than a day at the island. No one had set foot on the mainland.

The return voyage was a nightmare which ended in disaster. In thick weather and storms they lost track of their position, and scurvy and exposure debilitated everyone. On 6 November 1741 the *Sv Peter* drove ashore on an island over 100 miles offshore from Kamchatka, which Bering had mistaken for the mainland. There followed an appalling winter during which many died, including Vitus Bering. In the spring, from timber salvaged from the *Sv Peter* the survivors started building a 12-foot boat and in August they sailed to the mainland. A three-week voyage brought them to the shores of Kamchatka. The island where they endured a miserable winter and on which Bering died is named after the navigator.

In the *Sv Pavel* Chirikov had arrived on the American coast two weeks before Bering. South of Bering's landfall at L'tua Bay he attempted to send a party ashore, but lost both his boats and the men in them. Not knowing the fate of the party, and having no more boats, Chirikov had little alternative but to leave and return to Petropavlovsk. The voyage back against adverse winds took nine weeks, during which six men died of scurvy.

Steller, the scientist with Bering, bitterly claimed that the expedition had been organised 'merely to carry some water from America to Asia, while years of preparation led to ten hours of exploration'. However, although the sixth detachment bore little result, the other activities of the Great Northern Expedition were positive and valuable and a permanent port had been founded at Petropavlovsk.

The fur traders

During the two decades following Bering's expedition, Russia's proud navy fell into neglect and disrepair. Interest in the northeast waned in spite of disturbing reports filtering belatedly back to St Petersburg. Encouraged by the work of the Great Northern Expedition, the private hunter fur-traders pushed outwards from the mainland, island-hopping along the Aleutians in a variety of craft from *shitiki* to small, locally built galliots and hookers. The slaughter of the teeming seals and otters on the islands had begun in earnest. A reign of terror, brutality, rape and slavery descended on the Aleutian population. The *promyshlennik*, mainly Cossacks, were courageous men and made daring voyages. Some became wealthy, but their successes were often hidden from the eyes of the tax gatherers. Nothing, however, can excuse the brutality with which the Aleuts were treated. Outrages were committed to extract *iasak*, the fur tribute, and the traders used the local people mercilessly for their own ends. As Glynn Barratt records in his *Russia in Pacific Waters*,

'Slavery, extortion, murder, liquor and venereal disease – such were their gifts to them'.

By the mid 1760s the hunter-traders were operating on the Alaskan coast, and Spain, jealous of her claims, was beginning to show signs of nervousness. Under Catherine II, who came to the throne of Russia in 1762, interest was again revived in the Navy. It was not long before an effort was made to investigate the anarchy in the east and assess the territorial advance of the *promyshlennik*. An additional spur was a report that Britain's Commodore Byron and Captain Mouat, in the *Dolphin* and *Tamar*, had sailed for the region.

The result was the launching of two rather tentative expeditions which directed the naval officers concerned to accompany and make use of the *promyshlennik* and their craft. The first, between 1764 and 1767, was led by Lieutenant Ivan Sindt in a couple of galliots and resulted in the production of muddled and almost dangerous charts of the region about the Bering Strait. The second, under Captain Peter Krenitsyn and Midshipman Mikhail Levashev, was obliged to use their own craft as the *promyshlennik* had a natural reluctance to embark representatives of the Navy on their voyages.

Two ships were built, the *Sv Ekaterina*, styled a brigantine, and a hooker, *Sv Pavel*. Two galliots were also repaired and refitted and named the *Sv Gavriil* and *Sv Pavel* also. (Saint Gabriel and Saint Paul must have been considered very powerful influences.) They sailed from Okhotsk in October 1766 and within three days had lost all contact with one another. The *Sv Ekaterina* began to leak badly and Krenitsyn, her captain, tried to anchor, but high winds drove her ashore close to the Bol'shaia River where she went to pieces. The hooker *Sv Pavel* also anchored near the rivermouth and, in the same blow, parted her cables. Levashev managed to beach her without damage. The galliot *Sv Gavrill* also was thrown ashore, and the galliot *Sv Pavel* piled up halfway down the Kurile chain where her crew were rescued by the Ainu hunters.

After a hungry winter the shipwrecked crews at Bol'sheretsk repaired the *Sv Pavel* and *Sv Gavriil* and sailed around to Nizhne Kamchatsk on the east coast, arriving in mid September. Here they settled down to another winter. The following April Sindt arrived in a galliot named *Sv Ekaterina*. Krenitsyn refitted Sindt's ship and on 21 July Krenitsyn, with 72 men in the *Sv Ekaterina* and Levashev in the *Sv Pavel*, put out to sea; they were grossly overmanned.

After a stopover at Bering Island the two galliots sailed east, slowed by contrary winds. On 11 August they became separated, but rejoined again off Unalaska. In company they sailed on to Unimak and Alaska where they spent two days surveying before searching for a winter anchorage. They parted again on 5 September. Krenitsyn and his men spent a nervous, bleak winter on Unimak where after being attacked once by the natives who surrounded them, they lived in fear of further assaults. To add to their distress, scurvy enfeebled them and deaths began to occur regularly.

Happily, in May the *Sv Pavel* joined them at Unimak. Further explorations were abandoned and the two ships returned to Nizhne Kamchatsk after a long, hard voyage. Another gruelling winter was survived; this time beset by earthquakes in September and the following May. In 1770 the expedition was wound up. Unfortunately Krenitsyn drowned in June of that year while crossing a river in a dugout canoe. Levashev arrived back in St Petersburg in 1771 where he drew sympathetic attention to the predicament of the Aleuts from the Russian authorities.

The trials that Krenitsyn and Levashev faced demonstrate the effect of the appalling climate of the region. Unpredictable storms and fogs filled a summer so short that it seemed another harsh winter was upon them before they had recovered from the previous one. The *promyshlennik*, familiar with the seas and hardened to the climate, living on a similar diet to the indigenous people, fared better in that harsh environment than sailors from

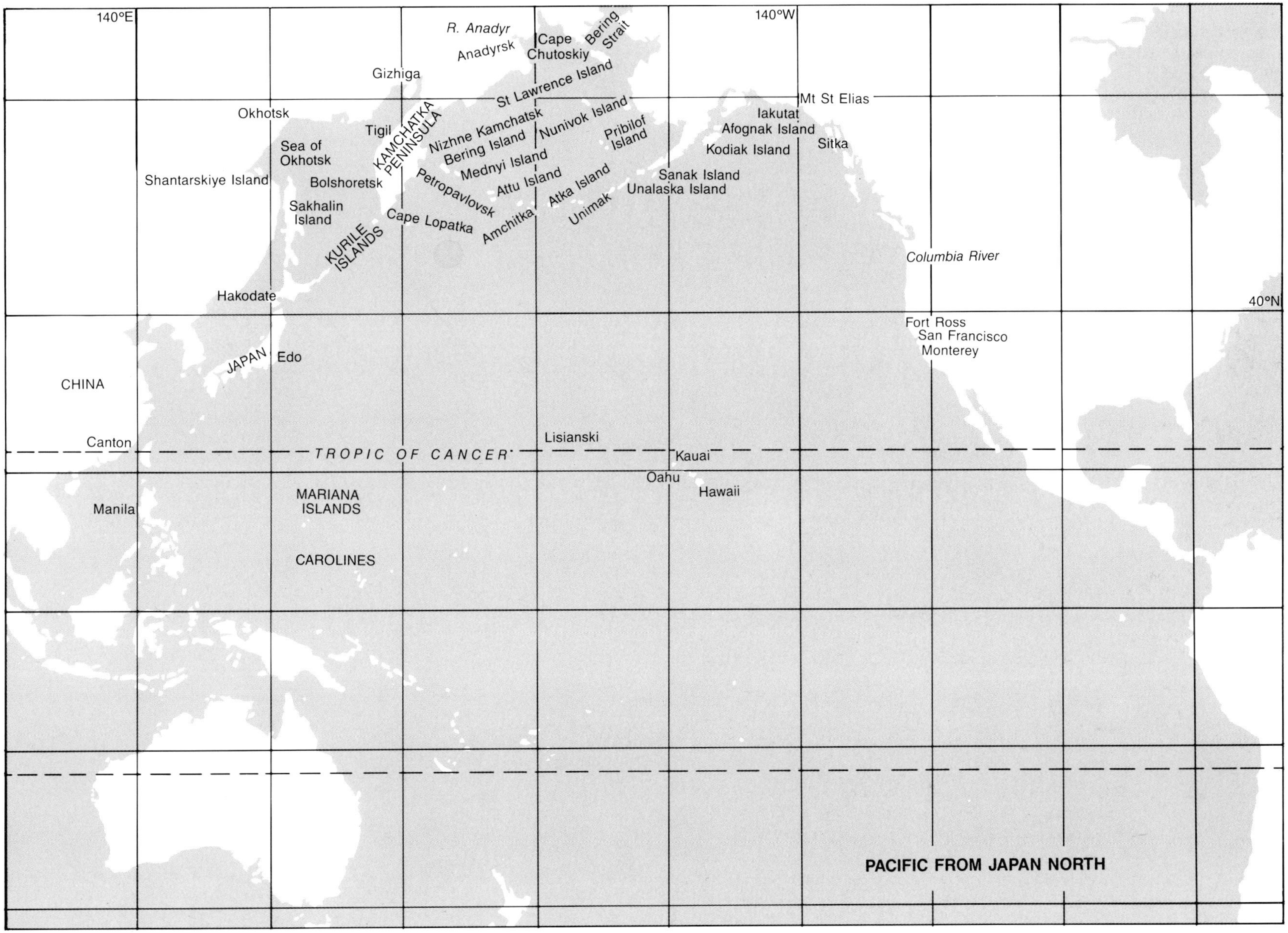
140°E
140°W
40°N
R. Anadyr
Anadyrsk
Cape Chutoskiy
Bering Strait
Gizhiga
St Lawrence Island
Mt St Elias
Okhotsk
Tigil
KAMCHATKA PENINSULA
Nizhne Kamchatsk
Bering Island
Nunivok Island
Pribilof Island
Iakutat
Afognak Island
Kodiak Island
Sitka
Sea of Okhotsk
Mednyi Island
Shantarskiye Island
Bolshoretsk
Petropavlovsk
Attu Island
Atka Island
Sanak Island
Unalaska Island
Sakhalin Island
Cape Lopatka
Amchitka
Unimak
KURILE ISLANDS
Columbia River
Hakodate
Fort Ross
San Francisco
Monterey
JAPAN
Edo
CHINA
Lisianski
Canton
TROPIC OF CANCER
Kauai
Oahu
Hawaii
Manila
MARIANA ISLANDS
CAROLINES
PACIFIC FROM JAPAN NORTH

the west, who all suffered abominably.

When the Kamchatkan commandant dined with Captain John Gore on board the *Discovery* on her way home to England after Captain Cook had been murdered in Hawaii, he expressed surprise

---

that all our people should look so well after being out near three Years, and said that from our Appearance he should have supposed that we had but just left England, nor was he less astonished to hear that we had lost but such a small Number of Men by sickness, telling us that the Russians send their small Sloops with about 60 Men on a Summer's Cruise to the Coast of America and the adjacent Isles & that it often happens that not more than 20 or 30 of them return home alive, the rest dying of the Scurvy & other Disorders; he was somewhat amazed to find that we carried only 112 Men in the *Resolution* & but 70 in the *Discovery*, for the Russian Sloops of one Mast and abt 70 tons Burden generally carry sixty Hands.

Soft gold

It was the speculative luck of Captain Gore that accelerated the flood of British and American traders into the north. Pelts which he casually acquired in the American northwest, he sold in Canton for £2000; a deal which was swiftly disseminated among the growing number of adventurous independent trading captains. John Gore, whose influence on the fur trade was inadvertent, was not the only member of Cook's company who left his mark in the Russian northeast. An AB in the *Discovery*, Joseph Billings, later joined the Russian Navy and rose to the rank of captain and commanded a major survey in the northern seas from 1786 to 1793.

Visits by Cook's ships and those of La Perouse in 1787, the reconnaissance voyage of a Spanish ship

San Carlos in 1788, and the increased poaching of foreign traders demanded some response from St Petersburg. Added to this was the continued mistreatment of the Aleuts, the understandable hostility of the American mainland Indians over which the Asian authorities had no control, and the appalling incompetence of the Cossack seamen. In *Russia in Pacific Waters*, Glynn Barratt writes:

All seven vessels used by the Shelikov Company during the 1790s had been lost. On average, they made only two voyages between Kamchatka and the coast. There were so many rotting vessels at Okhotsk that soon a commandant, Captain Minitskii, would be speaking of a regular museum of the shipwrights' art.

In 1799 a trading post and fort were established at Sitka Island, off the American coast, and proposals were made to send ships from the Baltic to establish a naval presence in the northeast – without stirring a hornet's nest of foreign protest. Also in 1799 the Rossiisko-Amerkanskaia Kompaniia was founded and granted its monopolistic charter by Tsar Paul I who succeeded Catherine II.

Kruzenshtern and Lisianskii

Ivan Fedorovich Kruzenshtern and Yuri Lisianskii were young Russian naval officers seconded to the British Navy for experience during the 1790s. Both were interested in improving Russia's position in the East and Kruzenshtern's visit to China, where he witnessed the fortunes being made by English and American fur traders, confirmed the need for Russian ships to carry the pelts direct to Canton. At that time the furs were landed at Okhotsk and transported overland to China. Obstructions to this trade were imposed at the whim of the Chinese. Kruzenshtern

considered it was necessary to get ships, expertise and materials to the American coast where suitable trading vessels could be built. Back in Russia, Kruzenshtern lobbied for his proposals and, after being ignored for a time, he was placed in command of a full-scale expedition to the Pacific. As second-in-command he selected Yuri Lisianskii.

Lisianskii was despatched to find suitable vessels abroad as none were to be had in Russia. He found what was required finally on the Thames in England and purchased two merchant ships, the two-year-old 450-ton *Leander* and the newly built 370-ton *Thames*. After organising some modifications and renaming them *Nadezhda* and *Neva*, he sailed these vessels to Kronstadt in May 1803.

The simple aims of the expedition as proposed by Kruzenshtern had become complicated. Firstly, for political reasons, the mission was to be a trading venture, therefore the Russian American Company shared the expense of the voyage and embarked their own freight for barter in the East. Two company clerks were to sail to handle these operations. The command and manning of the vessels were to be naval, and scientific and survey work was to be undertaken. Scientists were carefully chosen and briefed by Kruzenshtern.

A third objective turned out to be the source of discord on what was to be a superbly organised and executed voyage, a credit to the Russian seamen who had never till then sailed their own ships to the Pacific. Kruzenshtern was to embark an ambassador to Japan in the person of Count N.P. Rezanov and his entourage. He also had to find stowage for a barnful of delicate and precious gifts for the Mikado. In itself this would not overly complicate the whole venture, except that Rezanov, by virtue of his governmental rank and orders, claimed command over the whole expedition, apart from the immediate navigation and operation of the ships. As Kruzenshtern had very carefully selected his officers and men on the basis of their skill, compatability and loyalty, Rezanov had little chance of over-riding Kruzenshtern, but his attempts at asserting his authority and his churlishness when thwarted soured the shipboard climate until he left in Petropavlovsk.

The companies of both ships were well provided for; high pay, good food and extra comforts such as mattresses encouraged the crews to give of their best and set the Pacific service apart. Officers, highly paid by the Navy and contributed to by the company, had no cause for complaint. Should they survive and prove themselves, rapid advancement in the service was almost guaranteed.

On 7 August 1803 the *Nadezhda* and the *Neva* sailed from Kronstadt. Headwinds and delays at Copenhagen and Falmouth prevented Kruzenshtern from clearing the Channel sooner, but on 18 October they anchored at Tenerife. After Tenerife the scientific work began in earnest and a busy routine of observing, testing and collecting data was to continue for the rest of the voyage. In Brazil new masts had to be built for the *Neva* from the local timber. The delay delighted the botanists, who had a field day, but depressed their commander, who rightly worried about a late rounding of Cape Horn. As it transpired, although they had their share of severe weather when they rounded the Cape on 3 March 1804, conditions were kindly. Later the ships became separated, to meet again at their rendezvous in the Marquesas. Lisianskii raised Easter Island and managed to get a boat ashore in spite of high surf. His lieutenant bartered for provisions and noted the islanders' houses, banana groves and huge statues. Kruzenshtern made straight for the Marquesas and anchored at Nuku Hiva on 7 May; the *Neva* arrived on the eleventh.

Kruzenshtern, anxious to avoid the misunderstandings and unnecessary bloodshed that so frequently occurred when island cultures clashed with European, laid down strict but fair rules to his men. Their stay proved to be an exemplary one. Trading was fair and ordered (apart from an attempt by Rezanov to undermine Kruzenshtern by ignoring his regulations), valuable ethnic and scientific data was gathered, and not one sailor apparently succumbed to the readily available charms of the island girls.

It had been planned that, after leaving the Marquesas, the ships were to part company in the Pacific; the *Nadezhda* to steer directly for Japan, and the *Neva* for the Pacific northwest. For a variety of reasons Kruzenshtern determined to make straight for Petropavlovsk by way of the Hawaiian Islands where the ships could refresh and then go their separate ways. They found the Hawaiians disappointing; bartering for provisions was difficult as the islanders were not very interested in the Russians' trade articles. Kruzenshtern noted that the islands were ideal for a way-stop for ships bound from the south towards Russia or America.

The ships parted company on 10 June; Kruzenshtern was racing against time to make Petropavlovsk and then Japan before the onset of the northeast monsoon in September. The season might bring him a fair wind for the south but rather too much of it. The accompanying rain and thick weather would make navigation particularly uncomfortable. In light of the prevailing weather conditions about and northeast of Japan, one can understand his desire to visit Petropavlovsk first. Below, in the ship's hold, he carried supplies, some perishable, for the company. Should he have chosen to visit Japan first, as Rezanov still demanded, he could well have been held up there for months – as did in fact happen. In that event Kruzenshtern would have been unable to approach Kamchatka until after the ice retreated in May.

The only Japanese port open to them was Nagasaki in the far south, the intended base of the embassy. Even if Rezanov's task was completed with speed, it was likely they would not be able to clear Japanese waters before the northeast monsoon set in with stiff head winds and foul weather.

The *Nadezhda* arrived at Petropavlovsk on 15 July after a 35-day passage from Hawaii, during which, at Rezanov's request, they kept a lookout for the islands of gold and silver, the Rica de Oro and Rica de Plats of ancient Spanish legend. Kruzenshtern was certain that they did not exist.

At Petropavlovsk Rezanov did not participate in the celebrations surrounding their arrival. Instead he set about attempting to remove Kruzenshtern, ordering that troops should be sent from Bol'sheretsk. He involved the local commandant and the Governor of Kamchatka in the dispute, but fortunately the Governor was not to be bullied into a hasty decision. After reading both men's orders and mulling over them for a while, the Governor came to the conclusion that Kruzenshtern was in the right. Rezanov's attempt at subversion by offering the command to the lieutenants was met by point-blank refusal and the stay at Petropavlovsk, which should have been pleasant for all, resulted in a nightmare of contention for the officers. Some of the ambassador's suite left the ship, to be replaced by local men. Aside from the leaders' feud, Kruzenshtern's highly scathing comments sharpened up the management of the port and the servicing of the local craft, and a survey was completed of Avacha Bay.

Adverse weather prevented the *Nadezhda* leaving for Nagasaki before 7 September and they consequently experienced high winds, rain and fog. The ship sprang a leak in a storm off the Kuriles. However they managed to make a survey of the Japanese coast on their passage south, and anchored in Nagasaki Roads in October.

The Japanese reception was frosty. Since the sixteenth century the country had been committed to an isolationist policy and only the Dutch had permission to trade through their quarantined artificial island in Nagaskai Bay. As, claimed the Japanese, they were not Dutch and had no current permission to call, they had no business there; their miserable gifts were not wanted, so they were ordered to make a speedy departure. Rezanov's protestations that he was an ambassador were ineffectual and months dragged by while the Russians were confined to the ship and a fenced compound ashore. Rezanov, claiming illness, was grudgingly allowed to live ashore under guard. After five months waiting for a decision from the Shogunate, they were told they were not wanted and asked to depart, whereupon Rezanov undiplomatically lost his temper. The Japanese, to hasten his departure, offered the Russians a large quantity of provisions which Rezanov, in retaliation, tried to turn down. It was explained to him that should he refuse to accept the gifts, the insult to the Governor and all his officials would be such that it would necessitate the act of *seppuku*, or disembowelment by the Japanese. The gifts were accepted.

The Russians' visit was worse than just a failure. The Japanese, alerted and suspicious of their motives, had closed the door to trade even more firmly.

It would have been with some relief that the Russians sailed from Nagasaki on 18 April 1805. On board, while Rezanov fumed and schemed revenge for the insult to the Russian crown, Kruzenshtern was happily employed on the voyage north, charting the eastern shores of Japan, Sakhalin and the Kuriles. He observed that the Japanese in the north were virtually defenceless and he had friendly dealings with the kindly Ainu people. *Nadezhda* arrived back in Petropavlovsk on 6 June and the ship's company no doubt breathed a sigh of relief when the ambassador and his staff made their departure. On his return to Petropavlovsk, Rezanov took over the management of the Rossiisko-Amerkanskaia Kompaniia and as company representative and friend of the Russian monarchy, he exerted powerful influence in the East.

Kruzenshtern did not waste much time at Petropavlovsk but refitted the ship and on 9 July left to complete his survey of Sakhalin. He returned on 30 August, on time, to the surprise of the inhabitants of the port. A major overhaul was carried out during the following two months, for the damp climate had taken its toll of the rigging and spars. Then, shipshape and with a quantity of furs on board, the *Nadezhda* sailed for Macao on 4 October, anchoring in the Typa on 19 November 1805.

The voyage of the *Neva*

After the two ships had separated on 10 June 1804, Lisianskii continued in the Hawaiian Islands for a while, wisely turning down a request to assist in a revolt against Kamehameha in return for an offer by the insurrectionists to bring the islands under Russian domination. Reports had been filtering through to him that the settlement at Sitka had been taken by Indians and that the company was in trouble, therefore he sailed for Kodiak where he was to discharge the company's supplies. Their arrival, after a 20-day voyage, was greeted with joy and relief. The supplies of tools and food were welcomed and the strength represented by the *Neva* relieved the settlers of their fears of attacks by French or Spanish ships which had been reported on the coast. However, Lisianskii's first concern was to assist in the recapture of the settlement at Sitka – later to be known as Novo-Arkhangel'sk.

The fort had been overrun and burned by the Tlingit Indians within a year of its building. Out of 450 souls, less than 50 had survived and half the *baidarka* fleet from Kodiak had been destroyed. Without vessels, the company manager, Baranov, was unable to attempt a recapture of the settlement until he struck a deal with an American, O'Cain, to use his ship and crew. When the *Neva* arrived at Kodiak, Baranov, O'Cain, four small ships, 120 Russians and 800 Aleuts in 300 *baidarkas* were at Sitka attempting to retake the fort. Lisianskii immediately went to their assistance. Anchored by the ruined settlement waiting for Baranov to return from a hunting trip, he records –

I never saw a country so wild and gloomy; it appeared more adapted for the residence of wild beasts than of men . . . I learned that the inhabitants of Sitka had fortified themselves and were resolved not to suffer the Russians to make a second settlement amongst them without a trial of strength . . . . From the day of our pursuit of a canoe, no natives made their appearance till the 31st at noon, when a large boat was observed under the shore rowed by twelve naked men, whose faces and bodies were painted. In the meantime, Captain Okeen, returning from the woods, was attacked. I instantly sent the armed launch against the barbarians; but they escaped. Their skill as marksmen was apparent from the shattered state of Captain Okeen's launch, as well as from the collar of his coat, through which a bullet had passed . . . In the morning of September 8 Captain Okeen set sail on his voyage homewards.

Baranov was grateful to have the reinforcement of the *Neva*, but some unfortunate earlier experiences with naval officers made him reluctant to relinquish command. An attack organised by Baranov in mid September ended in almost a rout when the disciplined and warlike Tlingit, hidden in the fort, held their fire until the last moment, with devastating effect. The guns used in the attack were only saved by heroic efforts on the part of Lisianskii's sailors. Baranov then handed the command to Lisianskii. In early October he had his ship warped under the fort and opened fire. By 7 October, after negotiations with the Indians, the Tlingit deserted the settlement. The fort was well on the way to being rebuilt by the end of winter. That same winter and the following summer Lisianskii spent profitably in surveying and scientific work.

On 20 August 1805 the *Neva* sailed for China. The route that Lisianskii planned took the *Neva* south of a direct course and he hoped thereby to

The Russian fort of Novo Arkhangel'sk, situated on the island of Sitka on the Canadian shore of the Gulf of Alaska. The settlement was first founded in 1799 but was burned by the Tlingit Indians within 12 months. The fort was recaptured with the aid of Lisianskii in the *Neva* in 1804 and was rebuilt to become the main settlement for the Russians on the American coast. Here was based the Russian-American company trading in furs. The base had wharves and repair facilities for ships, but was described by a visiting Russian midshipman as a 'sorry place with a wretched climate—cruel winds, incessant rain. You can get practically nothing there, and even if you do, it's only for the highest price. No fresh food except fish, and precious little of that, during the winter.'

discover some hitherto unknown islands. He did just that – at 10 pm on 16 October the *Neva* ran on to a reef.

> All hands were summoned upon deck and set to work; and upon sounding, we found that we had touched on a coral bank. I now ordered the guns and the heaviest articles that we had stowed in the booms, to be thrown overboard, but with such precaution that they might be recovered should circumstances admit. The ship being thus lightened, we succeeded in getting her into deep water. Then we perceived, at a distance of about a mile, a small low island to be WNW, and to the SW some high rocks. . . . Desirous of examining the place which, by its situation, appeared to be of the greatest importance to navigation, I went on shore in the morning with several of my officers. . . . The surf was so great that we could only with difficulty land at a small bay, where we found numerous birds of different kinds and seals of an enormous size. . .Towards evening, having examined everything of worthy notice, we fixed a high pole in the ground and buried near it a bottle containing a description of our discovery.

If you look on a map, you will find the speck of Lisianskii Island far out to the west of the Hawaiian Islands.

A hurricane near Tinian was survived, and later their noses told them that all was not well in the hold. Over 30,000 putrid pelts had to be jettisoned. They anchored at Macao on 3 December 1805. Endless negotiations with the wily and difficult Chinese finally enabled them to sell their furs and load Chinese products for Russia. The ship sailed on 26 February 1806, only 24 hours before an order from Peking arrived for their arrest. They arrived home in Kronstadt in August 1806.

For tyros in the art of circumnavigation, the Russian sailors proved themselves equally as capable as the English and French. Their seamanship and shipboard organisation can hardly be faulted but the major achievement for those days was to bring their ship back without the loss of a single man.

Kruzenshtern later rose to the rank of admiral. The *Neva* made another voyage to the Pacific and Rezanov continued his governorship in the East. He had his revenge by organising a raid on the unarmed Japanese northern territories and died in 1807 on his way back to St Petersburg after becoming engaged to the daughter of the Spanish Governor of San Francisco. Later a Russian outpost was established at Fort Ross, just north of San Francisco. Although there was some improvement, the Rossiisko-Amerkanskaia Company's employees in the far north continued to suffer neglect and hardship. Frequently they had to rely on visiting American traders, who were only too willing to exchange food for fur, for their supplies. Nova-Arkhangel'sk became their main settlement on the American coast until Russian interest in the region declined.

After the Napoleonic wars the Russians carried out some successful and important scientific voyages. From 1815 to 1818 Otto Von Kotzebue sailed around the world and into the Arctic north of Bering Strait in a very small brig, the *Rurik*. Fabian Bellinghausen in the *Vostok* and *Mirny* explored the Antarctic in 1819-21. Fedor Lutke in a specially built barque, the *Senyavin*, in company with a similar ship, the *Moller*, commanded by a Captain Staniukovich, sailed to the Pacific on a highly successful scientific voyage from 1826 to 1829.

The Russians had made their mark in the maritime world.

FRENCH EXPLORATION

When the Seven Years War ended in 1763, France established a settlement in the Falklands on the initiative of Louis Antoine de Bougainville, a brilliant young officer and mathematician. Unfortunately the young colony soon had to be surrendered to the Spanish, and to carry out this distasteful task, Bougainville was placed in command of the 550-ton, 26-gun frigate *Boudeuse*. However, in an attempt to regain some foothold in the south, the French authorities, on Bougainville's own suggestion, ordered him to continue into the Pacific.

Bougainville (1767-9)

After Bougainville had completed the surrender of the Falklands he was joined at Rio de Janeiro by the 480-ton storeship *Etoile* and they set sail in November 1767 for the Magellan Strait. Because of the appalling weather, the passage took 52 days.

Once in the Pacific, Bougainville took some time searching for the land reported by the privateer Edward Davis, before continuing on through the Tuamotus until he raised a steep, small island they named Boudeuse Peak. This was Mehitia, and shortly afterwards, on 2 April 1768, they sighted Tahiti and came to anchor inside the reef in Hitiaa lagoon well south of Matavai Bay. Working the ships into the anchorage, towing and warping to their kedge anchors, was complicated by an armada of canoes filled with excited Tahitians. Friendly relations were soon established with the population and chiefs, but Hitiaa was not a good anchorage,

being exposed to the southerly storms which build a heavy swell. The seas piling over the reef cause fierce surges in the lagoons, putting at grave risk any ships at anchor, particularly should they be lying to hemp cables which become chafed and torn as they

scrape over the coral. *Boudeuse* parted both her cables and for two days they struggled to save the ship, losing four anchors in the process.

Bougainville resolved to sail earlier than he had originally planned. On 14 April the *Etoile* was safely worked clear out to sea while the *Boudeuse* completed watering. Before leaving, an oak plank was buried with an act of possession inscribed upon it, and, farewells completed, the *Boudeuse* got out to sea. While her boats were recovering the anchors used to work her out, the wind failed completely. The boats were only just got to her in time before the heavy swell piled her on to the reef. That night, while the boats' recovery of the anchors was continuing, the wind rose to gale force. Bougainville had to recall the boats and sail, leaving another two anchors in the lagoon. In all, during nine days six anchors had been lost and Bougainville bewailed the lack of iron chains.

The voyage continued across the Pacific but the ships kept further south than those of any previous navigators. Among other landfalls they visited the Samoas and Vanuatu, which Bougainville recognised as the *Australia del Espiritu Santo* of Quiros. Determined to get a sight of the east coast of New Holland, he ran his latitude down on about 15°South until he came upon the Great Barrier Reef, through which he was not prepared to take his ships. Steering north, they sighted New Guinea and had great difficulty in making out round the eastern extremity of the Louisiades, which Bougainville named. The east point of Rossel Island was named Cape Deliverance. On the coast of New Britain they discovered traces of a camp used by Carteret, who had recently been there in his decrepit ship *Swallow*.

The capstan. The large hemp or manila anchor cables were too large to pass around the capstan so a messenger—an endless lighter cable—was led around the deck and capstan. As the cable came in through the hawse the messenger was hitched to it by nippers which were removed as the cable passed into the cable tier. The riding bitts were used for passing a turn of the cable so that it could be surged and slacked away with some control. When at anchor, the cable was stoppered with a series of lines to ring bolts in the deck so as to take the weight off the bitts.

Warping ship. To move the vessel in confined waters when the wind was light or foul, a light kedge anchor was laid out in the direction the ship was

required to move. A second anchor was carried out beyond the first. The ship was warped to the first until hove short. The second anchor was then dropped and the first weighed and carried out again beyond the second. There were various methods of carrying the heavy anchors in the boats but the light kedges would be hung off the davit mounted in the stern of the launch *en cravette* as the French would say. Particularly if the anchors were being carried out up-wind, the warp would be flaked out in the boat and once the anchor was dropped, the end of the cable run back to the ship. In this case the launch would be towed as there would be no room to use the sweeps. A guesswarp, a light line, would be used to measure the distance needed to drop the anchors so that they would not exceed the distance the cable would span.

On 26 March 1769 Bougainville entered St Malo. On the voyage only nine men had died out of a total complement of 330.

La Pérouse (1785-8)

Bougainville, followed by the more extensive voyages of Cook, awakened the interest of France in the Pacific. Jean François Marie de Surville was on the coast of New Zealand at the same time as Cook, and Marion du Fresne, after calling at Tasmania, was killed by the Maoris in 1722 in the Bay of Islands, New Zealand. These two private voyages were disastrous, for both expeditions lost a large part of their crews to scurvy.

Under orders from the King of France, in 1785 Jean-François de Galaup, the Comte de la Pérouse, sailed for the Pacific in the *Boussole* and the *Astrolabe*, both 500-ton storeships. The mission was primarily scientific but also had important political and

The *Boudeuse* and the *Etoile* made Batavia where Bougainville kept his visit as short as possible owing to the sickness for which the place was notorious. After calling at Mauritius and the Cape, Bougainville came up with Carteret in the south Atlantic and

offered his aid. After they had parted he commented on the *Swallow*: 'His ship was very small, went very ill, and when we took leave of him he remained as it were at anchor. How much he must have suffered in so bad a vessel may well be conceived.'

commercial aims. The voyage took them to the Sandwich Islands, Alaska, Monterey, China, the Philippines and up the east coast of Asia as far as Kamchatka. Here La Pérouse was given instructions to sail to New South Wales to investigate the new British colony reported there. Sailing south, he called at Tutuila in the Samoas where twelve of his crew were killed. He reached Botany Bay on 26 January 1788 where he was courteously received by the British. On 10 March 1788 the two ships sailed for the Friendly Islands – and vanished.

The voyage of Chevalier d'Entrecasteaux (1791-4)

In the midst of the troubles presaging the Revolution, a worried French monarchy authorised an expedition to search for La Pérouse. Chevalier d'Entrecasteaux, a rear-admiral, was given command, with instructions to examine the east coast of New Holland and trace the possible track of La Pérouse through the Friendly Islands, New Caledonia, New Hebrides and the Solomons. Two ships, both 500-ton storeships, the *Recherche* and the *Espérance*, were allotted to the task. They proved to be slow, heavy sailers that handled badly. As with all expeditions, French and British, great emphasis was placed on gathering geographical and natural data. All commanders were skilled in some scientific field and each area of research was represented by either the ships' officers or scientists signed on for the voyage. On these expeditions the French in particular took along some very fine artists.

On 29 September 1791, three months after the royal family had been arrested, d'Entrecasteaux sailed. After calling at Cape Town on the basis of a vague report, the party decided to head directly to the Admiralty Islands through the Moluccas. However, adverse weather and poor supplies made

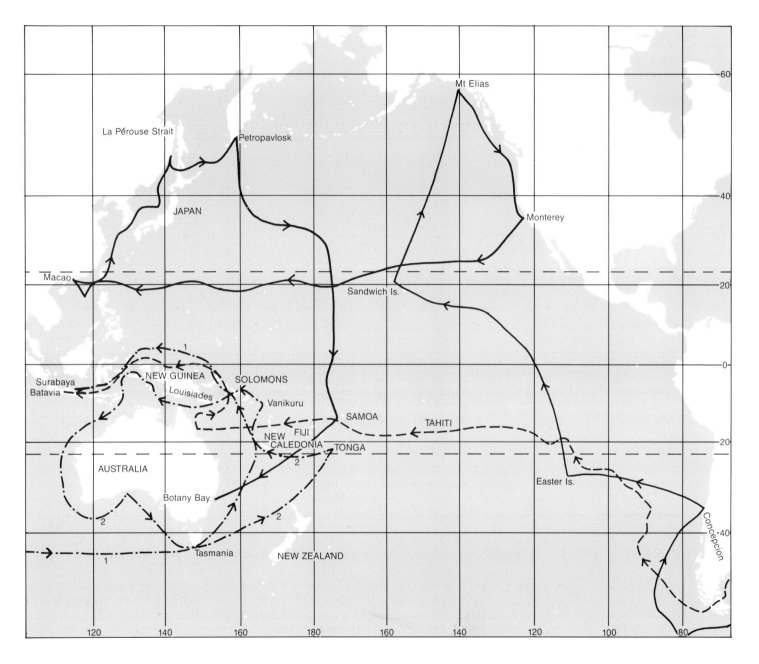

FRENCH ROUTES OF EXPLORATION IN THE PACIFIC

La Pérouse

Bougainville

d'Entrecasteaux

Mt Elias

La Pérouse Strait

Petropavlosk

JAPAN

Monterey

Macao

Sandwich Is.

Surabaya
Batavia

NEW GUINEA

SOLOMONS

Louisiades

Vanikuru

SAMOA

TAHITI

FIJI

NEW
CALEDONIA

TONGA

AUSTRALIA

Botany Bay

Easter Is.

Concepcion

Tasmania

NEW ZEALAND

60

40

20

0

20

40

120   140   160   180   160   140   120   100   80

d'Entrecasteaux change his mind and he sailed for Van Diemen's Land. Here he spent a month charting the coast. Continuing their voyage, the ships passed New Caledonia, made a call at Carteret Harbour in New Ireland and in July were in the Admiralty Group. No trace of La Pérouse was found. In view of the poor state of the health of the crew, a decision was made to go to the Dutch East Indies to convalesce. Subsequently they sailed clear round Australia back to Van Diemen's Land where, this time, they made the friendly acquaintance of the shy and doomed Tasmanians, the first Europeans to do so. Voyaging on, they called at New Zealand but did not stop, then carried on to Tongatapu, New Caledonia and the Santa Cruz Islands. Here they discovered an uncharted island and named it Ile de Recherche. Unable to anchor, they sailed on, unaware that they were within a few miles of their quest, for the island was Vanikoro where La Pérouse's ships had been wrecked.

In their search they wandered through the Solomons and Louisiades until finally they were forced to give up, exhausted. On their way to Java d'Entrecasteaux died. When the ships reached Surabaja the crews received the news that their king had been guillotined and the expedition disintegrated in political disarray.

Nineteenth-century French expeditions

Apart from an expedition commanded by Captain Nicolas Baudin which, during the years 1800-4 concerned itself with the Australian coast, no other French expeditions sailed to the Pacific until 1817. In that year the 350-ton corvette *Uranie*, under the command of Louis Claude de Freycinet, left on a scientific voyage eastbound round the world. Freycinet's resourceful wife, Rose Pinon, refused to be left at home and against all regulations, sailed in

Uranie disguised as a man until they were well out to sea. On the way home Freycinet's ship was wrecked in the Falklands, losing a large part of the scientists' collections. They were picked up by an American ship which they subsequently bought, renamed the *Physicienne* and sailed back to France in 1820.

Another scientific voyage followed in 1822 under command of the scientist-sailor Louis Isidore Duperrey, who had held the rank of ensign in *Uranie*. The *Coquille*, his 380-ton transport, designated a corvette, sailed westbound round the Horn, and for the first time since Bougainville, Tahiti was visited by the French. Anticipating the paradise described by their predecessor, they were disappointed. They found a literate but subdued population. Much of the blame for this transition has been placed on the London Missionary Society, but no doubt other factors contributed. After a 'scientifically exemplary' voyage, the *Coquille* returned to France in 1825.

Duperrey's second in command, Dumont d'Urville, took over the command of the *Coquille,* renamed her the *Astrolabe* after one of La Pérouse's ships, and sailed in 1826 for the Pacific. He cruised on the Australian coast and visited New Zealand – thereby possibly hastening the possession of the land by Great Britain.

At last the riddle of La Pérouse was solved. While in Hobart, Tasmania, in December 1827 and January 1828, d'Urville met the captain of an English ship, Peter Dillon, who said he had found the remains of La Pérouse's ships at Vanikoro. During their stopover at Tikopia in the Santa Cruz Group, Dillon had learned from one Martin Bushart, a Prussian living with the natives, that three years earlier, when Bushart had landed, he had seen several objects which could only have come from an European ship. An old sailor who had been on Vanikoro six years prior to Bushart had maintained he had met two very old white men, survivors of a shipwreck. Dillon and Bushart took a sword guard found on Tikopia to the Governor of Bengal, who gave them

a ship, the *Research,* to investigate if there were any survivors left. From some old men on Vanikoro they learned that long ago, one morning after a fierce storm, a large ship was seen on the reef. The survivors had got ashore, salvaged what they could from the wreck and built a small boat in which some months later they left, sailing west.

There were rumours also of another ship, the survivors from which had all been slaughtered. Of the two old men who had remained on the island, one had died and the other had left with some natives. Dillon departed Vanikoro on 8 October 1827, taking with him proof in the shape of two bells, one inscribed *'Bazin m'a fait',* and several other objects thought to have come from the wreck. After his meeting with d'Urville in Hobart, Dillon returned to Calcutta and sailed for France where Charles X paid his expenses, awarded him a pension for life and appointed him to the Legion of Honour.

Without delay d'Urville sailed in the *Astrolabe* for Tikopia where he met Bushart, who agreed to accompany him to Vanikoro. On Vanikoro they found final proof of the disaster. According to d'Urville, his party saw spread over the sea floor, at a depth of three or four fathoms, anchors, launches, cannonballs, ingots and a large amount of lead plates, indestructible proof of the tragedy which had taken place there 40 years before.

The *Astrolabe* returned to France on 24 February 1829. Ten of the expedition's 78 men had died, most of dysentery contracted in the East Indies. However, they had brought home a greater collection of scientific material than any other previous expedition and, in addition, 6000 drawings and their duplicates, an average of 12 drawings for each day of the voyage.

Other circumnavigations, with political intent, took place in the 1820s and thirties. None of these neglected the scientific possibilities, for this was the heyday of the exploration of natural history, exemplified by Darwin's voyage in the *Beagle*. (See page 141.)

Antarctic exploration

Dumont d'Urville was to make another voyage. In 1837 he sailed in the old *Astrolabe* in company with another 300-ton corvette, the *Zélée*. When the middle-aged and rather tired commander learned of the purpose of the expedition, which was to explore the South Pole, he was horrified, but resigned himself to the work. He made two forays into the Antarctic, the first into the Weddell Sea where the expedition very nearly got trapped in the ice, and the second south of Australia to Adélie Land, which he named after his wife. While in this region they came up with Charles Wilkes's expedition in the brig *Porpoise*. Apparently d'Urville failed to respond to Wilkes's signals and the incident gave rise to a controversy between the French and Americans over the priority of discovery of Adélie Land.

Among other places, d'Urville's voyage took the *Astrolabe* and *Zélée* to New Zealand where the Treaty of Waitangi had only very recently been signed in the Bay of Islands. Here they again came up with the *Porpoise* and both the American Wilkes and

The *Astrolabe* and *Zélée* in the Antarctic ice during Dumont d'Urville's last expedition

102

d'Urville indignantly refused to recognise the treaty and the authority of Governor Hobson, the British Crown representative.

On 7 November 1840 the *Astrolabe* and *Zélée* arrived home in Toulon. Twenty men had died and 20 deserted, but the voyage had worthwhile scientific results. The Americans finally conceded that d'Urville had priority in Adélie Land. Dumont d'Urville, after surviving the hazards of three circumnavigations, disease, ice and storm, was, with his wife and second son, killed in a railway accident in 1842.

The French ships

Of all the ships used by the French on their various expeditions, Dumont d'Urville's ship the *Astrolabe* (formerly the *Coquille*) must take the accolade for endurance. She survived three circumnavigations, ice (for which she was totally unsuited) and a severe grounding in Torres Strait. The *Coquille* was specially fitted out as an expeditionary ship for Duperrey's voyage. As a transport ship she was the universal type of carrier used throughout the period; flush decked, apart from a small raised poop level with the bulwarks, she was a spacious ship for her size and probably a good sailer. These transports were favoured by the French for exploratory work, just as the Whitby cats had been favoured by the English during Cook's time. When taken over by the government, they were redesignated either corvette or frigate, depending on their size. Corvettes themselves, handy small warships mounting about 18 guns, proved useful in this work. Freycinet's 20-gun *Uranie* was an example.

La Pérouse's ships were both 500-ton transports, redesignated frigates owing to their size. They were not frigates by definition. The only frigate used was Bougainville's *Boudeuse*. She measured 550 ton and 131 ft (40 m) on the gundeck, which mounted 26 cannon. As later frigates went she was small, but would have been a superb ship. When Bougainville sailed in her she was new and untried. He had doubts about her strength, for the French frigates were built for speed, with slightly inclined endposts and hollow waterlines and she would have carried a large spread of canvas on fairly light spars. In fact, when the *Boudeuse* first put out from Nantes she had immediately to return to Brest, having sprung her mainmast. Primarily she was an ocean-going fighting ship with a turn of speed which would allow her to chase or run with success. Carrying capacity, comfort and versatility would have been sacrificed to this end. Whatever Bougainville's doubts about her, she got around the world safely.

French frigates were superior in design to the frigates of any other nation, as were most of France's ships. These vessels were much valued during the Napoleonic Wars, when many French ships taken as prizes were turned against their builders.

From about 1760 the British began to use copper sheathing to protect their hulls but the French continued with *mailletage*, the covering of the sheathing with flat-headed iron nails which rusted together into a solid layer, easier to repair than copper sheathing, but presenting more surface resistance. Iron or lead was used as ballast, replacing sand and stone. This provided more compact and effective ballast and had the advantage that it could be traded in the islands.

Life on board the French ships is best described by the following extract from Jacques Brosse's *Great Voyages of Exploration*. The account was given by Captain Abel Aubert Dupetit-Thouars in 1840.

A drum awoke the crew, generally at 6 o'clock; after the morning call to quarters and stowing of hammocks came breakfast. The men were grouped into eights – into 'platters' or messes, each of which had a water can, a goblet, and a tin platter for meat. The morning ration consisted of a half-pound of bread or six ounces of biscuit with which to make a bread soup, and a quarter of a litre of wine or a tot of brandy. At 7 o'clock the ship was washed down. At half past eight, everybody got into the uniform of the day and the officers made an inspection. At 10 o'clock, there was gun drill. At 12, they had a meal of half a pound of bread, an equal amount of fresh beef or six ounces of salt pork, and a quarter litre of wine. From 2 to 4 o'clock, there was drill with the sails and weapons, and half an hour later came dinner: six ounces of biscuit and a soup of lima beans or other legumes, washed down with a quarter of a litre of wine. Then the men were free until the evening call to quarters, generally around sunset. Half the crew alternated with the night watch. Every day at sea was identical except for Sunday, when, after a general inspection – and Mass, if there was a chaplain on board – the men were free. Entertainments were organised, and in the evening there was dancing.

To maintain order among these 'demi-devils with rather rough ways', punishments were sometimes necessary. The most feared of these – not abolished until 1848 – was ducking: The guilty man was suspended from ropes at the end of the mainyard, weights were attached to his feet, and he was thrice plunged into the sea until almost suffocated. This was called wet ducking; in dry ducking, the victim's fall was arrested before he had touched the water; in keelhauling, the guilty man was passed under water from one side of the ship to the other. Clearly, this punishment was applied only in cases of serious infringements, but the whip was often used. The French Revolution had forbade it in principal, but until 1830 cabin boys were still whipped; the practice continued for a considerably longer time in the British navy.

Altogether, the French were very much more humane to their men than the British, a practice which was to continue to the end of the sailing-ship era.

THE EXPEDITIONS OF JAMES COOK

Captain James Cook was, there is no doubt, the supreme navigator and explorer of the Pacific. J.C. Beaglehole, in his definitive work *The Exploration of the Pacific*, devoted nearly a quarter of the space to the English captain and claimed that it was impossible to do him justice. With some trepidation, therefore, I must ask the reader's forebearance if I only briefly dwell on Cook's achievements and suggest you refer to some of the many fine books written on his voyages or, better still, his journals which are published in full by the Hakluyt Society.

The first voyage (1768-71)

Cook's first Pacific expedition in the cat-built *Endeavour* had the primary purpose of observing the transit of Venus from Tahiti, after which he was to explore the hitherto untraversed waters of the southwest Pacific as '. . .there is reason to imagine that a continent, or land of great extent, may be found.'

Sailing into the Pacific around Cape Horn, Cook successfully observed the transit at Tahiti, circumnavigated both main islands of New Zealand, charting them in outline, and made a landing on the east coast of Australia at Botany Bay. Exploring north up the coast, the expedition very nearly lost the ship on the Great Barrier Reef but managed to get her off and repair her in the Endeavour River. The subsequent navigation northwards through the labyrinth of reefs and in the Endeavour Strait could only have been completed safely by a navigator as competent as Cook.

The *Endeavour* returned to England by way of Batavia and Good Hope to complete a highly successful voyage, which, like most explorations of the time, posed more questions than it answered.

The Frenchman de Surville, who was on the New Zealand coast at the same time as Cook, had his crew decimated by scurvy; Cook had lost no one to the disease. His careful insistence on cleanliness and good diet successfully defeated the dreaded disease. However, as had happened to previous navigators, the fevers of Batavia caused havoc with the health of all on board and before Cook cleared the Cape of Good Hope homeward bound, 29 men had died from diseases contracted in the Dutch port.

It was not long before plans were made for a second voyage to the Pacific.

The second voyage (1772-5)

The purpose of Cook's second voyage was to circumnavigate the world in as high a southern latitude as possible. This was to be the first time a chronometer was carried on a circumnavigation. The invention of John Harrison worked well and eliminated the laborious calculation of longitude by lunar sights. The ships *Resolution* and *Adventure* called at Madeira and the Cape before launching out southwards to the Antarctic. For the first time the Antarctic Circle was crossed west of Enderby Land, then, as ice prevented further progress south, Cook worked eastward in high southern latitudes before slanting up to New Zealand to allow the crews to recuperate. On this passage the ships became separated but rejoined at Queen Charlotte Sound in the north of the South Island of New Zealand. The *Adventure,* under the command of Tobias Furneaux, had undertaken some exploration around Tasmania before continuing to the rendezvous. After completing their wooding and watering, both ships sailed east to 133°West, then north to the Tuamotus, Tahiti and Tonga. Before returning to Queen Charlotte Sound the ships once more became separated, this time for good.

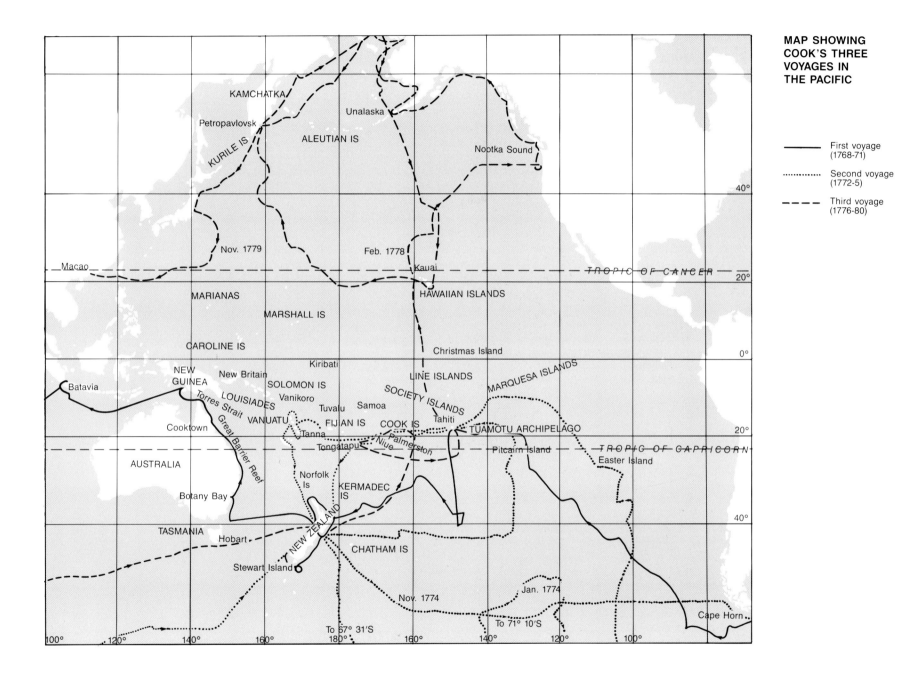

First voyage
(1768-71)

Second voyage
(1772-5)

Third voyage
(1776-80)

KAMCHATKA

Unalaska

Petropavlovsk

KURILE IS

ALEUTIAN IS

Nootka Sound

40°

Nov. 1779

Feb. 1778

Macao

Kauai

TROPIC OF CANCER

20°

MARIANAS

HAWAIIAN ISLANDS

MARSHALL IS

CAROLINE IS

0°

Kiribati

Christmas Island

NEW
GUINEA

New Britain

LINE ISLANDS

MARQUESA ISLANDS

Batavia

SOLOMON IS

SOCIETY ISLANDS

LOUISIADES

Vanikoro

Torres Strait

Tuvalu

Samoa

VANUATU

FIJIAN IS

COOK IS

Tahiti

TUAMOTU ARCHIPELAGO

20°

Cooktown

Great Barrier Reef

Tanna

Palmerston

Tongatapu

Niue

Pitcairn Island

TROPIC OF CAPRICORN

AUSTRALIA

Norfolk
Is

Easter Island

Botany Bay

KERMADEC
IS

40°

TASMANIA

Hobart

NEW ZEALAND

CHATHAM IS

Stewart Island

Nov. 1774

Jan. 1774

Cape Horn

To 67° 31'S

To 71° 10'S

100°   120°   140°   160°   180°   160°   140°   120°   100°

Cook's next foray traversed the southern reaches of the South Pacific in a series of huge zigzags, reaching his farthest south in 71°10′S and 106°54′W, where he was halted by ice. Once again he returned to New Zealand, taking a big swing north and calling at Easter Island, the Marquesas, Tahiti, Tonga, Vanuatu, New Caledonia and Norfolk Island. On this passage many new islands were found and previous discoveries confirmed, all of which were firmly placed on the developing chart of the Pacific.

From New Zealand he then sailed directly to Tierra del Fuego and into the Atlantic where he continued east, taking possession of South Georgia and on to complete the circumnavigation before heading north to the Cape of Good Hope and thence home. He had been away three years and 18 days and sailed 70,000 miles. Only four men were lost, none through scurvy. The *Adventure*, after some trouble with the New Zealand Maoris, had followed instructions and sailed east in a high latitude to the Cape and back to England.

The third voyage (1776-80)

This voyage in the *Resolution* and *Discovery* took the ships around the Cape of Good Hope to New Zealand, Tonga and Tahiti. From Tahiti they sailed northwards, discovering Hawaii, which Cook named the Sandwich Islands after the Earl of Sandwich. Here they paused for refreshment before commencing the main purpose of the voyage, which was to examine the American northwest coasts for a possible passage east. They made their landfall on the coast at about 45°N and cruised north, exploring and charting, until ice prevented progress beyond the Bering Strait in latitude 70°44'N. To winter, they returned to Kealakekua Bay in Hawaii. Good relations with the Hawaiians continued throughout their stay but, possibly because of depleted food resources, the islanders were happy to see them sail. Unfortunately the ships soon ran into a severe gale during which the foremast was sprung, enforcing a return for repairs. Relations with the Hawaiians deteriorated rapidly and in an effort to recover a stolen cutter, during which a chief was shot, Captain Cook was killed. The shocked and vengeful crews continued with preparing the ships, and by the time they sailed peace had been made and the Hawaiians mourned Cook as deeply as the sailors.

Command was taken over by Charles Clerke. On the return from Bering Strait after the next season's exploration, Clerke also died and Lieutenant John Gore took over leadership. He brought the ships home by way of Petropavlovsk and China.

The voyages of Captain James Cook were the grande finale of Pacific exploration; only a handful of reefs and islands remained to be discovered. His meticulous charting, seamanship, determination and care for his crews have become a legend.

The *Resolution* and the *Adventure*

Cook would have been happy to sail in the *Endeavour* on his second voyage but she had been sent to the Falkland Islands as a storeship. In September 1771 the Admiralty instructed the Navy Board to purchase 'two proper vessels for service in remote parts'. This task was given to Cook who found, in the Pool of London, two ships, the *Marquis of Granby* and the *Marquis of Rockingham*. They were both barques built at Whitby by Fishburn, who had built the *Endeavour*; both were less than 18 months old. The ships were purchased by the Navy and renamed the *Drake* and *Raleigh*, later changed to *Resolution* and *Adventure* when it was realised that the names might be taken amiss in the Spanish Americas. On the Navy Establishment they were classed 'sloops' and were rigged with a mizzen topsail. Cook said of the *Resolution*, '. . .that I do now, and ever did think her the most proper Ship for this service I ever saw, and that from the knowledge and experience I have had of these sort of Vessels I shall always be of the opinion that only such are proper to be sent on Discoveries to very distant parts'.

It was intended that the ships would sail in March 1772 but the unreasonable demands of Joseph Banks delayed the departure. He didn't approve of the *Resolution* from the first, thinking that a frigate would be more suitable to his now elevated station. The incredible amount of impedimenta, scientists, artists and thirteen draughtsmen, clerks and secretaries (including four horn players), Banks proposed to embark necessitated the building of an extra deck and the construction of a roundhouse. These can be seen if one looks carefully at the Admiralty draft.

When, in May, the *Resolution* was ordered to the Downs, the pilot gave up at the Nore for they could hardly set a sail on her without risking a capsize. Cooper, the first lieutenant, stated she was 'an exceeding dangerous and unsafe ship' and Clerke, speaking to Banks, burst out, 'By God, I'll go to sea in a grog-tub, if required, or in the *Resolution* as soon as you please, but I must say I think her by far the most unsafe ship I ever saw or heard of'.

Cook ordered the whole top hamper removed, the guns reduced in weight, and for good measure had the masts shortened. Banks, in a fury, refused to sail and removed all his equipment and people.

The *Resolution* proved to be Cook's favourite ship and lived up to his initial judgment of her. The *Adventure* also proved to be a good ship, but was more difficult in stays than the *Resolution*.

Ships of Cook's second expedition

	Tons	Length Lower Deck	Extreme Breadth	Depth of Hold
Resolution	462	110 ft 8 in. (33.75 m)	35 ft 5½ in. (10.81 m)	13 ft 1½ in. (4.0 m)
Adventure	336	97 ft 3 in. (29.66 m)	28 ft 4½ in. (8.65 m)	12 ft 8¾ in. (3.88 m)

The bottoms of both ships were sheathed and filled

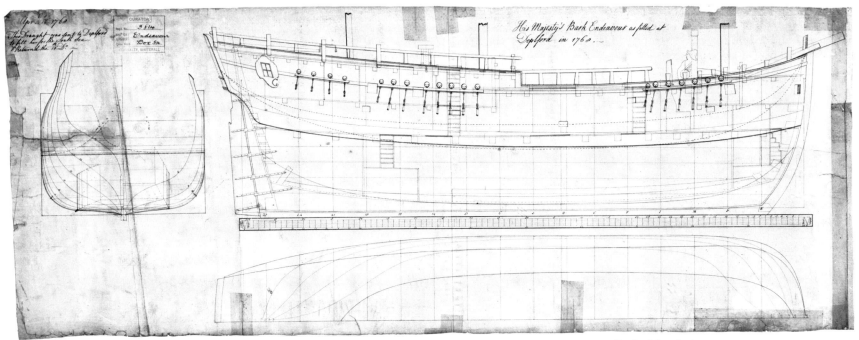

Draft of the *Endeavour*
(National Maritime Museum, Greenwich)

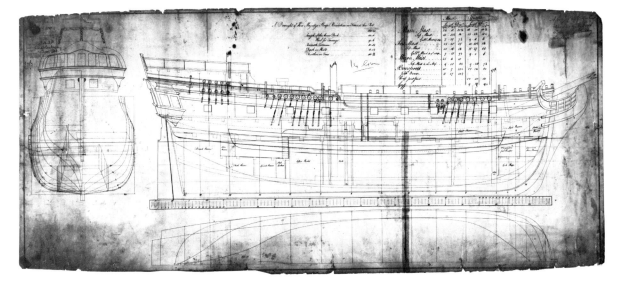

Draft of the *Resolution*
(National Maritime Museum, Greenwich)

WILLIAM BLIGH AND THE *BOUNTY*

Bligh, Christian and *Bounty* are three names which evoke a response even from those least versed in maritime history. The story, the facts woven into those names, form an epic hard to match by any writer of fiction. Three films, a musical and many books have hardly done justice to the truth and the personalities on which the tale hinges. Argument continues and a fairer judgment of the nature of William Bligh is gradually emerging. Maligned and cruelly satirised as Bligh often was, few questioned his seamanship and leadership in the face of Nature's hardships.

On 23 December 1787, after months of delays the *Bounty* put out into a stormy, wintry English Channel bound for the Pacific. Earlier that year, in response to a royal command, preparations were begun to send a vessel to sail via Cape Horn to Tahiti where breadfruit plants were to be embarked for shipment to the West Indies. Breadfruit, it was considered, would provide a cheap, ideal food for the slaves on which the economy of the islands depended. Instructions were given to sail from Tahiti through the strait between New Holland and New Guinea to Java, replacing any losses among the breadfruit with samples of local fruit-bearing trees. It was advised that September of 1787 would be the most suitable time to sail.

William Bligh had sailed with Cook and proved himself an able navigator and seaman. He was appointed to command the expedition through the influence of Joseph Banks. Bligh at the time was employed in the West Indian trade. Although he was a candidate for the position since May, he was not appointed and informed until August, and was not officially told of the purpose of the voyage until September; as a result, he had little influence on the preparation and manning of the ship.

In May, a small collier, the *Bethia,* had been purchased by the Navy for £1950 and moved into Deptford Dock for alterations and fitting out. The *Bethia* was small, measuring only about 215 tons and about 91 ft (27.75 m) on deck. Her diminutive size was to exacerbate the problem which Bligh and his complement had to face – it limited the number of crew she could carry to a precarious level for such a voyage and yet crowded the ship. No marines could be carried and the only commissioned officer was Lieutenant Bligh himself – a lonely command indeed. In fitting out the *Bethia,* or as she was renamed, the *Bounty,* all accommodation was removed from the after end of the maindeck. From the great-cabin windows to the foot of the quarter-deck companionway, shelving, lead guttering and waterways were constructed to contain and maintain a thousand-odd breadfruit plants. Bligh's cabin became a cupboard-sized space on the starboard side at the foot of the quarter-deck companion and crew space was correspondingly reduced.

Aloft, as a merchant ship and particularly if she was a collier, her rigging and spars would have been considerably modified for ease of handling with a scant crew. Once in the Navy dockyard, she would have been rerigged to Navy specifications. These would include larger tops, preventer stays, and a host of changes in the lifts, braces, trusses, slings, halliards and so on. She was provided with a full suit of studdingsails and booms. When she set out she would have probably carried more sail than a

merchantman but, for her voyage, the sail area was reduced from the rig which would have been provided for a Navy ship of her size.

On deck, the boat skids would have been strengthened to take the 23 ft (7.02 m) launch, 18

The *Bounty* replica's headgear

ft (5.49 m) cutter and 16 ft (4.88 m) jolly boat; the latter stowed inside one of the other two. These boats together and empty weighed over two tons. As their interiors formed a handy place to dump any loose gear and to house such things as chicken coops, and also the spaces on the skids between the boats formed a miniature spar-deck, the skids themselves were necessarily a powerful structure. The boats were firmly griped to the deck rather than the skids. Additional anchors, four four-pounders, and ten swivel guns, sweeps, spare spars, livestock housing and stores would have been a few of the items cluttering the decks, although the swivels, and for much of the voyage, the four-pounders, would have been stowed below. The wooden sheathing on her bottom was replaced with copper against the teredo worm.

The Admiralty manning scale for a ship of the size and class of the *Bounty* allowed for 25 able seamen. When Bligh sailed he had only 13 able seamen including Byrne, a partly blind Irish fiddler. The positions of the other 12 were either filled by 'young gentlemen' or midshipmen signed on as able seamen, as was common practice. Other able-seamen positions were filled by men assigned to tasks such as cook and steward. In normal conditions Bligh used a three-watch system, or four hours on, eight off, instead of the more normal four-on four-off port and starboard watches commonly practised. This would mean that a watch would only muster four or five able seamen along with a quartermaster. Perhaps the bosun and his mate stood a watch also, but even if this were so, the maximum number of hands in each watch would be six. The midshipmen and officers of the watch would not be expected, as in Drake's ships, to pull and haul with the seamen. From personal experience I can report that the *Bounty* replica could be sailed comfortably with six hands provided the weather was reasonable and

The *Bounty* off Matavai Bay

required not too much sail handling and trimming. However, if Bligh expected Navy standards of smartness and alacrity on his ship, the sailors would have been kept fairly jumping.

Bligh sailed two days before Christmas in 1787. To say that he was an irate captain at that time would be an understatement. However, his spleen was directed not at his men but at the Admiralty. He had left Deptford on 9 October and, after battling headwinds and dirty Channel weather, reached Spithead on 4 November. Here the Admiralty kept him waiting until the twenty-fourth while fair winds wasted. Foul weather and adverse winds then drove *Bounty* twice back to Spithead before she finally managed to claw out to sea, pounded by gales and heavy seas. Although her boats were damaged and some stores lost from the deck the ship and her crew were commended by Bligh. The delays had imposed a winter attempt at rounding Cape Horn and Bligh's scathing comment on Admiralty incompetence is aptly expressed in a letter to Duncan Campbell, his former employer in the West Indies trade:

> If there is any punishment that ought to be inflicted on a set of Men for neglect, I am sure it ought on the Admiralty for my three weeks' detention at this place during a fine fair wind which carried all outward-bound ships clear of the Channel but me, who wanted it most. This has made my task a very arduous one indeed for to get round Cape Horn at the time I shall be there. I know not how to promise myself any success & yet I must do it if the ship will stand it at all or I suppose my character will be at stake. Had Lord Home sweetened this difficult task by giving me promotion I should have been satisfied . . .

The subsequent voyage of the *Bounty* is better described elsewhere. Suffice to say that Bligh, in spite of a month of heroic effort in appalling

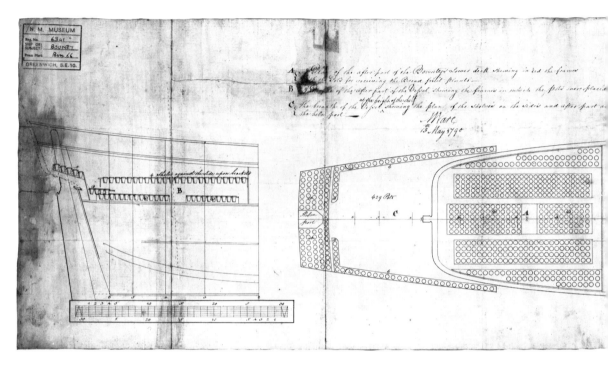

Drafts of the original *Bounty*
(National Maritime Museum, Greenwich)

conditions, failed to beat to windward around the Horn. During this time of hardship, he cared carefully for his men, providing hot food and dry clothes for the overworked and frozen sailors. Consistently throughout the voyage Bligh promoted the physical comfort and care of his people, an attribute gleaned from Cook but rare in the British Navy.

The helm was put up and the *Bounty* ran down her easting to the Pacific, stopping at Cape Town and Adventure Bay in Tasmania to recoup. She entered Matavai Bay on 26 October 1788

There had already been some friction in the ship, mainly, it seems, centred on William Purcell, the

carpenter, a cantankerous sea-lawyer, and the promotion of Fletcher Christian to acting-lieutenant. This put Christian in authority over John Fryer, the master, who would have been hoping to advance his own career on the voyage. Naturally Fryer resented the promotion of Christian, and this must in some measure explain the master's subsequent lack of interest and support for Bligh. According to Gavin Kennedy in his book *Bligh*, it was possibly Christian's failure to match Bligh's expectations that could have led to the traumatic events between them.

In Tahiti shipboard life became somewhat slack. Bligh was continually castigating his officers for incompetence. When moving the *Bounty* from Matavai Bay to Oparre, the ship ran aground due to carelessness on the part of both Christian and Fryer. Later it was discovered that many of the sails in the sail-room were mildewed and rotten, a serious business and the master's responsibility. A host of petty irritations such as thefts by the Tahitians and more serious troubles like those above, and attempts at desertion by the crew, led to a widening gulf between the captain and his men as Bligh's temper got shorter and shorter. Those who might have given him moral and physical support were outranked by the discontented and inefficient officers. The contrast between life among the friendly, easy-going islanders and the bitter wrangling in the ship must have played some part in the mutiny which was to follow.

With the breadfruit carefully installed, an unhappy crew, and to the accompaniment of grieving wails from their native wives, the *Bounty* left Tahiti on 4 April 1788, bound westward for Endeavour Strait. The mutiny took place before dawn on 28 April, shortly after visiting the island of Annamooka. Bligh, with 18 men, was launched on his epic three thousand-mile voyage to Timor and the mutineers returned to Tahiti. Attempts to settle on Tubai, 300 miles to the south of Tahiti, failed amid dissension and gross mistreatment of the islanders. The mutineers, divided among themselves, returned to Tahiti, from where the hard core, led by Christian, sailed for Pitcairn Island. They were not to be heard of again for 19 years until Captain Matthew Folger, of the Nantucket whaler *Topaz*, discovered the small colony whose sole survivor of the mutineers was a seaman, Alexander Smith. The *Bounty* had been deliberately or accidentally burned while at anchor offshore shortly after the mutineers' arrival. Throughout her voyage, whatever the tribulations of her complement and incompetence of her executive officers, the little ship had proved herself sound and weatherly.

Sailing the *Bounty* replica (1983-4)

The swing of masts and spars against the sky, the thud and hiss of a boarding sea and the reek of Stockholm tar are among a wealth of vivid memories I have of the *Bounty* replica, for I sailed in this ship as mate and master, spending three years tending her wants in port and at sea.

The modern replica was built by the Whangarei Engineering Company Ltd in Whangarei, New Zealand, in 1978 at the instigation of American film producer David Lean and the financier Dino de Laurentis. To all appearances she was constructed to be as closely as possible an exact replica of Bligh's *Bounty*, but was also provided with engines and modern equipment necessary to fulfil her role in film-making. Her steel hull was clad above the wales, contemporary fittings on deck were disguised or made removable, and any steel wire used in the rig was parcelled and served. The wheel and tiller line steering of the original was retained and working capstans and windlass provided. Two 23 ft (7.02 m) launches, identical with the boat in which Bligh made his remarkable voyage, were built.

However, the glory of the new *Bounty* was to be her rig which, apart from the discreet and mostly sensible use of wire here and there, and synthetic running rigging, would be almost identical with her predecessor – right down to the fourth reef in the main topsail, a modification which Bligh made from the three reefs of the usual Navy rig. The sails, as were the originals, were to be of Scottish flax canvas – strong and reasonably tame in a blow, but the subject of much cursing when wet as they take on the consistency of stiff cardboard and the weight of iron.

It was to be four years after launching that *Bounty* set out on her seagoing career. While she lay idle in Whangarei, the owner's representative, Lt Commander (Retired) J. McGuire, with true Tyneside tenacity, jealously guarded the ship from the depredations of time and officialdom while a small team of riggers and volunteers lovingly maintained her 11½ miles (18.52 km) of rigging, engines and equipment. From these enthusiasts the nucleus of the *Bounty*'s sailing crew was formed.

A new era for the *Bounty* was heralded on 1 January 1983, for on that day she possessed her first 'professional' crew who were to sail her to Tahiti for the making of the film 'The Bounty'. This was exciting stuff! Serious thought had previously been given to the problems of sailing the ship on a long ocean passage. Sure, we had sailed her on a coast-wise passage – once – and she had completed sea trials, but to sail her deepsea was something different. Some of us had experience in square rig, but how would the *Bounty* perform in Southern Ocean seas and storms? 'Well', we decided 'if Bligh did it, we can, so let's find out how...'.

Housing the foretopgallant mast at sea in the *Bounty* replica

113

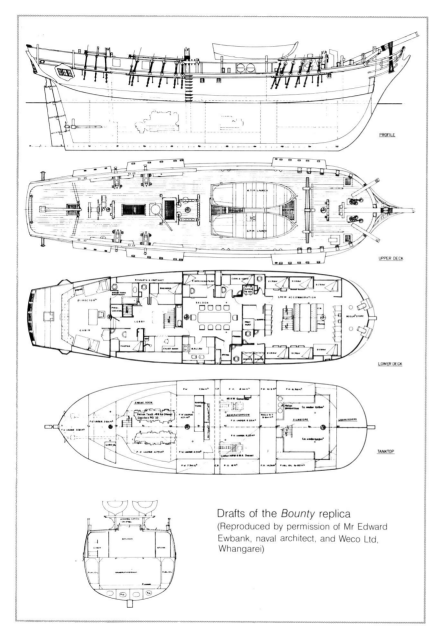

PROFILE

UPPER DECK

LOWER DECK

TANKTOP

Drafts of the *Bounty* replica
(Reproduced by permission of Mr Edward Ewbank, naval architect, and Weco Ltd, Whangarei)

Construction
Welded steel hull to Lloyds approved drawings. Oversheathed to w.l. in timber.
Deck planking N.Z. tanekaha
Hull planking African iroko
Masts & Spars British Columbian pine

Heights of masts
Fore	32.46 m
Main	33.94 m
Mizzen	22.24 m

Sails
Scottish flax	933 m²

Speed
Under power	9.3 k
Under 50% sail. 30 K wind	7.5 k

Capacities
Fuel oil	78.36 t
Fresh water	28.20 t

Accommodation
Director's cabin	2 berths
Master	Single cabin
Engineer	Single cabin
Watch Keepers	2 berth cabin
Cook & Bosun	2 berth cabin
Crew's Cabin	12 berths
Complement	20

Classification
Lloyds	100 A1 Yacht

Principal dimensions
Length o.a.	40.50 m
Length c.w.l.	26.48 m
Beam over channels	8.60 m
Depth mid.	5.49 m
Draft	3.79 m
Displacement	387 t

Machinery

Main engines 2 x Kelvin T.A.S.C. 8 diesels. Each developing 415 H.P. at 1200 R.P.M.
Auxiliaries 2 x Lister H.R.W. 6 MA diesels, direct-coupled to 2 x 49 Kw 60 Hz alternators. Voltages 415 — 220 — 110 AC.

Under the leadership of Paul Leppington, our Yorkshire dynamo of a captain, we delved into Bligh's logs and such archaic manuals as D'Arcy Lever's *Young Sea Officers' Sheet Anchor* and William Hutchinson's *Treatise on Practical Seamanship* which, incidentally, set us back on our heels with admiration for those old-time sailors who could 'right a ship on her beam ends' and sail up muddy creeks sideways using the tide.

'The way Grandfather did it' became our goal – 'Grandfather' of course being Bligh. Thus, only when short-handed would we use the power winches to sway up the one-and-a-half-ton launches or send up a yard. Safety harnesses were never used and work was done with a 'two six heave' or a shanty. After a while we were sending up and down topgallant masts and yards, running in the jibboom, reefing and setting stunsails – not with the expertise of the old sailors, but with some degree of confidence and efficiency.

We sailed for Tahiti in April 1983. A bleak fresh easterly wind bringing showers set the farewelling crowds on the wharf shivering as we let go the skirl of pipes. We were soon to find out what the Pacific could do to us, for that night and the next day it blew a gale and we spent three days battling to get clear of the coast. We found how the ship could roll;

Reefing the foretopsail on HMAT *Bounty*. The spritsail has been reefed so that it takes the form of a settee, a type of lateen sail. If the studdingsail booms were stowed on the yards, it was the practice to unlash the heel of the boom and trice it up out of the way. (On the *Bounty* replica it was found that this was unnecessary as the booms were small enough not to be a hindrance but an advantage, as they provided something to hang on to.)

indeed at times she rolled her gunn'ls under and we looked anxiously aloft, for we wondered how the masts could stand. Then, during the afternoon of the fourth day, an 'All hands!' call brought everybody scrambling out to bring the fore topsail on deck. The yard had broken clean in two. A spare yard was prepared and sent aloft as we fought south to find the westerlies, but they were not there. It was the year of El Ninos which fouled up weather patterns right across the Pacific, so we resigned ourselves to motor-sailing our easting down. Contaminated fuel made our engines anything but reliable and our track suffered a series of what we called 'hiccups'. Our first severe storm set us surfing off to the south soon after we had turned north for the trades.

I well remember that night, for we spent nearly three wild hours aloft reefing and furling, wrapping ourselves around the yards on the deeper rolls, for the ship had no jackstays. We finally had her snugged down to a reefed foresail and fore topmast staysail, scudding off before the gale. The *Bounty* gained our confidence that night, for her bluff and bouyant ends rose before every huge sea and although nobody could say she was comfortable, she was safe.

We made Papeete after a passage of 28 days and then went on to two months' filming around Moorea. There followed a fairly uneventful voyage back to New Zealand to complete filming, and then home to the port of Whangarei to undergo survey and refit. This was surely needed after the rigours of the last few months. Most of our crew had dispersed by this time and on our young rigger, Grey Hutchinson, fell the brunt of dismantling and overhauling the rig, which included the removal and regluing of the mainmast. On our equally young and incredibly industrious engineer Peter Kane fell the task of stripping and overhauling the engines and generators; he vanished into the bowels of the engineroom and was hardly to be seen for months.

What next? Rumours always rampant on the *Bounty* took her here, there and everywhere. A publicity tour of the United States? That faded. A

series on Cook? That was not to be. Then, out of the blue, early in February 1984 came word to get her to Los Angeles – allowing only three weeks to find our crew, send up our fore and main top and topgallant masts, cross most of the yards, bend on sail, reeve the running rigging, set up the standing rigging, store bunker and complete the multitude of details necessary for a long voyage. We made it after herculean efforts by the lads, putting to sea on 27 February 1984 with many of our old crew, some new, myself as master and Commander McGuire in overall charge.

It was going to have to be a motor-sailing passage; time allowed for nothing else. Tahiti first and then directly to Los Angeles. However, the gods decided otherwise. We made Tahiti in 15 days; good going with no problems except for the rig slackening up as it shook itself down, and bad leaks in the forward accommodation. We spent five days in Papeete and sailed for Los Angeles still desperately trying to fix those leaks. All credit must go to the crew who for days on end relaid the deck forward and discovered that an arc welder can be used under water if you do not mind a few belts here and there. A few days out, one of our engineers fell sick and got steadily worse. A decision was quickly made to divert to Honolulu. The monotonous slog, hard on the starboard tack, was forgotten as we bore away, piling on as much sail as we could. Our best day's run of 220 miles was made as we bowled along with the fresh trade wind just aft of the beam. Unfortunately we had to keep the engines going as our poor patient was in agony and the sooner we got him ashore the better.

Within five days we swept through the Kaiwi Channel and rounded Diamond Head before a 30-knot trade wind. The Hawaiians gave us a very warm welcome and were fascinated by the ship. With our patient in good medical hands, the lads set out to explore the town and island in the limited time allowed off from preparing the ship for the next leg. They would have been happy to stay, but

after a hectic week we were on our way. The wind was fair, so we sailed the *Bounty* off the wharf, swinging her head round with a backed fore topmast staysail and kedge anchor and, to the delight of the well-wishers ashore, hoisted our topsails as she came round. Never before had the ship had a fair wind to sail from a wharf! A fleet of yachts, pipes and trumpets accompanied us out of the harbour, the yachts staying with us until approaching night and a rising sea obliged them to leave.

We got on top of the North Pacific high at about 30° North and a good northwest wind got us to Los Angeles in 12½ days. We tidied the ship in the lee of Catalina Island and entered Los Angeles Harbour under full sail on 27 April. As the ship was to stay around Los Angeles for an indefinite time, most of the crew drifted away. Along with a few others, I stayed on until 4 July, when we sailed in the Los Angeles Parade of Tall Ships organised by the Port of Long Beach. This turned out to be a memorable day. We were placed second in a line of 27 ships, following 250 ft (75 m) behind the *Californian*. From Manhattan Beach to Seal Beach, thirty miles, the shore was lined with spectators and the ocean vanished under the swarms of small craft. Once round Palos Verdes, a freshening breeze and full sail made the *Bounty* a grand sight and kept the crew jumping around like monkeys, trimming for every course change.

I treasure the time I spent with the *Bounty* and miss the fine crews with whom I had the privilege of sailing.

SHIPHANDLING

Comments on the Whitby colliers

During the last half of the eighteenth century before iron came to be more widely used the technology of ships using wood and natural fibre had reached a peak. Iron was used for fastenings and some fittings but the whole rig of the ship, weighing many tons, was constructed and supported by wood and hemp. The ships sailed by Captain Cook and Lt Bligh for their work in the Pacific were examples of this technology. As a young man Cook had learned in the hard school of the British east coast colliers, hauling coal from the north to London. The type of work in which Cook was engaged is probably better described by his contemporary, William Hutchinson, who also had experience of these ships and referred to them often in his *Treatise on Practical Seamanship.*

On ships' sails

To endeavour to make a ship sail by the wind, and turn well to windward, deserves the greatest regard, because safety as well as many other great benefits depend upon it. The good effects of deep and narrow squaresails, can't be better recommended to answer this purpose, than by the performance of ships in the coal and timber trades to London, tho' the design'd properties in building and fitting these ships are, burden at a small draft of water, to take and bear the ground well, and to sail with few hands, and little ballast, yet these ships perform so well at sea, that the government often makes choice of them for store ships, in the most distant naval expeditions; and in narrow channels among shoals, and turning to windward in narrow rivers, there are no ships of equal burthen can match them. . . .

On making passages in the coal trade

In the navigation from Newcastle to London, two thirds of the way is amongst dangerous shoals, and intricate channels, as may be seen by the chart of the coast, and the ships are as large as the shoal channels will admit them to get through with the flow of the tide, which requires to be known to a great exactness to proceed in proper time, and dexterous pilots to navigate through those channels with safety and expedition, to make so many voyages in the year, that they may be gainers by their ships, which are numerous as well as large, and

managed by the fewest men and in a more compleat manner than in any other trade that I know of in the world, considering the difficulty of the navigation, and how deep the ships are loaded, and how lightly they are balasted, yet they meet with very few losses in proportion to the number of ships, which the owners generally run the risque of, and thereby save the expence of insurance, by which means they can afford to freight their ships cheaper than others, so that they are become the chief carriers in the timber, iron, hemp, and flax trades.

Blowing weather and contrary winds, often collect a great many of these colliers together, so that they sail in great fleets, striving with the utmost dexterity, diligence and care, against each other, to get first to market with their coals, or for their turn to load at Newcastle, where at the first of a Westerly wind, after a long Easterly one, there are sometimes two or three hundred ships turning to windward in, and sailing out of the harbour in one tide; the sight of so many ships, passing and crossing each other in so little time and room, by their dexterous management, is said to have made a travelling French gentleman of rank, to hold up his hands and exclaim, 'that it was there France was conquered'; the entrance into the harbour being so very narrow, with dangerous rocks on one side, and a steep sand bank on the other, with a hard shoal bar a-cross, where the waves of the sea frequently run very high, and puts them under the necessity of being very brisk and dexterous.

What is most worthy remarking here when they are going out with a fair wind in their great deep loaded ships, and the waves running high upon the bar, that they would make the ship strike upon it, if she was to sail out pitching against the head waves, to prevent which when they come to the bar, they in a very masterly manner bring the ship to, and she drives over, rolling broad side to waves, which management preserves her from striking.

I have heard of a bold single adventurer getting to sea out of this harbour, when many ships lay windbound with the wind and waves right in, and right upon the shore without the harbour; he having a small handy ship, and no doubt, materials and men that could be depended upon, made every thing snug and ready, as the occasion required, and got as near the bar as she could ride with safety, and had the sails, that were designed to be carried, furled with rope yarns that would easily break; he then took the advantage as may be supposed, of the first of the ebb of a high strong spring tide when there was water enough and so drove over the bar, stern foremost, with the sails all furled and the yards braced sharp up. . . . by the strength of the tide out of the harbour, 'till they reached the sea tide from the southward along the coast, then put the helm hard a-starboard, and brought the ship by the wind on the larboard tack, and expeditiously set all the sails they could carry; the tide checking the ship two points on the lee bow helped her to get to windward off the lee shore, so that they made their course good along the coast, and got their passage.

–William Hutchinson, *A Treatise on Practical Seamanship*

These collier cats, descendants from the Dutch fluyts, ranged in size from 5 to 300 tons and some were fine, well kept ships in spite of the dirty cargo they carried. They were all capacious ships for their size; they could take the ground well and were weatherly – important attributes for a ship that was to be alone for years on end.

When the British Navy bought these vessels for the expeditions they were re-rigged to Navy specifications. As colliers they had a simplified rig that could be handled by a few men. There was ample manpower on their voyages to the Pacific and the Navy rig enabled the ships to spread more canvas to make long passages faster. It is not possible here to go into the details of the whole rig, involving miles of cordage and hundreds of tackles, but having sailed a ship equipped with all this gear, I feel that some of our experiences on the *Bounty* replica may be worth recording.

For the newcomer the first task was to 'learn the ropes'. Being a good yachtsman was not much help here, although it did have its value in wind and weather sense. As an exercise I counted the lines on the pinrails when everything to topgallant studdingsails was rigged. The total came to 119, and this counting lines such as the main port and starboard clew garnets as one line. One would see a new recruit wandering around the deck oblivious to everything but remembering. He would approach a pin, place his hand on it and gaze aloft as if asking the help of the Almighty. After a tense minute he would then check with his pinrail diagram which he had put out of temptation behind his back. Success or otherwise could be read from the expression on his face. Some people were quicker than others, but a few weeks, providing the gear was being used, would fix every line in his mind so that he could find it in the dark. Heaven help anybody who, when coiling down, led a line to the wrong pin! Nothing can be more frustrating on a wet, dark, stormy night than trying to haul out a reef tackle which on investigation turns out to be a stunsail halliard belayed aloft, then having to find out where the blazes the reef tackle fall has got to.

Our main worries concerned our lack of practical experience with the rig and in the event we were probably inclined to be overcautious. We found the topgallant sails gave us the most problems, particularly the foretopgallant, which whipped about horribly in a seaway. The foretopgallant stay led down to the jibboom end, which in turn was only held down by the guys led to the forecastle through thimbles on the spritsail yard. If these were not set up taut the stay slackened and so did the topgallant shrouds and backstays. We suspect that this problem was alleviated on the original *Bounty* which had light rope stays and shrouds. Ours were wire, served the whole length, and were too heavy. At sea the fore topgallant mast was on deck more than it was aloft. As in the days of Cook, it became our practice at the onset of possible heavy weather to send down the fore topgallant mast and main topgallant yard and run in the jibboom.

The *Bounty* replica had two large propellers under

The jibboom and bowsprit

Rigging to the spritsail yard on the *Bounty* replica

her stern and it would be unfair to compare her sailing ability with the original ship. We found the screws had an enormous effect in handling under sail and she would lose her way too soon in stays. I am positive the original ships would have come about easily. With the wind a point or so free she would sail well and by bracing sharp up and sometimes counterbracing the lower yards, we could get her within 67° of the wind but she made an awful lot of leeway. Counterbracing was done by leading forward the yardtackles used for lifting boats and heavy gear on and off the ship, so that the yard could be braced more sharply.

The sail which impressed us most was the spritsail, the yard of which braces in a vertical plane.

Very few sailors today have handled a ship setting this sail and it is often referred to somewhat dubiously in contemporary books relating to ships of the past. We found that it was a very useful sail, setting well even with the wind slightly forward of the beam, especially if it was reefed. When reefed it took the form of a type of lateen sail known as a settee (see page 114) and the low weather clew was lifted well clear of the water. With the wind aft of the beam, when the fore topmast staysail was becalmed by the squaresails on the foremast, the spritsail collected the wind glancing from the ship's side and always remained full. The spritsail yard served not only to spread the sail but also acted as a spreader for the jibboom guys and a lead for the fore lower studdingsail boom guy, as you can see if you examine the illustration of the *Bounty*'s foremast and head gear on page 110.

I should mention here that the arrangement of the jibboom guys in the replica, according to John Harland in his book, *Seamanship*, did not come into use until 1815, but the principle was the same. The holes in the clews were to let water drain from the sail when it dipped into the sea. Reefing the spritsail was a fairly hair-raising operation in a moderate sea when the yard plunged within a three feet or so of the water. The only time the spritsail became a problem was in narrow waters when the sail effectively screened off any forward vision.

By far the heaviest work we found was furling the bunts of the courses, particularly when they were wet. The biggest and strongest manned the bunt to heave the sail on to the yard while the bunt gasket was passed around the huge belly of canvas. The bunt of the courses were so large that our arms were not long enough to pass the gasket under the yard and up before the sail. The method arrived at was for someone to sit on the footrope, jam the gasket between his toes and execute a slow high kick forward. It was always hilarious to see a darned great horny foot rising out of nowhere before the yard. On large ships jigger tackles hitched under the

top were used to get the bunt on to the yard.

The flax canvas may have been heavy to handle, but it had advantages. When properly controlled, its weight made the sails quite tame in the wind, unlike light modern sails which thrash and bang around. If it became necessary to take in a sail in, say, a rising sea breeze, we found it unecessary to furl the sail. We would clew and bunt it and let it hang in its gear until we required to set it again, sometimes making an 'end furl' or just furling along the yards to the bunt. The sail would hang quite quietly in fairly strong winds.

On departure deepsea, when all our gear was on board, we appreciated the difficulties of stowage. The ship was stiff, that is, she would not heel easily and would right herself violently, initiating sharp, quick rolls which at times would get synchronised, each roll getting deeper. This was not only very uncomfortable but frightening, and a great danger to the spars. To overcome this, we made the ship's centre of gravity higher by stowing gear as high as possible. On deck we had two 23 ft (7.02 m) launches on the skids. Into these we stowed, piggyback, a 16 ft (4.88 m) work boat, and a lot of spare line such as studdingsail gear. Under the boats on the main hatch went warps, bags of sand and anything else suitable. On the skids and alongside them went spare spars and oars and in the channels the large sweeps and more spare spars. Studdingsails were kept on deck ready for use.

At sea an anxious eye was always kept on the rig. First light always saw the watch examining the gear for chafe, undue working or damage. We had some wire in the standing rigging and this did not stretch like the hemp, but a week at sea would have the topmasts beginning to flop about and the stays pumping. Getting the standing rigging set up was a tricky and skilled job in port, but at sea it was even more difficult. If set up too hard, the mast would bow; too slack and the mast would work. An overly set up maintopmast backstay could result in the stay taking the whole weight of the mainmast and some of the foremast to which, apart from the mainstay, the mainmast stays were secured. Nothing at all could be done if the deadeye lanyards were wet. After a week at sea we generally had swifters rigged to bowse in the backstays to take up the slack.

However, the strength of the rig was tremendous, as can be demonstrated by an incident at Opunohu Bay, Moorea. For filming purposes we had just made fast to an old tank landing-barge anchored close to the reef when the wind swung right round and set the barge down on the reef. Green water turned to white as the water shallowed, and to prevent stranding we had to let go very fast, using the engines to back her off. In the manoeuvre, with 80 film crew on deck, the main topmast backstay fouled a protruding davit on the barge. The stay stretched like a bowstring, but it was not the stay or the mast which failed; the four inch (10 cm) solid steel davit snapped clean off!

The ship was remarkably dry apart from leaking decks. Only in heavy weather would water come aboard, and then mainly at the waist where it would sweep across the deck and off to leeward. The quarter-deck hatch, just aft of the mainmast, was the only access to the deck in rough weather, therefore it had to be left open. We rigged dodgers to prevent torrents of seawater getting below but these made an obstacle course of the hatch. I would be interested to know what arrangements were made on the original ship, for the same problem would have existed.

A task almost forgotten by modern sailors was the absolute necessity to air the sails in port whenever possible. With our short-handed crew this was always a job which frustrated the mate. Loosing the sails completely or to the bunt was quick and easy. If it looked like rain or was late afternoon, furling was a two-hour job for four men who had to be taken from the multitudinous tasks requiring attention in the ship. Flax canvas rots very quickly if stowed damp. Even a spot of damp can destroy a sail stowed in the sail locker; Bligh lost a whole suit of sails when they were not looked after properly and water got to them.

I have selected these observations to highlight a few of the almost forgotten wrinkles in sailing and maintenance of old ships. In *Bounty* we experimented with handling under sail and tried to do everything 'right'. We hove to, tacked, and wore; in heavy weather we scudded before a gale and lay to under a mizzen staysail. We once managed to sail her out of port, and Captain Paul Leppington once lifted the one-and-a-half ton bowsprit ashore and back again by hand using a spare topmast as a derrick. We raised and lowered the 23 ft (7.02 m) launches using the stay and yard tackles, and sailed the boats. We sent topgallant and topmasts up and down as well as every yard on the ship. Unfortunately we never got around to such skills as working the ship in a tideway, backing and filling as the tide drifts the ship sideways against the wind up a narrow channel. We missed the original ship's 11 ft (3.36 m) anchors, the security they offered, and there were occasions when we wished we had the four-pounders on the quarterdeck!

We learned a lot and wished we could have done more with the *Bounty*, but the complications of insurance, the expense of maintenance and demands of time prevented this. Unfortunately today's high costs and hustle are not the environment in which an eighteenth-century east coast collier can profitably operate.

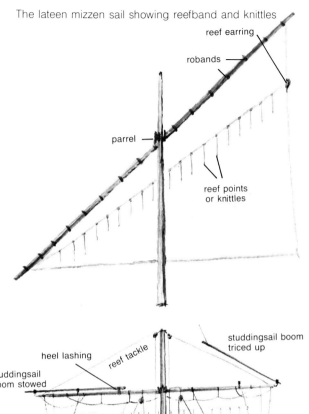

The lateen mizzen sail showing reefband and knittles

reef earring
robands
parrel
reef points
or knittles

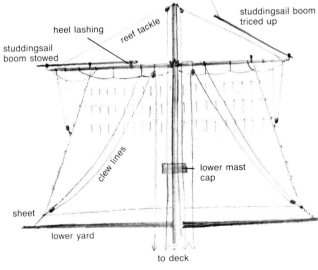

heel lashing
reef tackle
studdingsail boom triced up
studdingsail boom stowed
clew lines
lower mast cap
sheet
lower yard
to deck

Some of the gear handled in reefing a topsail

Shortening sail and reefing

Up to the mid eighteenth century, seamen relied on the courses as their heavy-weather sails. Their centre of effort was low and the lower masts were strong and well supported, so as the wind increased, the high, light sails such as the royals and topgallants were taken in first, followed by the topsails, until the ship was reduced to her lower sails. Further reduction was made by removing some of the area of the courses. Up to about 1660 this was done by lowering the yard and unlacing one or two panels at the foot of the sails. These were known as the 'bonnet' and the 'drabbler'. The heavy yard was raised and lowered by powerful jeer tackles and a downhaul and the sail confined in the process by clew garnets and martnets. Martnets were replaced early in the seventeenth century by buntlines and leechlines.

It is clear that a topsail cannot be reefed in this manner. During the seventeenth century, topsails increased in size and a method of reefing became necessary. Reef points in bands across the upper part of the sail were introduced and the same method came to be used on the courses. The courses still continued to be the last sails taken in until the mid eighteenth century, but there were problems. In very high seas these lower sails would lose the wind, with subsequent loss of control of the ship and the sails' steadying influence. It became the practice to weather a gale under reefed topsails rather than the courses, as these sails were high enough to keep the wind. There was much argument in those days as to the best sail to carry in a storm, but if the ship was off the wind, it was usually a close-reefed maintopsail and reefed forecourse that was carried.

In the nineteenth century the topsails and, later, the topgallants, were divided into upper and lower sails. The lower topsail – a broad, narrow and strong sail – could not be reefed and was usually the last squaresail handed. The upper topsails continued to carry reefbands except on some of the later large steel ships such as the *Pamir*. The upper topgallants rarely carried reefbands.

To reef a topsail, the yard is braced so that some of the wind is spilled from the sail and the yard either lowered to the cap or to a position below where the reefed sail will set. The reef-tackles, hitched to the leech of the sail below the lowest reefband, are hauled out from the deck and the yard firmly steadied by lifts and braces. Then it is 'lay aloft' and pass the earrings. The sail has been hauled up to and stretched along the yard by the reef-tackles and the whole area above the reefbands falls in a bag before the sail. Aloft, the men lay out along the yard, the strongest and best seaman going to the weather earring. When everyone is ready in position, gripping the sail at the selected reefband, a concerted effort, often with a two-six heave or a chorus of *Paddy's Boots*, lights the sail to windward and the weather earring is lashed around cleats at the end of the yard; three turns round the cleat and four around the yard.

It remains to pass the lee earring and tie off the reef points. The latter are taken round the yard or later the jackstay and secured with, of course, a reef knot. Care is taken that each reef point takes an equal strain as the sail could be torn by the stress coming on a single point. This completed, the men leave the yard, the mate checks the reef points and, leaving one man aloft to overhaul the buntlines, it's down to the deck, cast off the reef-tackles, man the halyards and braces and hoist away. It sounds straightforward, but try it in a gale of wind when you wish you could use one hand for yourself and one for the ship but cannot because each task requires two hands!

The two poems which follow describe reefing. The first, *Shortening Sail*, describes reefing in the early eighteenth century. At the beginning the ship is under topsails and courses, but with the increasing wind the topsails are handed and rolling tackles clapped on the yards. These tackles, set up between the mast and a position a few feet or so out along the weather yard-arm, prevent the topsail yard from sawing backwards and forwards across the mast as the ship rolls. Next the topgallant yards are sent down. As the weather worsens, it becomes necessary to reef the courses. In the poem the conservative Rodmond disputed the wisdom of the new method of clewing up by taking up the weather clew first; this argument continued throughout the period of sail, but it seems that the 'weather-clew-first' advocates generally won out as far as handling the courses went. 'He who strives the tempest to disarm, will never first embrail the lee yard-arm' became an adage known by most square-rig seamen. It is apparent that the courses had reefbands but no reefpoints or knittles. A line was passed hand to hand through eyelets in the reefband and instead of around the yard, through the lashings known as 'robands' which secured the head of the sail to the yard.

Still the storm increases and the mainsail is furled. 'Four men are lost when the ship rolls the lee yard-arm under.' Next the fore and mizzen courses are taken in; the mizzen course is the old lateen mizzen and has a reefband running from the tack to the leech. It has knittles or reefpoints, and to reef the sail the yard is lowered to the deck. The mizzen reef was often referred to as the 'balance reef' because it was used to balance the sail trim of the ship. With the mizzen reefed and set, the ship lies 'a-try' with the wind and seas on the weather bow.

Shortening Sail

As the proud horse with costly trappings gay,
Exulting, prances to the bloody fray;
Spurning the ground he glories in his might,
But reels tumultuous in the shock of fight·
E'en so, caparison'd in gaudy pride,
The bounding vessel dances on the tide.
  Fierce and more fierce the gathering tempest grew;
South, and by west, the threatening demon blew;
Auster's resistless force all air invades,
And every rolling wave more ample spreads.
The ship no longer can her top-sails bear;
No hopes of milder weather now appear.
Bow-lines and halyards are cast off again,
Clew-lines haul'd down, and sheets let fly amain.
Embrail'd each top-sail, and by braces squared,
The seamen climb aloft, and man each yard;
They furl'd the sails, and pointed to the wind
The yards, by rolling tackles then confined,
While o'er the ship the gallant boatswain flies;
Like a hoarse mastiff through the storm he cries,
Prompt to direct the unskilful still appears,
The expert he praises, and the timid cheers.
Now some, to strike top-gallant-yards attend,
Some, travellers up the weather-back-stays send,
At each mast-head the top-ropes others bend;
The parrels, lifts, and clew-lines soon are gone,
Topp'd and unrigg'd, they down the back-stays run;
The yards secure along the booms were laid,
And all the flying ropes aloft belay'd.
Their sails reduced, and all the rigging clear,
Awhile the crew relax from toils severe;
Awhile their spirits with fatigue opprest,
In vain expect the alternate hour of rest –
But with redoubling force the tempests blow,
And watery hills in dread succession flow:
A dismal shade o'ercasts the frowning skies,
New troubles grow; fresh difficulties rise;
No season this from duty to descend,
All hands on deck must now the storm attend.
  His race perform'd, the sacred lamp of day
Now dipt in western clouds his parting ray.
His languid fires, half lost in ambient haze,

Refract along the dusk a crimson blaze;
Till deep immerged the sickening orb descends,
And cheerless night o'er heaven her reign extends;
Sad evening's hour, how different from the past;
No flaming pomp, no blushing glories cast,
No ray of friendly light is seen around;
The moon and stars in hopeless shade are drown'd.
  The ship no longer can whole courses bear,
To reef them now becomes the master's care;
The sailors, summon'd aft, all ready stand,
And man the enfolding brails at his command:
But here the doubtful officers dispute,
Till skill, and judgment, prejudice confute;
For Rodmond, to new methods still a foe,
Would first, at all events, the sheet let go;
To long-tried practice obstinately warm,
He doubts conviction and relies on form.
This Albert and Arion disapprove,
And first to brail the tack up firmly move;
'The watchful seaman, whose sagacious eye,
On sure experience may with truth rely,
Who from the reigning cause foretells the effect,
This barbarous practice ever will reject;
For, fluttering loose in air, the rigid sail
Soon flits to ruins in the furious gale;
And he, who strives the tempest to disarm,
Will never first embrail the lee yard-arm,'
So Albert spoke; to windward, at his call,
Some seamen the clew-garnet stand to haul.
The tack's eased off, while the involving clew
Between the pendent blocks ascending flew;
The sheet and weather-brace they now stand by,
The lee clew-garnet, and the bunt-lines ply:
Then, all prepared, 'Let go the sheet!' he cries.
Loud rattling, jarring, through the blocks it flies!
Shivering at first, till by the blast impell'd;
High o'er the lee yard-arm the canvas swell'd;
By spilling lines embraced, with brails confined,
It lies at length unshaken by the wind.
The fore-sail then secured with equal care,
Again to reef the main-sail they repair;
While some above the yard o'er-haul the tye,
Below, the down-haul tackle others ply;
Jears, lifts, and brails, a seaman each attends,

Reefing the main topsail

122

And down the mast its mighty yard descends.
When lower'd sufficient they securely brace,
And fix the rolling tackle in its place;
The reef-lines and their earrings now prepared,
Mounting on pliant shrouds they man the yard.
Far on the extremes appear two able hands,
For no inferior skill this task demands.
To windward, foremost, young Arion strides,
The lee yard-arm the gallant boatswain rides.
Each earring to its cringle first they bend,
The reef-band then along the yard extend;
The circling earrings round the extremes entwined,
By outer and by inner turns they bind
The reef-lines next from hand to hand received;
Through eyelet-holes and roband-legs were reefed;
The folding reefs in plaits inroll'd they lay,
Extend the worming lines, and ends belay.

   Hadst thou, Arion! held the leeward post
While on the yard by mountain billows tost,
Perhaps oblivion o'er our tragic tale
Had then for ever drawn her dusky veil;
But ruling Heaven prolong'd thy vital date,
Severer ills to suffer, and relate.

   For, while aloft the order those attend
To furl the main-sail, or on deck descend;
A sea, upsurging with stupendous roll,
To instant ruin seems to doom the whole.
'O friends, secure your hold!' Arion cries –
It comes all dreadful! down the vessel lies
Half buried sideways; while, beneath it tost,
Four seamen off the lee yard-arm are lost.
Torn with resistless fury from their hold,
In vain their struggling arms the yard enfold;
In vain to grapple flying ropes they try,
The ropes, alas, a solid gripe deny.
Prone on the midnight surge with panting breath
They cry for aid, and long contend with death;
High o'er their heads the rolling billows sweep,
And down they sink in everlasting sleep.
Bereft of power to help, their comrades see
The wretched victims die beneath the lee,
With fruitless sorrow their lost state bemoan,
Perhaps a fatal prelude to their own!

   In dark suspense on deck the pilots stand,
Nor can determine on the next command.
Though still they knew the vessel's armed side

Impenetrable to the clasping tide;
Though still the waters by no secret wound
A passage to her deep recesses found;
Surrounding evils yet they ponder o'er,
A storm, a dangerous sea, and leeward shore!
'Should they, though reef'd, again their sails extend,
Again in shivering streamers they may rend;
Or, should they stand, beneath oppressive strain,
The down-press'd ship may never rise again;
Too late to weather now Morea's land,'
And drifting fast on Athens' rocky strand'–
Thus they lament the consequence severe,
Where perils unallay'd by hope appear.
Long pondering in their minds each fear'd event,
At last to furl the courses they consent;
That done, to reef the mizzen next agree,
And try beneath it sidelong in the sea.
   Now down the mast the yard they lower away,
Then jears and topping-lift secure belay;
The head, with doubling canvas fenced around,
In balance near the lofty peak they bound;
The reef enwrapp'd, the inserting knittles tied,
The halyards throt and peak are next applied –
The order given, the yard aloft they sway'd,
The brails relax'd, the extended sheet belay'd;
The helm its post forsook, and lash'd a-lee,
Incline the wayward prow to front the sea.

–William Falconer, in *The Eternal Sea*

Reefing Topsails

Three hand-spike raps on the forward hatch,
   A hoarse voice shouts down the fo'castle dim,
Startling the sleeping starboard watch,
Out of their bunks, their clothes to snatch,
   With little thought of life or limb.

'All hands on deck. D'ye hear the news?
   Reef topsails all –'tis the old man's word.
Tumble up, never mind jackets or shoes!'
Never a man would dare refuse,
   When that stirring cry is heard.

The weather shrouds are like iron bars,
   The leeward backstays curving out.
Like steely spear-points gleam the stars
From the black sky flecked with feathery bars,
   By the storm-wind swerved about.

Across the bows like a sheeted ghost
   Quivers a luminous cloud of spray,
Flooding the forward deck, and most
Of the waist; then, like a charging host,
   It rolls to leeward away.

'Mizzen topsail, clew up and furl;
   Clew up your main course now with a will!'
The wheel goes down with a sudden whirl
'Ease her, ease her, the good old girl,
   Don't let your head sails fill!'

'Ease off lee braces; round in on the weather;
   Ease your halyards; clew down, clew down;
Haul out your reef tackles, now together.'
Like an angry bull against his tether,
   Heave the folds of the topsails brown.

'Haul taut your buntlines, cheerly, men, now!'
   The gale sweeps down with a fiercer shriek;
Shock after shock on the weather bow
Thunders the head sea and below
   Throbbing timbers groan and creak.

The topsail yards are down on the caps;
   Her head lies up in the eyes of the blast;
The bellying sails, with sudden slaps,
Swell out and angrily collapse,
   Shaking the head of the springing mast.

Wilder and heavier comes the gale
   Out of the heart of the Northern Sea;
And the phosphorescent gleamings pale
Surge up awash of the monkey rail
   Along our down pressed lee.

'Lay aloft! Lay aloft, boys, and reef,
   Don't let my starbolines be last,'
Cries from the deck the sturdy chief;
'Twill take a man of muscle and beef
   To get those ear-rings passed!'

Into the rigging with a shout
  Our second and third mates foremost spring;
Crackles the ice on the ratlines stout,
As the leaders on the yards lay out,
  And the footropes sway and swing.

On the weather end of the jumping yard,
  One hand on the lift, and one beneath,
Grasping the cringle, and tugging hard,
Black Dan, our third, grim and scarred,
  Clutches the ear-ring for life or death.

  'Light up to windward!' cries the mate,
  As he rides the surging yardarm end;
And into the work we throw our weight,
Every man bound to emulate,
  The rush of the gale, and the sea's wild send.

'Haul out to leeward!' comes at last,
  With a cheering from the fore and main;
'Knot your reef-points, and knot them fast!'
Weather and lee are the ear-rings passed,
  And over the yard we bend and strain.

'Lay down men, all; and now with a will,
  Swing on your topsail halyards and sway;
Ease your braces and let her fill,
There's an hour below of the mid-watch still,
  Haul taut your bowlines-well all-belay!'

–Walter Mitchell, in *The Eternal Sea*

Tacking

To tack, stay or come about is to bring the wind on the other side of the ship by turning to windward. Anyone who has sailed even a small fore-and-aft-rigged craft will know the momentary confusion, banging and effort in coming about. Imagine then the rumpus and organisation involved in tacking a square-rigged ship carrying perhaps dozens of sails, both square and fore and aft, tons of gear aloft and a multitude of lines to handle.

All sailing ships have different sailing characteristics and to stay, or come about, easily is a valued ability enabling the ship to make well to windward on short tacks. A ship that does not stay well may point satisfactorily and at the end of long tacks, wear ship without losing appreciable ground, but given the allotted six points, or 67½ degrees, which a square-rigged ship may point to the wind, a good part of a twenty mile board may be lost in wearing.

Sea and wind conditions variously affect a ship's chance of tacking. A light wind and heavy swells are anathema to her as she will not carry enough way and the swells will stall her. Likewise, heavy seas and high winds may have the same effect with the additional danger of carrying away gear as the sails spill the wind and flog. The master's ability to judge under what conditions of weather, sea and sail his ship will stay can be critical. The *Forest Hall*, bound from Newcastle, Australia, to Chile, ran ashore on the northwest coast of New Zealand. In broad daylight her master stood in too close, tried to come about, missed stays and ran on to a weather shore. Visibility and wind conditions were good, but Captain Collins had been in ill health, which may have accounted for the mishap. This example is extreme, but many ships have been lost through missing stays when sea-room was scant.

The evolution of bringing a square-rigged ship about has been established for hundreds of years with little variation. In a ship of the *Pinmore*'s era (late nineteenth century), the procedure was as follows:

All hands are rousted out with the call, 'All hands 'bout ship!'
The watch on deck, joined by those below as they tumble out, throw off its pin every coil which will be handled – taking special care to fake down the braces so that they will run without fouling. The main tack will have been unhooked and the main-bowline, if carried, cast off by the watch. The mate forward, and the second mate in the waist, call back,

'All clear for running!' as soon as their respective domains are ready. The apprentices and third mate will have readied the after gear.

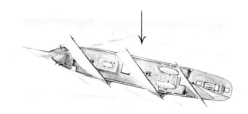

A clean full starboard tack

A call from the master, 'Stations 'bout ship!' will send each hand to his post for tacking. On most British ships, give or take the apprentices, the mate and port watch are on or about the fo'c's'le, the bosun is standing by the fore tack, the cook traditionally will be at the fore sheet, the second mate at the main tack, the starboard watch, the carpenter and sailmaker at the mainsail gear, the third mate and an apprentice at the main sheet and the remainder of the apprentices at the mizzen. This was, if you like, the start line for tacking. Each hand must perform many tasks and the watchword is 'Be handy'. With an experienced crew no orders other than those by the master should be necessary, and from now on the only voices heard will be that of the master and the replies of the helmsman, and maybe a short-haul shanty for the heavy work. While this preparatory work is being carried out the ship will have been given a good, or clean, full; she has been sailed slightly free thereby increasing her speed. It is the inertia of the ship's movement which enables her to stay. An empty or light ship is always difficult.

The ship is now eased into the wind and at the first tremble of the weather leeches, the order 'Lee oh!' is given and the helm is put down, the helmsman reporting 'Helm's a-lee' once the wheel is over.

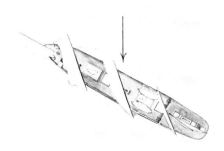

Lee oh!

It may be a good idea to clarify these terms relating to steering. Until the middle of this century, confusion often arose from different methods of giving steering orders. For instance, an old seaman, given the order, 'Put your helm to starboard', may well steer the ship to port. This dates way back to when even large sailing ships were steered by a helm or tiller. Pushing to starboard will turn the ship to port. Nowadays orders are given always relating to the rudder, such as 'Starboard ten', or 'Hard a starboard'. The Americans allow no confusion, with the, 'Ten degrees right rudder', or 'Full right rudder'. Now consider a sailing ship heeling with the wind on her port side. The helmsman is given the order, 'Put your helm down'. He will then push it down to leeward and the ship will turn into the wind to starboard. Similarly, if the helm is put up, the ship will turn away from the wind to port. These steering instructions are still used on yachts today, to the utter confusion of the novice, and continue to be used on all sailing ships, whether steered by wheel or not.

To continue; at the order 'Lee oh!' the headsail sheets and fore sheet are let go and the spanker is hauled hard in. The combined effect of the rudder, the spanker pushing the stern downwind and the release of pressure forward swings the ship up into the wind, accompanied by the thunder of slatting sails and the clatter of blocks. As the ship turns to windward the order, 'Raise tacks and sheets!' is given and the mainsail is clewed up and quietens, as do the other squaresails as they come aback.

As the ship approaches the eye of the wind, it's 'Mainsail haul!' and all the main and mizzen yards are slewed swiftly round, given a boost by the wind in their weather leech. The other parts of the main and mizzen sails will have been partly blanketed by the foremast sails. The yards are swung by means of the main and cro'jack braces, the upper yards being freed to follow.

For an observer, now is a comparatively quiet time and there is a tension in a ship that has problems staying. The headsails will still be slatting or aback but the squares will be quiet; creaks and groans emanate from the spars as they protest the

Mainsail haul

unaccustomed forces of the sails. The hands not on the fo'c's'le will be getting over the main and mizzen staysails and hardening up the main and mizzen braces.

As the ship passes through the eye of the wind she has probably lost, or is about to lose, her headway. The master watches overside and as soon as the ship stops, the helm is put amidships and

then, as the ship begins to make a sternboard, put over the other way.

The foresails, aback, are pushing or 'boxing' the ship's head around and the aftersails begin to fill.

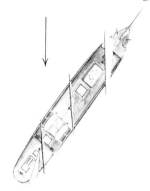

Let go and haul!

'Fore bowline!' followed immediately by, 'Let go and haul!' come the next orders. The hands are ready, both watches now standing by the fore lee braces, and as the mates let go the weather braces, the yards are hauled round against the pressure of the wind. With a wallop the foresails fill and the yards are braced up sharp. The port watch haul aft the fore

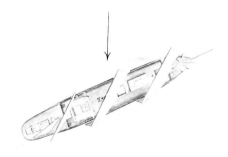

Port tack

sheet and heave down the fore tack, the starboard watch set the mainsail and attend to its sheet and tack and the apprentices, now forward, haul aft the jib and staysail sheets.

The ship has now successfully stayed and will be gathering steerage way. All that remains is for the watch to coil down and give the odd brace a swig as the mate casts his critical eye on the trim of the yards.

(*Left*) The *Grace Harwar* shortened down in heavy weather

The *Pinmore* in stays. A frequent visitor to the North American west coast was this large steel four-masted barque, built in 1882 as the *Pass of Balmaha*. She was a fairly typical British 'limejuicer' sailing under the Red Ensign until she had the distinction of being sunk by Graaf Felix von Luckner in 1917. The Count had made two voyages in her during 1902, and when his raider, the sailing vessel *Seeadler*, came up with her in the Atlantic he soon recognised his old ship. He boarded her alone and wandered around nostalgically, finding his initials still remained scratched on the wheel rim. Before he reluctantly sank the *Pinmore*, von Luckner, with his characteristic daring, had some of his own seamen aboard posing as her former crew and sailed her into the neutral port of Rio de Janeiro. There he picked up stores and mail before sailing out to rejoin the *Seeadler* some hundred miles off-shore.

Earlier, in 1901, the *Pinmore*'s career nearly came to an end when her cargo shifted on a voyage from Santa Rosalia in Mexico to Portland, Oregon. As she lay on her beam ends, the crew hastily abandoned her and were picked up by a passing steamer. The *Pinmore* was made of sterner stuff and survived to be taken in tow to Astoria the following day by another steamer, the delighted captain of which collected a large sum in salvage. The crew of the *Pinmore*, who had been taken to the same port, were startled and I imagine somewhat chagrined to see their ship riding safely at anchor; more so when they found that their personal effects had vanished from the ship.

Wearing ship

The alternative to tacking is to turn the ship away from the wind until the wind is aft, then bring her up on to the other board. This is a much easier evolution than staying the ship and can be carried out by the watch on deck if sharpness is not necessary and conditions are reasonable. Timing is not critical except in heavy seas where there can be a risk of pooping or broaching.

As in tacking, ships vary in their steering performance under various sail combinations, and although what is described here is common practice, it may not pertain to all ships.

As has been said before, sailing craft, large ones particularly, rely on a good balance of sail to steer, and different sail combinations are used on different points of sailing. A ship under all plain sail on a windward board will have all her squares and fore and aft-ers set. To wear, the spanker is brailed in and perhaps some of the mizzen squaresails clewed down; the mizzen staysails also may be run down. The mizzen and mainyards are checked in and the helm is put up. The foresails, drawing well, help to push the ship's head off the wind and as she bears away, the main and mizzen yards are squared. With the wind aft, the foreyards are squared and the headsails and staysails got over. As she comes round towards the wind, the mizzen yards are braced up and the spanker and mizzen staysail set to assist in turning the ship. The foreyards are braced up before there is any chance of them coming aback and the ship is brought on the wind and the sails trimmed accordingly.

As can be gathered, provided there is not a big ugly sea running, the ship can be held on any point while sheets and braces are handled, and a kindly ship will come round easily. In certain very heavy conditions, however, reduced sail and big seas can make this operation tricky, and there have been ships unable to sail themselves around.

It was our watch on deck. As the port watch for'ard was being called I hooked open the berth door of Parsons and Tosswill and howled out, 'Show a leg, show a leg, show a leg! Rouse and shine, you sleepers! All hands about ship!' in approved nautical style, then pattered around the decks after Stringer, assisting him to coil the braces down clear on deck, so that presently they would run out freely and not check the yards swinging as we tacked the ship.

'Watch this,' said Stringer as he threw off some turns of the weather main brace from its belaying-pin. He next hitched it with two turns only, but in such a way that the brace could neither fall off the pin nor render around it. 'When she tacks in five minutes,' he said, 'and the weather braces are hauled in, they will be belayed over these hitches instead of throwing them off. Then when she goes about a second time the top turns are thrown off, the braces run right out until the hitches are tautened up again as they are now. That saves the trouble of measuring and slacking braces every time you tack ship.'

The helmsman was keeping her clean full – there was not even a wrinkle in the weather-leach of the skysail, the gleaming snow-white bellies of the sixteen square sails strained out to leeward, and the *Wairoa* was dancing along at 8 knots. The watch had just unhooked the main-tack tackle and let go the main bowline. The mate on the forecastle-head and the second mate in the waist sang out, 'All clear for running'.

'Stations about ship', came the answering order from the master on the poop, and all hands took up their stations. The mate and his watch were on the forecastle-head, bos'n at the fore-tack, 'Doctor' at the fore-sheet, Chips and Sails and the starboard watch at the gear ready to haul the mainsail up, the second mate at the main-tack, third mate and an apprentice at the main-sheet, three apprentices at the spanker-boom sheet. Captain Bungard made a slight movement of his forefinger to windward, in response to which the man at the wheel eased the helm down.

'Ready about,' the mate reported.

'Lee oh!' came from the master in high, ringing tones which resounded all over the ships – a clear, unmistakable order. The fore-sheet and head-sheets were let go. Collins steadily but quickly hauled over on the spokes of the wheel until the helm was hard down. 'Helm's a-lee, sir,'

he reported to the master, as we apprentices hauled in smartly on the spanker. The rudder, the release of pressure forward and the increased pressure of the spanker aft, all conspired at an increasing rate to swing the ship's bows towards the wind. For'ard the jibs were slatting, the sheet-blocks banging about and the foresail was thudding. As she came flying up into the wind all the sails flapped and pounded like thunder.

'Raise tacks and sheets!' The master's order rose clear above the tumult. Up went the clews and the great mainsail flapped and fell aback against the mast. 'Cro'jack braces,' Stringy hissed, and Tosswill and I fled to the main fife-rail, leaving him to handle the spanker-sheet with a little surreptitious help from Collins.

'Mainsail haul!' sang the master, and the lofty, vertical canvas planes of the main and mizzen swung swiftly from the port tack to the starboard tack as the apprentices hauled madly on the cro'jack braces, racing the frenzied starboard watch as they hauled on the main braces. The sails flat aback on the foremast were boxing the ship's head off on to the starboard tack.

By this time the ship, unlike a fore and aft-er, had lost her way through the water – the helm had no effect, but the pressure of the for'ard canvas was making her head pay off correctly. 'Midships' was the next order from the master, and Collins swung the wheel until the rudder was amidships. As the *Wairoa*'s head fell away from the wind, the after-sails began to fill. The master was waiting for this, and the orders, 'Fore bowline!' and 'Let go and haul!' followed like pistol shots. The mates let go to starboard, both watches hauled furiously on the port against the pressure of the wind. Meantime the ship had gathered a little sternway and the master signalled to Collins, who had stepped across to starboard, to 'put the helm down'. When a ship has sternway the effect of the helm is reversed, so the *Wairoa* paid off more and the foreyards came round with a fullock and were braced sharp up. The port watch hauled aft the fore-sheet and hove down the fore-tack, while the starboard watch set the mainsail in similar fashion and the apprentices hauled aft the staysail sheets. The ship lost sternway, forged ahead and heeled over on the starboard tack. In other words, she had been put about. The master had succeeded in staying her. 'That'll do, the watch,' said the mate.

'Coil up the ropes', commanded the second mate. After this had been done Stringer pointed out to me that the weather braces on the starboard side had all been hitched in readiness for again tacking ship if necessary in similar fashion to which the port braces had been hitched before tacking.

–Frank Worsley, *First Voyage in a Square-rigged Ship*

Hauling down

Since ships have sailed the seas it has been necessary to keep their bottoms clean of growth and, in the case of wooden vessels, protect them against the ravages of shipworm. In the Pacific, where shipyards capable of hauling out a ship were at first non-existent and later few and far between, alternative methods had to be used to get at her underwater parts. Providing the tides had a wide range, a ship could be careened. To carry out this operation, the ship was emptied as far as possible, and the yards and topmasts sent ashore. The ship would be run gently ashore on a firm, shelving beach and an anchor carried out to port or starboard to haul her over as the tide fell. Once the tide had fallen, the bottom was cleaned by scrubbing or, if the growth was very bad, by burning or breaming. Willem Schouten's *Hoorn* was destroyed at Port Desire when the breaming fires got out of control. The ship in the painting has been careened without beaching. A powerful steam winch on the dockside and tackles stropped at the lower mastheads have hove the ship down to allow a dockyard gang to clean her off from floating stages.

Keeping a clean bottom was essential, for any growth slowed the ship down and should it become excessive, the vessel would handle poorly and might be endangered. An extreme case was an iron ship,

A ship hauled down in San Francisco

the *Hellas*. With 16 ft (4.9 m) of growth on her bottom, she wouldn't sail any further and had to be abandoned in mid Pacific.

With wooden ships a running battle was maintained against shipworm or teredo, some tropical species of which can grow to 6 ft (1.8 m) with a girth as thick as a man's arm. Unprotected wood could become honeycombed in weeks. Various methods were used to combat the worm. Some Spanish ships in the sixteenth and seventeenth centuries sheathed their bottoms with lead, a practice which was experimented with by the British. This added a lot of weight to the ship and the lead was inclined to tear loose easily. A light

sheathing of a suitable wood such as elm over a mixture of tar and hair proved effective.. In time the sheathing would be eaten away and have to be replaced, but the tar and hair presented a barrier to the worm. Another method used by Cavendish was to char the planking and then coat it with pitch. Lime, among other more exotic materials, proved repellent to teredo. I have read somewhere that the Arabs apply a mixture of lime, camel fat and some other ingredient to their ships. Some vessels in the East Indies hung over the bow a bag of lime which would wash back in solution over the hull.

Mailletage or nailing was common practice before copper came into more general use. Large, flat-headed nails were hammered into the sheathing so close together that when they rusted a sheet of iron oxide would cover the hull. Cook's ships were treated in this way. Cook also used a coating of white lead to protect his boats.

Copper sheathing was introduced into the British Navy in the 1760s. The third ship to be coppered was the sixth-rate frigate *Dolphin*. She sailed around the world twice, once under the command of John Byron and secondly under Samuel Wallis, who discovered Tahiti. Coppering, it was found, reacted with the iron fastenings, causing rapid corrosion by electrolytic action, but once this was realised, it became the favoured means of protection. It retarded weed growth and allowed ships to stay longer at sea. The *Bounty* was coppered and some of the original sheets have been recovered from Pitcairn Island.

The 24-gun frigate *Pandora* shortly before foundering on the Great Barrier Reef. Under Captain E. Edwards, she was sent out to Tahiti to find the *Bounty* mutineers and bring them back to England for trial. Fourteen *Bounty* crew were apprehended in Tahiti and incarcerated in an 11 by 18 ft (3 by 5.5 m) box built on the *Pandora*'s afterdeck.

After a futile search for the *Bounty*, Edwards steered for Cook's Endeavour Passage through the Torres Strait where he was to make a survey. The *Pandora* never reached the strait; trying to find a passage through the Great Barrier Reef, she was driven upon it and foundered with the loss of many of her crew and four mutineers.

In 1977 two Australian divers found the wreck in 110 ft (33 m) of water near the tip of Cape York in northern Queensland. Under the supervision and direction of the Queensland Museum of Brisbane, many artifacts have been recovered from the wreck. The project director, Ron Coleman, hopes that one day the hull may be recovered, for the *Pandora* is considered the most important wreck in the Southern Hemisphere.

PANDORA HUNTS THE MUTINEERS

Eight months after Bligh reported to the Admiralty, the *Pandora*, under the command of Captain Edward Edwards, sailed for Tahiti where he was to commence a search for the *Bounty* mutineers. He would be faced with an almost impossible task if, as was likely, the *Bounty* was not found at Tahiti. He comments in his report:

Christian had been frequently heard to declare that he would search for an unknown or uninhabited island in which there was no harbour for shipping, would run the ship ashore, and get from her such things as would be useful to him and settle there, but this information was too vague to be followed by me in an immense ocean strewed with an almost innumerable number of known and unknown islands.

As it happened, on their way across the Pacific after rounding Cape Horn, passing Easter Island and discovering Ducie Island, the searchers subsequently

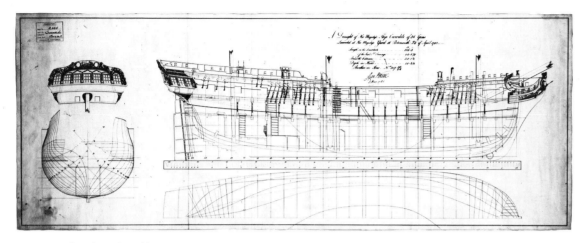

Draft of a *Pandora*-class frigate
(National Maritime Museum, Greenwich)

sailed very close to their quarry at Pitcairn.

At Tahiti 14 'pirates' were apprehended and, although some of them were innocent of any part in the mutiny, Edwards treated them all alike. He placed them in irons and, to the heartbreak of their Tahitian wives, incarcerated them in a roundhouse built on the afterdeck of the *Pandora*. The surgeon, George Hamilton, writes:

> A prison was built for their accommodation on the quarter deck that they might be secure and apart from our ship's company; and that it might have every advantage of a free circulation of air which rendered it the most desirable place in the ship. . . . Orders were likewise given that they should be victualled in every respect the same as the ship's company, both in meat, liquor and all the extra indulgencies with which we were so liberally supplied, notwithstanding the established laws of the service which restricts prisoners to two-thirds allowance; but Captain Edwards very humanely commiserated with their unhappy and inevitable length of confinement.

James Morrison, one of the inmates, gave a different tale:

> When the poop or roundhouse was finished, we were conveyed into it and put in irons as before. This place we stiled Pandora's Box, the entrance being a scuttle on the top, of 18 or 20 inches square, secured by a bolt on the top thro' the coamings; two scuttles of nine inches square in the bulkhead for air, with iron grates and the stern ports barrd inside and out with iron. The centrys were placed on the top, while the midshipman walked across by the bulkhead. The length of this box was 11 feet upon deck, and 18 wide at the bulkhead. No person was suffered to speak to us but the master-at-arms, and his orders were not to speak to us on any score but that of our provisions. The heat of the place when it was calm was so intense that the sweat ran frequently into the scuppers, and produced maggots in a short time, the hammocks being dirty when we got them we found stored with vermin of another kind which we had no method of erradicating but by lying on the plank; and tho' our friends would have supplied us with plenty of cloth, they were not permitted to do it, and our only remedy was to lay naked; these troublesome neighbours and the two

necessary tubbs which were kept in the place helped to render our situation truly disagreeable.

Morrison's statements, however, should be treated with caution as, although he claimed his account of both the *Bounty*'s and *Pandora*'s voyage was compiled from notes written during the course of events, it is more likely that the *Journal of James Morrison* was cobbled together several years later, mainly from memory.

Edwards appears to have possessed much of the merciless traits later attributed to Bligh but lacked the latter's superb skill in seamanship. Bligh commented that Captain Edwards was 'not seaman enough' to take his ship through the Endeavour Strait towards which, after a fruitless search for the *Bounty*, the *Pandora* set course.

Edwards had been instructed by the Admiralty to make a survey of the strait and, to give him some credit, the captain of the *Pandora* did have a formidable task. Cook had only achieved it after the greatest of difficulty, nursing the *Endeavour* through the reefs and currents in the stiff southeast trades. On 25 August 1791, the *Pandora* was off the Great Barrier Reef and began her search for a passage through to the Endeavour Strait. Of the twenty-eighth Hamilton wrote:

> At five in the afternoon a signal was made from the boat, that a passage through the reef was discovered for the ship. But wishing to be well informed in so intricate a business and the day being far spent, we waited the boat coming on board and made a signal to expedite her.
> . . . False fires were burnt, and muskets fired from the ship and answered by the boat reciprocally; and as the flashes from their muskets were distinctly seen by us, she was reasonably soon expected on board. We sounded and had no bottom with a hundred and ten fathom line, til past seven o'clock when we got ground in fifty fathom.

The boat was now close under our stern. We were lying to to prevent the ship fore-reaching.

Immediately on sounding this last time, the topsails were filled.

Before way could be got on the ship, she struck the sheer coral ledge of the Great Barrier Reef. The heavy swell drove the *Pandora* across the reef, pounding her bottom apart as the swells dumped her on the coral. Here is Surgeon Hamilton's description:

All hands were turned to the pumps and to bale at the different hatchways. Some of the prisoners were let out of irons and turned to the pumps. At this dreadful crisis, it blew very violently, and she beat so hard upon the rocks that we expected her every minute to go to pieces. It was an exceeding dark stormy night; and the gloomy horrors of death presented us all round, being everywhere encompassed with rocks, shoals and broken water. About ten, she beat over the reef and we let go the anchor in fifteen fathom of water.

The guns were ordered to be thrown overboard; and what hands could be spared from the pumps were employed thrumbing a topsail to haul under her bottom, to endeavour to fother her. To add to our distress one of the chain pumps gave way, and she gained fast upon us. The scheme of the topsail was now laid aside, and every soul fell to bailing and pumping. All the boats, except one, were obliged to keep a long distance off on account of the broken water and the very high surf running near us. We baled between life and death, for had she gone down before daylight, every soul must have perished. She now took a heel and some of the guns they were endeavouring to throw overboard run down to leeward, which crushed one man to death; a spare topmast came down from the booms and killed another man.

The people now became faint at the pumps and it was necessary to give them some refreshment. We had luckily between decks a cask of excellent strong ale which we brewed at Anamooka. This was tapped and served regularly to all hands which was much preferable to spirits as it gave them strength without intoxication. During this trying occasion the men behaved with the utmost intrepidity and obedience, not a man flinching from his post. We continually cheered them at the pumps with the delusive hopes of it soon being daylight.

About half an hour before daybreak, a council of war was held. As she was then settling fast down in the water, it was their unanimous opinion that nothing further could be done for the preservation of the ship; and it was their next care to save the lives of the crew. To effect which, spars, booms, hencoops and everything buoyant was cut loose that when she went down, they might chance to get hold of something. The prisoners were ordered to be let out of irons. The water was now coming faster in at the gunports than the pumps could discharge, and to this minute the men never swerved from their duty. She now took a very heavy heel, so much so that she lay quite down on one side.

Three prisoners had been taken out of the 'box' to man the pumps, leaving 11 inside as the *Pandora* foundered. Morrison takes up the story:

At daylight, the boats were hauled up and most of the officers being on top of the box, we observed that they were armed and preparing to go into the boats by the stern ladders.

We begged that we might not be forgot when By Captn. Edwards' order Josh Hodges the armourer's mate was sent down to take the irons off Muspratt, Skinner and Byrn and send them up, but Skinner, being too eager to get out, got hauled up with his handcuffs on, and the other two following him close, the scuttle was shut and barred before Hodges could get to it . . . . He knocked off my hand irons, and Stewarts. I begged the master-at-arms to leave the scuttle open when he answered: 'Never fear, my boys, we'll all go to Hell together.' The words were scarcely out of his mouth, when the ship took a sally and a general cry of 'There she goes' was heard. The master-at-arms and the centinels rolled overboard and at the same instant we saw through the stern ports Captain Edwards astern, swimming to the pinnace which was some distance astern . . . .

Burkitt and Hillbrant were yet handcuffed and the ship under water as far as the mainmast and it was now beginning to flow in upon us.

Now the Devine providence directed Wm. Moulter (boatsn's mate) to the place. He was scrambling up on the box and hearing our cries, took out the bolt and threw it and the scuttle overboard. Such was his presence of mind, tho' he was forced to follow instantly himself. On this, we all got out except Hillbrant. It was as much as I could do to clear myself before she sank . . . .

Seeing one of the gangways come up, I swam to it and saw Muspratt on the other end, having brought him up with it, but falling on the heads of several others, it sent them to the bottom.

The top of our prison having floated, I saw Heywood, Burkitt and Coleman and the first lieutenant (John Larkan).

After having been about an hour and a half in the water, I reached the blue yawl and was taken up with several others.

Four of the mutineers had been drowned.

Surprisingly, very little effort had been made to provision the boats and the 1100-mile voyage to Coupang was made that much harder. Although among the most epic of small-boat voyages, it did not gain much publicity. All Edwards wrote was:

It is unnecessary to retail our particular sufferings in the boats during the run to Timor. Sufficient to observe that we suffered more from heat and thirst than from hunger and that our strength was greatly decreased. At seven o'clock in the morning of the 13th September we saw the island of Timor bearing N.W.

The four boats, the pinnace, the launch, and two yawls reached Coupang on 18 September 1791.

AUSTRALIA'S FIRST FLEET

The arrival of the First Fleet in Port Jackson, New South Wales, was the result of Britain's attempts to clear her overcrowded gaols and convict hulks by deportation of the prisoners to other parts of the world. Although there is some doubt as to the actual figures, 568 male and 191 female prisoners were embarked in the six transports. The voyage out was remarkably free of navigational problems and the ships arrived in Botany Bay within 48 hours of each other. Considering the already debilitated condition of the convicts when they were embarked, the state of health maintained on the voyage was surprisingly good. From embarkation to arrival at Port Jackson, 36 men and 4 women had died. Most of these deaths were from diseases brought into the ships by convicts infected before boarding. The *Scarborough*, which sailed with a healthy complement, lost not a single prisoner.

In some of the ships, problems were caused by the women. Lieutenant Clark in the *Friendship* exploded, 'They are a disgrace to the whole sex, b......s that they are. I wish all the women were out of the ships'. Harsh measures such as flogging and ironing were imposed to control the violent and foul-mouthed ladies.

The transportation of convicts to Australia continued until 1868 when the *Hougemount* brought the last prisoners to Fremantle in Western Australia.

After the convicts had been landed, the *Charlotte*, *Lady Penrhyn* and *Scarborough*, under charter to the East India Company, sailed to China where they loaded tea for England. The *Lady Penrhyn* is remembered by Penrhyn Island which was discovered on her voyage home across the Pacific.

The other three transports and the *Borrowdale* left Port Jackson in July 1788. Scurvy soon reduced the crews to the extent that the *Friendship* had to be scuttled in the Straits of Macassar and her survivors put into the *Alexander*.

The *Prince of Wales* sailed home by way of Cape Horn. She arrived in Rio with her crew so distressed from scurvy that men from the boats which came out to her had to bring the ship to anchor. Her master, John Mason, had died on the passage.

Ships of the First Fleet

There is some doubt about the exact tonnages but the figures here are those of Philip King, the second lieutenant of the *Sirius* and are generally accepted.

HMS *Sirius* was the larger of the two escort vessels accompanying the nine transports. She perhaps measured in length 98 ft 4 in. (30 m), breadth 32 ft 9 in. (10 m), depth 13 ft (4 m), with a tonnage of 612 tons. She carried 20 guns, 10 of which were stowed below for the voyage. In the painting I have shown her with 14 gun ports on a side as is depicted in the only existing sketches, which are contained in the journal of Lieutenant William Bradley of the *Sirius*. As an officer and a seaman he would be unlikely to err in this detail. The October after escorting the fleet to Australia, the *Sirius* sailed for Cape Town by way of Cape Horn to obtain provisions for the new colony, thus becoming the first ship to make this passage. After loading at Cape Town she continued east to Port Jackson, arriving there in May 1789. She had sailed entirely around the world using the strong winds of the roaring forties and crossing the Southern Pacific, Atlantic and Indian oceans.

On 19 March 1790 she became embayed in Sydney Bay, Norfolk Island and drove ashore where she became a total loss.

A second escort vessel was provided by a small brig, rated as a sloop and measuring only 170 tons. She was named the *Supply*.

This painting represents a typical British merchantman of about the 1820s. These were the vessels which were engaged in the transportation of convicts during the first half of the nineteenth century. As can be seen in this example, some of the ships of the time had become more wall-sided and, after the Napoleonic Wars, had ceased to carry heavy armament. The object on the fore lower studdingsail boom is a bag of sand, hung there to stop the boom lifting. The main topmast studdingsail is being hauled down.

First fleet transport and store ships

	Tons	Length	Beam
Alexander	452	114 ft 3½ in. (34.86 m)	31 ft (9.46 m)
Scarborough	430	111 ft 6 in. (34.0 m)	30 ft 2 in. (9.2 m)
Charlotte	335	105 ft (32.03 m)	28 ft 3½ in. (8.63 m)
Lady Penrhyn	333	103 ft 11 in. (31.69 m)	27 ft 6 in. (8.39 m)
Prince of Wales	350	103 ft (31.42 m)	29 ft 3½ in. (8.94 m)
Friendship (probably a snow brig)	274		
Borrowdale (store ship)	275		
Fishburn (store ship)	378		
Golden Grove (store ship)	375		

The First Fleet at anchor in Port Jackson, evening, 26 January 1788. HMS *Sirius* and the brig-rigged sloop *Supply* accompanied the nine transports carrying the first convicts from England to Australia. After assembling in Botany Bay, the fleet moved to Port Jackson to found the first settlement at Sydney Cove. The ships had sailed from England on 13 May 1787 and had made calls at Tenerife, Rio de Janeiro and the Cape. After a voyage of nine months the crew must have felt a sense of security and relaxation once they were at anchor and a harbour furl had been put on the sails. I have tried to capture the atmosphere in the painting with the officers at dinner in the great cabin of the *Sirius* and an officer in a gig on his way to visit another ship.

All the transports, apart from the *Friendship*, were three-masted vessels probably carrying a mizzen topsail. Some of them were described as barque built or rigged, but at this period it did not necessarily mean the absence of squaresail on the mizzen but seemed to define more the placement of the mainmast well aft with a relatively small mizzen mast. Most small English three-masted ships were similarly rigged.

All these ships were two-deckers and some had in addition a quarter-deck. The height between decks would have been about 4 ft 6 in. (137 cm), cramped quarters for the convicts confined to the 'tween deck.

DANA AND THE *PILGRIM*

Thanks to the replica at Dana Point in California, designed by Captain Ray Wallace of San Pedro and skippered by him on her maiden voyage, and clues given by Richard Henry Dana, it was not difficult to paint a fair representation of the brig *Pilgrim*. The replica falls short of perfection in details such as the use of wire standing rigging in place of rope, and placement of some of the deck fittings. The windlass, for instance, should be in its traditional position aft of the foremast instead of on the fo'c's'le as it is in the replica. I suspect the original carried a flying jibboom (as Dana refers to 'jibbooms' in his description of tarring down) and had skysail masts above the royal and topgallant masts – each of which was one spar: '. . .all the rest of the top hamper remained aloft, even to the skysail masts and studding-sail booms'.

When in the Atlantic, the *Pilgrim* was chased by what may have been a pirate; to escape they ran off before the wind, wetting their sails and rigging oars for stunsail booms. Dana mentions ten stunsails, which would have been lower, topsail and topgallant on the fore, and topsail and topgallant on the main. In addition it seems that a ringtail aft of the trysail was carried, for the young English sailor, George Ballmer, was drowned after falling from aloft where he was rigging the ringtail halyards.

Dana refers to the mizzen as a 'trysail' and in the replica both the trysail on the main and the spenser on the fore are set on their own masts. These are stepped immediately abaft the lower masts and are supported at the head by trestle-trees. Apart from the trysail boom, the *Pilgrim* had all the features of a *snow brig*, the true brig having a much larger mizzen with a gaff and boom.

Down-east American sailing ships became notorious among seamen for their hard-driving masters and officers, and Dana's cantankerous and tyrannical captain was no exception; on occasion he took his ill humour out on a sailor by having him flogged. Dana's laconic record of the manner in which a delegation from the crew was received is classic:

He was walking the weather side of the quarter-deck, and seeing us come aft, stopped short in his walk, and with a voice and look intended to annihilate us, called out, 'Well, what the d–l do you want now?' Whereupon we stated our grievances as respectfully as we could, but he broke in upon us, saying that we were getting fat and lazy, didn't have enough to do, and that made us find fault. This provoked us, and we began to give word for word. This would never answer. He clenched his fist, stamped and swore, and sent us all forward, saying, with oaths enough interspersed to send the words home, 'Away with you. Go forward every one of you. I'll haze you. I'll work you up. You don't have enough to do. If you a'n't careful I'll make a hell of the ship. . . .You've mistaken your man. I'm F–T–, all the way from down east. I've been through the mill, ground, and bolted, and come out a *regular-built down-east johnny-cake, good when it's hot*, but when it's cold, sour and indigestible – and you'll find me so.' The latter part of this harangue I remember well, for it made a strong impression, and the 'down-east johnny-cake' became a by-word for the rest of the voyage.

Apart from his irascibility, Captain F–T–'s character possessed other traits which could create problems for his crew. As she rounded windy Point Conception on her passage up the coast to Monterey, the *Pilgrim* came on the wind. Skysails and lee studdingsails were taken in but F–T– hung on to the weather studdingsails and everything else. The following was the result of his bravado:

As the brig came more upon the wind, she felt it more, and we doused the skysails, but kept the weather studding-sails on her, bracing the yards forward so that the swinging-boom nearly touched the spritsail yard. She now lay over to it, the wind was freshening, and the captain was evidently 'dragging on to her'. His brother and Mr R–, looking a little squally, said something to him, but he only answered that he knew the vessel and what she would carry. He was evidently showing off his vessel, and letting them know how he could carry sail. He stood up to windward, holding on by the backstays, and looking up at the sticks, to see how much they would bear, when a puff came which settled the matter. Then it was 'Haul down!', and 'Clew up!' royals, flying-jib, and studding-sails, all at once. There was what the sailors call a 'mess'– everything let go, nothing hauled in, and everything flying. The poor Spanish woman came to the companion-way, looking as pale as a ghost, and nearly frightened to death. The mate and some men forward were trying to haul in the lower studding-sail, which had blown over the spritsail yard-arm and round the guys, while the topmast-studding-sail boom, after buckling up and springing out again like a piece of whalebone, broke off at the boom-iron. I sprang aloft to take in the main top-gallant studding-sail, but before I got into the top, the tack parted and away went the sail, swinging forward of the topgallant-sail, and tearing and slatting itself to pieces. The halyards were at this moment let go by the run; and such a piece of work I never had before, in taking in a sail. After great exertions I got it, or the remains of it, into the top, and was making it fast, when the captain, looking up, called out to me, 'Lay aloft there, d–, and furl that main royal.' Leaving the studding-sail, I went up to the cross trees, and here it looked rather squally. The foot of the topgallant-mast was working between the cross and trussel trees, and the royal mast lay over at a fearful angle with the mast below, while everything was working and cracking, strained to the utmost.

There's nothing for Jack to do but to obey orders, and I went up upon the yard; and there was a worse 'mess', if possible, than I had left below. The braces had been let go, and the yard was swinging about like a turn-pike gate, and the whole sail having blown over to leeward, the lee leach was over the yard-arm, and the sky-sail was all adrift and flying over my head. I looked down, but it was in vain to attempt to make myself heard, for everyone was busy below, and the wind roared, and the sails were flapping in every direction. Fortunately, it was noon and broad daylight, and the man at the wheel, who had his eyes aloft, soon saw my difficulty, and after numberless signs and gestures, got someone to haul the necessary ropes taught. During this interval I took a look below. Everything was in confusion on deck; the little vessel was tearing through the water as if she were mad, the seas flying over her, and the masts leaning over at

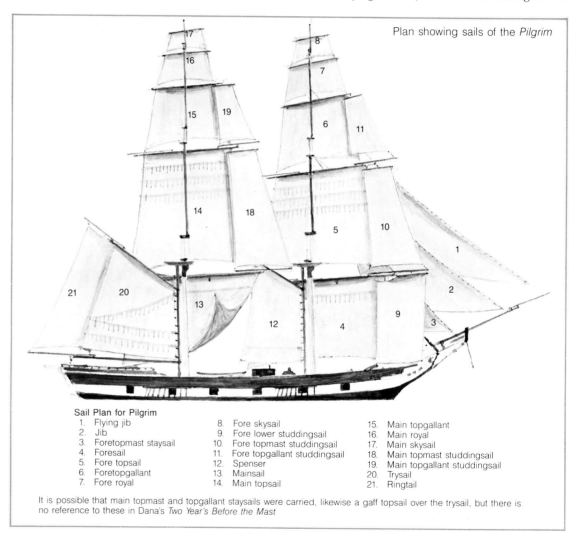

Plan showing sails of the *Pilgrim*

Sail Plan for Pilgrim

1. Flying jib	8. Fore skysail	15. Main topgallant
2. Jib	9. Fore lower studdingsail	16. Main royal
3. Foretopmast staysail	10. Fore topmast studdingsail	17. Main skysail
4. Foresail	11. Fore topgallant studdingsail	18. Main topmast studdingsail
5. Fore topsail	12. Spenser	19. Main topgallant studdingsail
6. Foretopgallant	13. Mainsail	20. Trysail
7. Fore royal	14. Main topsail	21. Ringtail

It is possible that main topmast and topgallant staysails were carried, likewise a gaff topsail over the trysail, but there is no reference to these in Dana's *Two Year's Before the Mast*

an angle of 45° from the vertical. At the other royal-mast-head was S–, working away at the sail, which was blowing from him as fast as he could gather it in. The topgallant-sail below me was soon clewed up, which relieved the mast, and in a short time I got my sail furled, and went below; but I lost overboard a new tarpaulin hat, which troubled me more than anything else. We worked for about half an hour with might and main, and in an hour from that time the squall struck us; from having all our flying kites abroad, we came down to double-reefed topsails and stormsails.

–Richard Henry Dana, *Two Years Before the Mast*

In 1836 Dana returned to Boston after transferring to a happier ship, the *Alert*. He studied law, published his *Two Years Before the Mast* and later, in 1841, the *Seaman's Friend*, both books establishing his reputation. His experience at sea motivated him to use his influence and profession to improve the hard lot of American seamen.

Richard Henry Dana's little brig *Pilgrim* is seen here ghosting over the swell to a faint breeze which hardly touches the surface. All sail is set to skysails and weather topsail and topgallant stunsails. The fore lower stunsail is being readied for setting. In 1834 Dana shipped in the brig as a foremast hand on a voyage from Boston around Cape Horn to California to load hides. The *Pilgrim* was built at Metford, Massachusetts, for the smuggling trade and was therefore fast and handy, measuring 87 ft (26.54 m) in length and 180 tons.

Moored at the Orange County Marine Institute, Dana Point, California, is a replica of the brig which, with some changes, I have used as a model for this painting. The original ship was lost by fire at sea in 1856.

CHARLES DARWIN AND THE *BEAGLE*

Of all the ships of the nineteenth century that played a part in the development of human thinking, none is so well known as the little *Beagle*. The ship in which Charles Darwin circumnavigated the world was about the same size as Bligh's *Bounty*, measuring 90 ft (27.45 m) on deck and 242 tons. She carried a barque rig.

The *Beagle* made two voyages to the Pacific, the first under the command of Captain Pringle Stokes in company with the *Adventure* (330 tons), commanded by Captain Parker King. From 1826 to 1828 these two ships surveyed the southwest coast of South America, the Magellan Strait and Tierra del Fuego. Most of the work in the intricate channels and iron-bound shores of Tierra del Fuego fell to the handy *Beagle*, which, to the credit of her sailors, survived the williwaws, storms, rocks and rips to return to England with the first comprehensive survey of the region. Captain Stokes, depressed by the continual anxiety and lack of any rest, committed suicide. The command was taken over by Captain Robert FitzRoy, a brilliant officer who had entered the Royal Naval College at the age of fourteen. The *Beagle* returned to England with not only the fruits of her survey, but with four young Fuegians. One of these died in England, but the others were returned to their homeland on the *Beagle*'s second voyage.

Before this second and most famous voyage, the ship underwent a complete refit, for she was found to be badly rotted. In his *Narrative of the Surveying Voyages of HMS Adventure and Beagle...*, FitzRoy describes some of the preparations:

The *Beagle* was commissioned on the 4th of July 1831, and was immediately taken into dock to be thoroughly examined and prepared for a long period of foreign service. As she required a new deck, and a good deal of repair about the upper works, I obtained permission to have the upper-deck raised eight inches abaft and twelve forward which proved to be of the greatest advantage to her as a sea boat, besides adding so materially to the comfort of all on board. While in dock, a sheathing of two-inch fir plank was nailed to the vessel's bottom, over which was a coating of felt, and then new copper. This sheathing added about fifteen tons to her displacement, and nearly seven to her actual measurement. Therefore, instead of 235 tons, she might be considered about 242 tons burthen. The rudder was fitted according to the plan of Captain Lihoux [for ease in unshipping]: a patent windlass supplied the place of a capstan: one of Frazer's stoves, with oven attached, was taken instead of a common 'galley' fireplace; and the lightning-conductors, invented by Mr Harris, were fixed on all masts, the bowsprit, and even the flying jib-boom . . . .Our ropes, sails and spars, were the best that could be procured; and to complete our excellent outfit, six superior boats beside a dinghy were built expressly for us, and so contrived and stowed that they could be carried in any weather.

From December 1831 to October 1836 the barque was the home and laboratory for Charles Darwin. The revolutionary theories later expounded in the *Origin of Species* and the *Descent of Man* set the scientific and religious world on its ear.

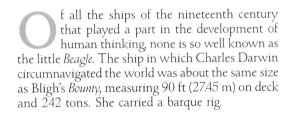

The *Beagle* anchored at Albemarle Island in the Galapagos Group. 'From the regular form of the many craters they gave the country an artificial appearance, which vividly reminded me of those parts of Staffordshire where the great iron-foundries are most numerous,' wrote Charles Darwin of these islands.
(After an etching in the Mansell Collection, Mitchell Library, Sydney, State Library of New South Wales)

THE NINETEENTH-CENTURY WHALERS

These were the circumnavigators
Who thought themselves but mere harpooners
Nor dreamed that the malodorous schooners
Were the galleons of creators
Who seeking whales with single heart,
Starred with names the rude sea chart.
– Nantucket Whalers, Daniel Henderson

Apart from Herman Melville's *Moby Dick* (1851), probably the most well known book on whaling is Frank T. Bullen's *The Cruise of the Cachalot.* Bullen's first-hand account of a whaling voyage around the world is packed with detail and incident, but of all the tales told in his book, my favourite is his account of Captain Paddy Gilroy who, in his decrepit whaler *Chance,* fished the Solander Grounds off the stormy southwest coast of New Zealand.

The *Cachalot* had just put in to Port William in Stewart Island, the southernmost island of New Zealand.

Two whale-ships lay here – the *Tamerlane,* of New Bedford, and the *Chance,* of Bluff Harbour. I am bound to confess that there was a great difference in appearance between the Yankee and the colonial – very much in favour of the former. She was neat, smart, and seaworthy, looking as if just launched; but the *Chance* looked like some poor old relic of a bygone day, whose owners, unable to sell her, and too poor to keep her in repair, were just letting her go while keeping up the insurance, praying fervently each day that she might come to grief, and bring them a little profit at last.

But although it is much safer to trust appearances in ships than in men, any one who summed up the *Chance* from her generally outworn and poverty-stricken looks would have been, as I was, 'way off'. Old she was, with an indefinite antiquity, carelessly rigged, and vilely unkempt as to her gear, while outside she did not seem to have had a coat of paint for a generation. She looked what she really was – the sole survivor of the once great whaling industry of New Zealand.

Bullen goes on to describe the *Chance's* captain:

He was a queer little figure of a man – short, tubby, with scanty red hair, and a brogue thick as pea-soup. Eccentric in most things, he was especially so in his dress, which he seemed to select on the principle of finding the most unfitting things to wear. Rumour credited him with a numerous half-breed progeny – certainly he was greatly mixed up with the Maories, half his crew being made up of his dusky friends and relations by *marriage.* Overflowing with kindliness and good temper, his ship

was a veritable ark of refuge for any unfortunate who needed help, which accounted for the numerous deserters from Yankee whalers who were to be found among his crew. Such whaling skippers as our late commander hated him with ferocious intensity; and but for his Maori and half-breed bodyguard, I have little doubt he would have long before been killed. Living as he had for many years on that storm-beaten coast, he had become, like his Maories, familiar with every rock and tree in fog or clear, by night or day; he knew them, one might almost say, as the seal knows them, and feared them as little. His men adored him . . . .

There were sixteen white men on board the *Chance,* including the skipper, drawn as usual from various European and American sources, the rest of her large crew of over forty all told being made up of Maories and half-breeds. One common interest united them, making the jolliest crowd I ever saw – their devotion to their commander. There was here to be found no jealousy of the Maories being officers and harpooners, no black looks or discontented murmuring; all hands seemed particularly well satisfied with their lot in all its bearings; so that, although the old tub was malodorous enough to turn even a pretty strong stomach, it was a pleasure to visit her cheerful crowd for the sake of their enlivening society.

Four days later the *Chance* and other ships left for the whaling grounds. Bullen describes their departure:

Characteristically, the *Chance* was away first, before daylight had quite asserted itself and while the bases of the cliffs and tops of the rocks were as yet hidden in dense wreaths of white haze. Paddy lolled on the taff-rail near the wheel, which was held by an immense half-breed, who leant back and carried on a

desultory, familiar conversation with his skipper; the rest of the crew were scattered about the decks, apparently doing what they liked in any manner they chose. The anchor was being catted, sails going up, and yards being trimmed; but, to observers like us, no guiding spirit was noticeable. It seemed to work all right, and the old ark herself looked as if she was as intelligent as any of them; but the sight was not an agreeable one to men accustomed to discipline. The contrast when the *Tamerlane* came along an hour or so after was emphatic. Every man at his post; every order carried out with the precision of clockwork; the captain pacing the quarter-deck as if she were a line-of-battle ship – here the airs put on were almost ludicrous in the other direction. Although she was only 'a good jump' long, as we say, whenever an order was given, it was thundered out as if the men were a mile away, each officer appearing to vie with the others as to who could

The whalers *Charles W. Morgan* and (*left*) *Kutusoff* are shown here cutting in their catch in the icy waters of the far northern Pacific where the baleen or right whale was hunted. Apart from a low grade oil, this species provided baleen or whalebone for hats and corsetry.

The ships are hove to on the port tack so as to headreach offshore in the light wind. It was normal practice to heave to on the starboard tack with the foresail aback, the fore topsail yard on the cap and the topsail hanging before the foresail. With her main and mizzen topsails drawing, the ship would make steady but slow headway, keeping the whale on the windward side firmly in position while her crew 'cut in' from stages rigged out from the waist. Most whalers cut in on the starboard side, possibly because this enabled them to cut in on the starboard tack, thus giviing them right of way. The

whale being taken in tow has been flagged to mark it should the boat have to leave it adrift.

The whaler *Kutusoff* is remembered in the paintings of the artist Benjamin Russell, who shipped out in her during 1871. After his return from the voyage around the world, Russell and another artist painted a panorama of whaling scenes 8 ft 6 in. (2.59 m) high and 1275 ft (388.9 m) in length. Russell became the most famous of whaling artists; he died in 1885.

The *Charles W. Morgan,* now preserved in Mystic, Connecticut, hunted whales for 80 years and earned $2,000,000 for her owners. She was built in New Bedford in 1841 and from 1887 to 1904 she worked out of San Francisco; her last voyage was in 1921. After the end of her whaling career and before being preserved in a dry berth, she was used in the production of films.

143

bellow the loudest. That was carrying things to the opposite extreme, and almost equally objectionable to merchant seamen.

Sometime later, after Paddy had been bringing in whale after whale while the Americans struggled to hold on to their catch in the teeth of the frequent gales, Bullen sighted the *Chance* and three Yankees, each with a whale alongside. They were in the western approaches to Foveaux Strait between the South Island and Stewart Island and making for shelter to cut in their catch. A change of wind ot the north put them all on the lee shore:

As the devoted craft drifted helplessly down upon that frowning barrier, our excitement grew intense. Their inability to do anything but drift was only too well known by experience to every one of us, nor would it be possible for them to escape at all if they persisted in holding on much longer. But it was easy to see why they did so. While Paddy held on so far to leeward of them, and consequently in so much more imminent danger than they were, it would be derogatory in the highest degree to their reputation for seamanship and courage were they to slip and run before he did. He, however, showed no sign of doing so, although they all neared, with an accelerated drift, that point from whence no seamanship could deliver them, and where death inevitable, cruel, awaited them without hope of escape. The part of the coast upon which they were apparently driving was about as dangerous and impracticable as any in the world. A gigantic barrier of black, naked rock, extending for several hundred yards, rose sheer from the sea beneath, like the side of an ironclad, up to a height of seven or eight hundred feet. No outlying spurs of submerged fragments broke the immeasurable landward rush of the majestic waves towards the frowning face of this world-fragment. Fresh from their source, with all the impetus accumulated in their thousand-mile journey, they came apparently irresistible. Against this perpendicular barrier they hurled themselves with a shock that vibrated far inland, and a roar that rose in a dominating diapason over the continuous thunder of the tempest-riven sea.

High as was the summit of the cliff, the spray, hurled upwards by the tremendous impact, rose higher, so that the whole front of the great rock was veiled in filmy wreaths of foam, hiding its solidity from the seaward view. At either end of this vast rampart nothing could be seen but a waste of breakers seething, hissing, like the foot of Niagara, and effectually concealing the *chevaux de frise* of rocks which produced such a vortex of tormented waters.

Towards this dreadful spot, then, the four vessels were being resistlessly driven, every moment seeing their chances of escape lessening to vanishing-point. Suddenly, as if panic-stricken, the ship nearest to the *Chance* gave a great sweep round on to the other tack, a few fluttering gleams aloft showing that even in that storm they were daring to set some sail. What the manoeuvre meant we knew very well – they had cut adrift from their whale, terrified at last beyond endurance into the belief that Paddy was going to sacrifice himself and his crew in the attempt to lure them with him to inevitable destruction. The other two did not hesitate longer. The example once set, they immediately followed; but it was for some time

doubtful in the extreme whether their resolve was not taken too late to save them from destruction. We watched them with breathless interest, unable for a long time to satisfy ourselves that they were out of danger. But at last we saw them shortening sail again – a sure sign that they considered themselves, while the wind held in the same quarter, safe from going ashore at any rate, although there was still before them the prospect of a long struggle with the unrelenting ferocity of the weather down south.

Meanwhile, what of the daring Irishman and his old barrel of a ship? The fugitives once safe off the land, all our interest centred in the *Chance*. We watched her until she drew in so closely to the seething cauldron of breakers that it was only occasionally we could distinguish her outline; and the weather was becoming so thick and dirty, the light so bad, that we were reluctantly compelled to lose sight of her, although the skipper believed that he saw her in the midst of the turmoil of broken water at the western end of the mighty mass of perpendicular cliff before described. Happily for us, the wind veered to the westward, releasing us from the prospect of another enforced visit to the wild regions south of the island. It blew harder than ever; but being now a fair wind up the Straits, we fled before it, anchoring again in Port William before midnight. Here we were compelled to remain for a week; for after the gale blew itself out, the wind still hung in the same quarter, refusing to allow us to get back again to our cruising station.

But on the second day of our enforced detention a ship poked her jibboom round the west end of the little bay. No words could describe our condition of spellbound astonishment when she rounded-to, cumbrously as befitting a ship towing a whale, and revealed to us the well-remembered outlines of the old *Chance*. It was like welcoming the first-fruits of the resurrection; for who among sailor men, having seen a vessel disappear from their sight, as we had, under such terrible conditions, would ever have expected to see her again? She was hardly anchored before our skipper was alongside, thirsting to satisfy his unbounded curiosity as to the unheard-of means whereby she had escaped such apparently inevitable destruction. I was fortunate enough to accompany him, and hear the story at first-hand.

It appeared that none of the white men on board, except the redoubtable Paddy himself, had ever been placed in so seemingly hopeless and desperate a position before. Yet when they saw how calm and free from anxiety their commander was, how cool and businesslike the attitude of all their dusky shipmates, their confidence in his ability and resourcefulness kept its usual high level. It must be admitted that the test such feelings were then subjected to was of the severest, for to their eyes no possible avenue of escape was open. Along that glaring line of raging, foaming water not a break occurred, not the faintest indication of an opening anywhere wherein even so experienced a pilot as Paddy might thrust a ship. The great black wall of rock loomed up by their side, grim and pitiless as doom – a very door of adamant closed against all hope. Nearer and nearer they drew, until the roar of the baffled Pacific was deafening, maddening, in its overwhelming volume of chaotic sound. All hands stood motionless, with eyes fixed in horrible fascination upon the indescribable vortex to which they were being irresistibly driven.

At last, just as the fringes of the back-beaten billows hissed up to greet them, they felt her motion ease. Instinctively looking aft, they saw the skipper coolly wave his hand, signing to them to trim the yards. As they hauled on the weather braces, she plunged through the maelström of breakers, and before they had got the yards right round they were on the other side of that enormous barrier, the anchor was dropped, and all was still. The vessel rested, like a bird on her nest, in a deep, still tarn, shut in, to all appearance, on every side by huge rock barriers. Of the furious storm but a moment before howling and raging all around them, nothing remained but an all-pervading, thunderous hum, causing the deck to vibrate beneath them, and high overhead the jagged, leaden remnants of twisted, tortured cloud whirling past their tiny oblong of sky. Just a minute's suspension of all faculties but wonder, then, in one spontaneous, heartfelt note of genuine admiration, all hands burst into a cheer that even overtopped the mighty rumble of the baffled sea.

Here they lay, perfectly secure, and cut in their whale as if in dock; then at the first opportunity they ran out, with fearful difficulty, a kedge with a whale-line attached, by which means they warped the vessel out of her hiding-place – a far more arduous operation than getting in had been. But even this did not exhaust the wonders of that occasion. They had hardly got way upon her, beginning to draw out from the land, when the eagle-eye of one of the Maories detected the carcass of a whale rolling among the breakers about half a mile to the westward. Immediately a boat was lowered, a double allowance of line put into her, and off they went to the valuable flotsam. Dangerous in the highest degree was the task of getting near enough to drive harpoons into the body; but it was successfully accomplished, the line run on board, and the prize hauled triumphantly alongside. This was the whale they had now brought in. We shrewdly suspected that it must have been one of those abandoned by the unfortunate vessels who had fled, but etiquette forbade us saying anything about it. Even had it been, another day would have seen it valueless to any one, for it was by no means otto of roses to sniff at now, while they had certainly salved it at the peril of their lives.

When we returned on board and repeated the story, great was the amazement. Such a feat of seamanship was almost beyond belief; but we were shut up to believing, since in no other way could the vessel's miraculous escape be accounted for. The little, dumpy, red-faced figure, rigged like any scarecrow, that now stood on his cutting-stage, punching away vigorously at the fetid mass of blubber beneath him, bore no outward visible sign of a hero about him; but in our eyes he was transfigured – a being to be thought of reverently, as one who in all those qualities that go to the making of a man had proved himself of the seed royal, a king of men, all the more kingly because unconscious that his deeds were of so exalted an order.

I am afraid that, to a landsman, my panegyric may smack strongly of gush, for no one but a seaman can rightly appraise such doings as these; but I may be permitted to say that, when I think of men whom I feel glad to have lived to know, foremost among them rises the queer little figure of Paddy Gilroy.

– Frank T. Bullen, *The Cruise of the Cachalot*

Captain Paddy Gilroy died in 1902.

THE SAN FRANCISCO GOLD RUSH

An extraordinary combination of circumstances in the late 1840s was to have enduring repercussions in the Pacific. Australia and New Zealand were firmly within the British Empire and slowly and hesitantly being settled. California was in a state of desultory flux, still under the domain of the Spanish Mexicans, when famine in Ireland and the discovery of gold near San Francisco created the greatest migration the world had yet seen.

On 24 January 1848 when James Wilson Marshall found gold in the tailrace of John Sutter's mill on the Sacramento, the population of San Francisco was less than 1000. Sutter tried to suppress the discovery which might compromise his grants with the Mexicans, but the word soon got out. First to Californians, who flocked to Sutter's Mill, and then around the world the news was spread, borne literally on the wind, as sailing ships completed their long voyages. There followed a stampede to California which employed any vessel that could float – and some that could not. On everything from the graceful and fast early American tea clippers to the oldest, worm-eaten brig, the 'Forty-niners' found transport to San Francisco round Cape Horn.

In spite of its hazards, the sea route was certainly safer than the waggon train overland, and healthier than the fever-blighted route by way of Panama. Many ill-found ships were lost and the overcrowded vessels could take on average about four months. The extreme clippers, which bettered 110 days from New York or Boston in 1850 and 1851, averaged 104 days, but there were passages of over 200 days, including a paddle-wheel steamboat which took the best part of a year – 300 days.

Ships bound for San Francisco, apart from their aspiring and impatient passengers, freighted all the requirements of the gold towns – tools, food, luxuries – to the extent that the market was soon glutted. However, a successful voyage could pay for the cost of a vessel in one trip. In San Francisco a $5 barrel of flour could fetch $50 and an egg $1. Any shipowner who could judge the commodity that would be in short supply in the tent cities was certain to make a handsome profit. If, however, he misjudged, he could end up with a ship with no crew, a hold full of pickaxes and nowhere to ship them to.

Nothing demonstrates the sheer craziness of the San Francisco gold rush more than the old daguerreotypes of the rotting ships abandoned after their arrival. It has been told that ships making the port would anchor and before a furl could be made

The Californian gold rush brought the 'forty-niners' flocking to San Francisco overland and by sea. Many ships were abandoned after their arrival, their officers and crews hotfooting it to the goldfields. Hundreds of vessels, many battered and unseaworthy after their voyage around Cape Horn, lay at anchor or were beached to become hotels and stores.

on the yards, abandoned. Many, arriving in after a battering round the Horn, were leaking and unfit for sea again without a refit, but even sound ships were trapped. A master wishing to return would be hard put to find a crew in spite of the bloody efforts of the crimps and boarding-house masters. To get out, his only recourse was to pay exorbitant wages to a skeleton crew and sail for Hawaii or China where a normal crowd could be engaged. Many of the derelict ships sank at their moorings or drove ashore. Others were converted to warehouses, hotels and gambling dens after being beached and roofed.

The gold rush boosted the population of California from its initial 15,000 to hundreds of thousands. Between 1848 and 1851 inclusive, 412,942 people arrived by sea from the East, either round the Horn or across the Isthmus. Many more came overland, and thousands arrived from Europe, Australia and New Zealand. News of the find reached southern British colonies late in 1848 and in no time a motley collection of craft was on its way, carrying optimistic diggers to California. In 1851 the tide turned; gold was discovered in Australia and there began a race to the Victorian gold fields which eclipsed the lure of California and ironically brought most of the Australian migrants back to their own doorstep.

The demand for fast passages around Cape Horn to San Francisco provided the spur to realise the remarkable talents of America's most famous and able shipbuilder and designer, Donald McKay. McKay was born in Nova Scotia in 1810 and left home at the age of 16 to take up an apprenticeship as a shipwright in New York. The young apprentice's talent, industry and ambition soon made a favourable impression in the yards, where he was given tasks normally outside the competence of an apprentice, and he was freed from his indentures to start out as a freelance shipwright. In 1832 he married Albenia Martha Boole, the eldest daughter of a shipbuilder. This well educated young woman knew a great deal about ship construction and design and was able to draft and lay off lines. These skills she imparted to Donald, along with the sciences and maths to which his primary-level education did not aspire.

Eager to learn, the ambitious McKay was soon in partnership as a shipbuilder, first at Newburyport in Massachusetts and then, at the age of 34, he founded his own yard at the foot of Border Street, East Boston. By this time a revolution in ship design was starting and the progenitors of the true clippers were beginning to come off the New York slipways. The leading designer of these ships, a friend of McKay, was John Willis and his ideas strongly influenced the shipbuilder. John W. Griffiths' prototype clipper, the *Rainbow*, was launched in 1845 and the *Seawitch* the following year. Both ships proved fast and weatherly in spite of their sharp lines and towering rig.

Until that time the ideal lines for a ship had continued to be based on the 'codfish' principal –

THE AMERICAN CLIPPERS

bluff bows with the maximum beam well forward and a long run aft. The clippers broke away from this ancient concept. Their entry was sharp, with a fine run to their maximum beam about amidships. A great deal of attention was given to their lines, both fore and aft, so as to attain the maximum speed without sacrificing seaworthiness. Waterline models first invented by Orlando B. Merrill of Newburyport in 1796 were used to develop their lines. These models were much more efficient and versatile than the frame models previously used. The waterline model was faired out of horizontal slabs of wood – each interface between the slabs representing a waterline. The slabs were either dowelled or screwed together and could be separated, enabling the lines to be transferred to plans. The hydro-dynamics of the new lines were tank-tested and refined, with the result that American designers soon led the rest of the world.

As for Donald McKay, his ability was already in demand, particularly by the Boston merchant and shipowner, Enoch Train, for whom he built Atlantic packet ships employed in the freight and immigrant trade. In 1849, the *Rainbow*, the first of McKay's ships for the California trade, was launched. McKay vainly tried to persuade her owners to build a sharp ship along the lines pioneered by Griffiths. *Rainbow*'s first passage to San Francisco cannot be compared with the run of McKay's later ships.

The *Staghound*

McKay's first ship to make a notable contribution to the vessels now distinguished by the name 'California clippers' was the *Staghound*, launched in December 1850. She was totally designed and drafted by McKay and was larger, longer and sharper than any other merchant ship in the world. Although the *Staghound* was designed for speed, stability and strength had not been neglected. She lacked the ornamentation of many ships of her time and was impeccably finished with the finest quality woods and fittings. Her appearance in New York drew much comment. Her sharpness was criticised – she would bury herself in heavy weather. Aloft she was the most heavily sparred ship yet seen in New York. Her 8000 yards (6690 m) of canvas caused a deal of wonder.

The *Staghound* left New York on 1 February 1851 and silenced her critics. Her captain, Josiah Richardson, who had been in the demanding trans-Atlantic packet ships, was of a breed of shipmasters who drove their ships to the limit. There is no doubt that the skills of such masters in the art of carying sail in all weathers combined with the revolution in ship design to make resounding successes of the clippers. The ship's lives were short and glorious, for no matter how well built, no wooden ship could for long stand the strains suffered by the stresses of sail carrying and pounding imposed by their demanding captains. It was often claimed that the Yankee skippers and their crews were past masters at the art of clapping on a fish, stoppering a shroud and making do to carry on. Six days out of New York the *Staghound*'s maintopmast and all her topgallants went by the board in a southeast gale. It took 12 days to repair the damage. In spite of this, she arrived in Valparaiso under jury rig in 66 days. Captain Richardson had no doubt about his ship:

Gentlemen:- Your ship the *Staghound* anchored in this port this day after a passage of sixty-six days, the shortest one ever made here; and if we had not lost maintopmast and all three topgallantmasts February 6th, our passage doubtless would have been the shortest ever made....The ship is yet to be built to beat the *Staghound*. Nothing that we have fallen in with as yet could hold her play. I am in love with the ship; a better sea boat, or better working ship, or drier, I have never sailed in.

She spent five days at Valparaiso and continued to San Francisco, making the Golden Gate in 21 days. *Staghound* was 108 days at sea from New York; her total time was 113 days and her best day's run was 358 nautical miles – a record voyage.

The *Flying Cloud*

Before the *Staghound* had completed her first voyage, McKay had started building a ship which was to become a byword in maritime history. *Flying Cloud* was twice as large as Griffiths' *Seawitch* and larger again than the *Staghound*. She measured 1783 tons, 229 ft (69.85 m) in length, 41 ft (12.5 m) in breadth and 21 ft 6 in. (6.56 m) in depth. Her main truck rose 200 ft (61 m) from the keel, she crossed three skysail yards and set every imaginable sail from watersails to royal studdingsails. The ship was ordered by Enoch Train, but she attracted so much attention while she was being built that offers to purchase her poured in. Train succumbed to an offer of $US90,000 from Grinnell and Mintura, who operated the New York Swallow Tail Line. It was a sale that Enoch Train always afterwards regretted.

The *Flying Cloud* was launched on 15 April 1851 and sailed from New York bound for San Francisco on 3 June. Command had been given to Captain Josiah Creesy from Marblehead; he had commanded ships for a number of years in the China and East India trade. With him sailed his wife, Eleanor, an able navigator in her own right. In the true style of down-east captains, Creesy drove *Flying Cloud* with all she could carry. Three days out, he lost the main topsail yard and main and mizzen topgallant masts. One can imagine in a gale of wind the shambles created by such a partial dismasting; the unrestrained canvas slatting and blatting, heavy spars and blocks swinging wildly about and the mess of standing and running rigging. Attempts to save a spar had to be weighed against its murderous tendency to demolish the remaining rig or stove in the ship's side. Little could be done except to clear the wreck as quickly as possible, axing shrouds and cutting clear sails and gear, saving as much as possible. However, most ships of this period were well provided with spare spars and within a day the topgallants were back in place and another day saw a new maintopsail yard crossed, the sails bent and the ship flying on southwards. A few days later, on the fourteenth, it was discovered that the mainmast had sprung near the hounds. This was fished but an anxious eye was kept on the mast for the rest of the voyage. There was to be no returning to a handy port for repair and some of the green hands and hardcases among the crew were terrified.

Creesy would have shipped the usual mixture of bums and layabouts and others who had signed on only to get to California and would not have known a brace from a bowline. This brawling, bemused, seasick crowd would have been leavened by a sprinkling of first-class sailors, often company men. On them and the hard-riding mates depended the safety of the ship and the swiftness of the voyage. Belaying pins and knuckle dusters were not just sadistic instruments used by the mates of the down-easters; without the certainty of instant reprisal, the ship could not be managed – the lazy longshore tough, seasick and scared, found it safer to lay out and secure a berserk topgallant than face the wrath of the mate on deck.

Creesy had trouble with his crew in a near mutiny, and as they fought on south towards the Horn, two men were ironed for attempting to sabotage the ship so as to force a diversion to a port for repair. They had drilled and opened up a leak in the fo'c's'le, causing a fair amount of water to get below and damage the cargo. The saboteurs were soon released as they were sorely needed on deck. Later Creesy suspended the mate from duty for 'arrogating to himself the privilege of cutting up rigging contrary to my orders, and long continued neglect of duty'.

The following are extracts from the *Flying Cloud*'s log from 11 July when they were well south towards the Horn:

July 11 – Very severe thunder and lightning. Double-reefed topsails. Latter part blowing a hard gale, close reefed topsails, split fore and main-topmast staysails. At 1 p.m. discovered mainmast had sprung. Sent down royal and topgallant yards and studding sail booms off lower and topsail yards to relieve the mast. Heavy sea running and shipping large quantities of water over lee rail.
July 12 – Heavy South-West gales and sea. Distance 40 miles.
July 13 – Let men out of irons in consequence of wanting their services, with the understanding that they would be taken care of on arriving at San Francisco.
At 6 p.m. carried away main-topsail tye and truss band round mainmast. Single-reefed topsails.
July 19 – Crossed latitude 50°South.
July 20 – At 4 a.m. close-reefed topsails and furled courses. Hard gale with thick weather and snow.
July 23 – Passed through Straits of Le Maire. At 8 a.m. Cape Horn North 5 miles distant, the whole coast covered with snow.
July 26 – Crossed latitude 50°South in the Pacific, 7 days from same latitude in the Atlantic [a record for the Horn].
July 31 – Fresh breezes and fine weather. All sail set. At 2 p.m. wind South-East. At 6 p.m. squally; in lower and topgallant studding sails; 7 p.m. in royals, 2 a.m. in fore topmast studding sail. Latter part, strong gales and high sea running, ship very wet fore and aft. Distance run this day by observation 374 miles. During the squalls 18 knots of line were not sufficient to measure the rate of speed. Topgallant sails set.

Aug. 1 – Strong gales and squally. At six p.m. in topgallant sails, double reefed fore and mizzen topsails. Heavy sea running. At 4 a.m. made sail again. Distance 334 miles.

On 12 August the *Flying Cloud* crossed the equator and during the next 12 days averaged runs better than 200 miles each day. A couple of days of 'Light baffling breezes' had Creesy champing at the bit for he knew he stood a chance of breaking all records for the voyage. The wind returned fresh and strong. On the twenty-ninth, within almost a day's run of the Golden Gate, the fore-topgallant mast went overboard. The crew now were caught up in the race and set too with a will. In 24 hours the mast was back up in spite of the squally northwester blowing. Creesy drove his ship for the line with everything she could carry, raising the South Farallones at 6 a.m. on the thirtieth, a brief pause for the pilot an hour later, and on through the Gate and to anchor at 11.30 a.m. – only 89 days and 8 hours from New York. Her passage times were as follows:

Sandy Hook to Equator ....21 days
Equator to 50°South ....25 days
50°S. Atlantic to 50°S. Pacific 7 days
50°S. Pacific to Equator ....17 days
Equator to San Francisco ......19 days
Distance run ....15,452 nautical miles
Daily average ....195 nautical miles

Crowds swarmed to see the record-breaking new clipper. Seamen noted the fished spars, frappings, stoppered shrouds and seizings which all told of a hard-won victory.

Captain Creesy lost most of his crew in San Francisco and sailed to China short-handed. The *Flying Cloud* still tramped along, equalling her best day's run of 374 miles the first day out and making Honolulu in 12 days. However, her passage time from China took 96 days, ten days more than her rival, the *N.B. Palmer* which sailed from China ten days after her. The *Flying Cloud* did not give her best in light winds.

The *Flying Cloud*, Donald Mckay's first extreme clipper which set the record of 89 days and 8 hours from New York to San Francisco.

Creesy made five voyages in the *Flying Cloud*. On the fourth, in 1854, he beat his previous record from New York to San Francisco by 13 hours and showed a clean pair of heels to another rival, the new clipper *Archer*, which was on her maiden voyage. Sailing home from China on this voyage, the *Flying Cloud* ran hard on to a coral reef. Creesy managed to get her off. She was leaking badly, with her shoe missing and her keel severed, but Captain Creesy refused to run the expense of putting in for repair. In very creditable time he sailed her back to New York, winning the effusive gratitude of the owners and underwriters.

On Creesy's final voyage his wife endeared herself to all sailors by being instrumental in the rescue of a man lost overboard off Madagascar. She was below when the sailor fell and saw him tumble past the port. She rushed on deck, called 'Man overboard' and threw over the life ring. A boat was put over, but an hour's search failed to find him. Eleanor Creesy had worked out the drift and direction to search and persuaded her husband to continue the search until dark. The sailor was found, at dusk, hardly able to keep afloat any longer, and two miles away from the ship. In Mrs Creesy's care the sailor was nursed back to health and the story of Eleanor's humanity later spread among sailors round the world.

For her sixth voyage to San Francisco, Creesy handed over command to a Captain Reynard. Creesy was in need of a rest and the *Flying Cloud* was also getting tired. Captain Reynard attempted to drive her and is credited with a day's run of 402 miles but a sprung bowsprit and a very shaky rig forced him to put into Rio for repair.

Depression and the Civil War badly affected the flourishing American shipping. About 1863 the *Flying Cloud* was sold to James Baines of Liverpool, under which flag she traded to Australia, carrying emigrants. She ended her days in the Atlantic timber trade, got ashore on the New Brunswick coast in 1874, but was refloated and taken to St John for repair. While on the slip she caught fire, causing such damage that little could be done except break her up for her metal.

The *Flying Cloud* continues to hold the record sailing passage of 89 days 8 hours, from New York to San Francisco.

Ships, all of them renowned, continued to come off the ways of Donald McKay's yard. The *Flying Fish*, launched in 1851, the same year as the *Flying Cloud*, on her maiden voyage was beaten by William H. Webb's *Swordfish* by eight days to San Francisco, but won her second race against the clippers *Wild Pidgeon, John Gilpin* and *Tradewind*; a race which was much publicised. *Flying Fish* won this in the time of 92 days and 4 hours.

The *Sovereign of the Seas*

The *Sovereign of the Seas* followed in July 1852. She was built entirely on McKay's account and also made her first voyage freighted with her builder's cargo. She was the largest ship to that date, measuring 2421 tons and shipped the largest cargo ever out of New York, amounting to 2950 tons of general merchandise. McKay ran her out to San Francisco with a hand-picked crew of 103. Her master, Captain Lauchlan McKay, Donald's brother, belied the usual stamp of a down-east captain. His leadership, skill and care inspired his crew to the heights of effort. 'Captain Lauchlan McKay's skill as a sailor, his dauntless energy as a man, his kindness to his crew, and his entire abnegation of self, all stamped him a truly great commander...' wrote one of the *Sovereign's* crew.

On this voyage head winds and contrary gales were the lot and after rounding the Horn the maintopmast went overboard, followed by the fore topmast, foreyard, and mizzen topgallantmast. By herculean efforts everything was saved and brought inboard. While the ship continued to make 12 knots under mainsail, cro'jack and mizzen topsail, the whole rig was restored within 12 days. The *Sovereign*

of the Seas made San Francisco in 103 days and claimed to have beaten every ship which sailed within a month of her. Instead of continuing to China, McKay sailed to Honolulu and lifted a cargo of whale oil from the Yankee whalers, creating a boom in that industry. She sailed home with a crew of only 34 – apart from 'one large grizzly bear, a rainbow bear, a wolf, coyote, wildcat and leopard'. With her reduced crew, and still partly crippled fore and main topmasts, she ran 6,245 statute miles in 22 days and for eleven consecutive days averaged 354 statute miles. During four of these days, also consecutively, she averaged 394¾ statute miles; another record for the day. She made New York in 82 days.

The *Sovereign of the Seas* continued as a record-breaker, cleaning up the New York-to-Liverpool record and, under James Baines' Liverpool Blackball Line, showing herself a flier on the Australian run. She was finally wrecked in the Strait of Malacca in August 1859.

Servicing the 'Coolie Trade'

The *Westward Ho* was appropriately named; she was launched in September 1852. She was a beautiful ship which racked up no new achievements but didn't disgrace her builder. As did a number of American clipper ships, *Westward Ho* engaged in the shipping of Chinese from Swatow to the guano deposits in the Chincha Islands off Peru. This trade, as inhumane as the African slave trade, exploited poverty-stricken Chinese by offering contracts for five years at $US8 per month on payment of $US50 passage money – which amounted to the poor man buying his way to Hell. The British Government had forbidden traffic from any port with a consul in residence, but Swatow and other ports were outside their jurisdiction. McKay's next ship, the 1704-ton *Bald Eagle*, also engaged in the 'Coolie trade' about 1854. Captain Hayes of the *Otrant*, running between Singapore and San Francisco, describes the recruitment of the Chinese:

All men over 35-years old, or after they have been stripped stark naked show the least sign of disease upon their persons are rejected, and these poor creatures, brought a long way from the interior by 'crimps' of their own nation – who got $10 for bringing down all of what they term healthy cattle – are turned ashore to perish of starvation or die a lingering death by exposure. Great numbers, says Captain Hayes, are seen along the beach in this horrible state. Perhaps, he added, they are far better off than those poor wretches who have been led to suppose they are bound to the golden regions of California or Australia, or some pleasant land in the China or Indian Seas.

The *Great Republic*

One more ship, the *Empress of the Sea*, 2200 tons, left McKay's yard before his masterpiece, the colossal *Great Republic* slid into the water in October 1853. She was the largest merchant ship in the world, registering 4555 tons and able to stow 6000 tons. McKay built her on his own account in spite of the prophets of doom who claimed she would bankrupt him. He spared no expense on his mighty ship, which was the largest clipper ever built. A description was given in a pamphlet written by a friend of McKay, Duncan McLean:

She is 325 feet long, has 53 feet extreme breadth of beam, and 39 feet depth of hold, including 4 complete decks. The height between her spar and upper decks is 7 feet, and between the others 8 feet; and all her accommodations are in her upper between decks. The crew's quarters are forward; and aft she has sail rooms, store rooms, accommodations for boys and petty officers, and abaft these, two cabins and a vestibule. The after cabin is beautifully wainscotted with mahogany, has recess sofas on each side, ottomans, marble-covered tables, mirrors and elliptical panels ornamented with pictures. She has also a fine library for the use of her crew, and spacious accommodations for passengers.

On the spar deck there are five houses for various purposes, but such is her vast size, that they appear to occupy but little space. She has an eagle's head forward for a head, and on the stern, which is semi-elliptical in form, is a large eagle with the American shield in his talons. She is yellow metalled up to 25 feet draught, and above is painted black. Instead of bulwarks, the outline of her spar deck is protected by a rail on turned stanchions, which, with the houses, are painted white. Of her materials and fastenings we cannot speak too highly. She is built of oak, is diagonally cross-braced with iron, double ceiled, has 4 depths of midship keelsons, each depth 15 inches square, three depths of sister keelsons, and 4 bilge keelsons, two of them riders, and all her frames are coaged, also the keelsons and waterways, and she is square fastened throughout. She has three tiers of stanchions, which extend from the hold to the third deck, and are kneed in the most substantial style. She also has many long pointers and 10 beamed hooks forward and aft. In a word, she is the strongest ship ever built.

The *Great Republic* stepped four masts, the aftermast, which would later be called the 'jigger', was named the spanker and sometimes called the 'McKay mast'. She was also provideed with double topsails and a 15 horsepower steam engine. The latter could be used for a variety of purposes such as pumping, hoisting sails and even, it was claimed, transferred to a large longboat where it provided power for towing.

Unfortunately the great ship was never to prove herself. In New York, when she was nearly ready for sea, a fire ashore sent sparks into her rigging and she took fire. Water couldn't be got to the burning sails aloft and the fire got out of control. She was virtually destroyed. The underwriters paid $US235,000 to McKay, who had nothing more to do with her. While the *Great Republic* was being rebuilt to the orders of N.B. Palmer for Messrs A.A. Low and Brothers, McKay continued to build ships such as the *Lightning* and the *James Baines*.

When the *Great Republic* sailed in February 1855 she was still the largest sailing ship ever built, although her tonnage was reduced to 3357 tons and her rig cut down by 25 per cent. Her arrival in Great Britain caused a sensation and until 1856 she was employed by the French, transporting troops between Marseilles and the Crimea. She returned to New York in 1856 and was put into the California trade, sailing on her first voyage to San Francisco in December 1856. With a rough crew and the officers always armed, she made the Golden Gate in 92 days without once clewing up her topgallants. On her fifth day out she logged 413 statute miles, outsailing the Bostonian favourite *Westward Ho*. The *Great Republic* continued running to California and carried one of the first large grain shipments from San Francisco to Liverpool in 1861. She was involved in the Civil War on government service, but returned to the Pacific afterwards. In 1869 she was sold to the Merchant Trading Company of Liverpool and renamed *Denmark*, to be generally employed in the East India trade. She foundered near Bermuda in 1872 as a result of a leak caused by the stresses imposed upon her by a hurricane.

Donald McKay's first wife, Albenia, had died of a sudden illness in 1848. He remarried, to Mary Cressy Litchfield, who survived McKay's death in 1880 and lived until 1923. To her, apparently, are attributed many of the lovely names of her husband's ships. After the brief era of the extreme clippers such as the *Flying Cloud*, McKay's yards continued to build famous and fast medium clippers, many to be employed by the British on the Australian run.

The successful and revolutionary ships of the American builders, of whom Donald McKay is probably the most well known, spurred Britain to

compete. Not having the softwoods of the Americans, the British had to conceive a new method of construction. In the early 1860s, the first successful British composite clippers slid off the ways.

The *Great Republic* was designed and built by Donald Mckay for the California trade. The largest ship of her time, she was 325 ft long (99.1 m) and could stow 6000 tons of cargo. Unfortunately, she caught fire in New York just before her maiden voyage. She was sold and rebuilt and although much reduced from her former dimensions, she remained the largest ship built to that date and gave good service until she foundered in 1872.

THE *CUTTY SARK*

During the early 1950s, when I was a raw young cadet in the Thames Nautical Training College HMS *Worcester,* I had the privilege of having the *Cutty Sark* in my charge. Admittedly all I had to do was to ensure that she was kept clean, a bit of rust-busting here and there and enough care in the stripped-down rig to make certain someone didn't break their neck falling from aloft. My close acquaintance with the beautiful ship was brief, for that year she was towed away to be restored and preserved at her present site at Greenwich. Before she went I had poked my nose into every corner of her, imagining what life was like in the cramped, dark fo'c'sle and comparing it with the bird's-eye-maple luxury of the accommodation under the poop. I would pull under her bow, which at a close perspective was so fine that it resembled a knife. Aft, the fine run to her fairly square counter belied the power designed into her powerful quarters which enabled the ship to rise before the huge seas of the Southern Ocean and carry sail as well as the later large iron and steel ships.

The *Cutty Sark,* along with her rival the *Thermopylae* and other British tea clippers, were Britannia's answer to the American challenge flaunted by McKay's splendid *Oriental* way back in 1850. The American clipper had arrived in London 97 days out of Whampoa, China, and had been declared '. . .a menace and a challenge' in the London *Times.*

The *Cutty Sark*

It was 19 years later before the keel of the *Cutty Sark* was laid. During those years the British had caught up with American designers. The days of the large extreme clippers had passed and the British ships were small; the *Cutty Sark* and *Thermopylae* grossing 963 and 991 tons respectively. In Europe good shipbuilding timber had become a scarcity and what was used was mostly imported. A method of construction was developed whereby the ships were framed in iron and sheathed in wood. This 'composite' construction had first been tried out in a ship, the *Marion McIntyre*, in 1851, but the method was not successfully employed until the early 1860s after the introduction of diagonal iron webb plates inside the planking. This finally produced probably the most enduring method of ship construction ever, as the longevity of the *Cutty Sark* has demonstrated. Many of the British tea clippers were built in this manner.

The *Thermopylae* had sailed on a record-breaking voyage in 1868. The shipowner, Captain Jock Willis, or 'Captain John' in shipping circles, whose attempts at building ships to beat his rivals had met with little success, determined to build a vessel to outclass the green Aberdeen clipper. Employing a young designer, Hercules Linton, and using the successful Indian-built ship *Tweed* as a guide, the lines of the *Cutty Sark* were produced and building started at Scott and Linton's yard at Dumbarton. The demand for nothing but the best in materials and craftsmanship strained the resources of the small shipyard, which went bankrupt. The hull, sheathed in rock elm and teak, was moved to William Denny and Bros yard and the clipper was completed.

To appreciate the *Cutty Sark* in her youthful days calls for a quick glance at the China clippers, which do not really come within the scope of this book. During the 1860s these ships, plying between England and China around the Cape of Good Hope, were as smart, well handled and competitive as any vessels in seafaring history, including yachts. Indeed, the beautiful little ships were as indulged as any

yacht. Owners took inordinate pride in their crack ships and lavished infinite care in their appearance, fittings, gear and decoration. Captains, carefully chosen for their ability to get the best out of a ship, inspired or drove their crews to heights of seamanship and pride in their craft rarely matched in any ships, and vast sums of money were laid out in wagers by nearly every soul engaged in the tea trade. The ships' names were a poem – *Ariel*, *Serica*, *Taeping*, *Fiery Cross*, *Titania*, *Flying Spur* and *Thermopylae* – and poems the ships were, at sea and in port. It was customary, after anchoring with all the smartness usually associated with men-of-war, to immediately unbend every sail, reeve off all inessential running gear, and square every yard to an inch. Spotless awnings were spread taut over the equally immaculate decks. Painted panels, sometimes displaying landscapes or flowers, were fitted on the inside of the bulwarks, and the copper sheathing above the waterline was burnished. All the ships abounded in brass. *Ariel* had a brass strip let in the entire length of her bulwark rail, and this, with all her guns, bells, binnacles, capstan caps, cask hoops, door handles, belaying pins, etc., is said to have employed four men for a 12-hour day. The *Cutty Sark* was built to outclass these thoroughbreds.

Her name derived from Robert Burns' poem *Tam O'Shanter*, in which Tam, on his mare, Meg, is pursued by Nannie, a beautiful young witch, after he unwisely drew attention to himself by bellowing 'Weel done Cutty Sark' in praise of Nannie's dancing in her short chemise. The original trail-boards illustrated the naked witches following Nannie represented by the original superbly carved figurehead. Unfortunately the boards were condemned as indecent and soon replaced. It became the custom, while in port, to place a horse's tail in Nannie's outstretched hand – the only trophy she managed to claim from Tam and his mare.

The *Cutty Sark* was launched on 22 November 1869 and towed to Greenock for rigging. Her lower masts and bowsprit were of iron, all the rest of her

spars being oregon pine. She was more heavily sparred and carried a greater sail area than any comparable ship in the tea trade. Although setting a skysail only on the main, an idea of the power of the rig can be gained by considering her fore yard. This was 78 ft (23.79 m) over a deck of 30 ft (9.15 m). On this yard, her fore-topmast stunsail booms were each 47 ft (14.34 m), extending 33 ft (10.07 m) beyond the yard arms, giving an entire spread of 144 ft (43.92 m).

From loadline to main truck she rose 151 ft (46.06 m) and from the flying jibboom to the end of the spanker boom measured 280 ft (85.4 m). The fore lower stunsail swinging booms each extended 30 ft (9.15 m) and to these the triangular lower stunsails were sheeted and the foot of the foresail extended by means of a parsaree. She could set every imaginable sail from a Jamie Green and watersails to a ringtail. On the mainmast she carried a spencer which apparently was rarely used.

On her maiden voyage under Captain F. Moodie the *Cutty Sark* disappointed Jock Willis. Light winds and probably caution incurred by faulty ironwork aloft prevented the ship from showing her paces. In fact, throughout her career in the tea trade she never broke a record, although it was generally agreed that she was a very fast ship. In this trade occurred her famous race with the *Thermopylae*. In 1872 the two ships put out over the Woosung Bar on 18 June. Unfortunately, before the *Cutty Sark* reached the Cape, her rudder carried away and she lost probably 13 days while, with superb seamanship, Captain Moodie rigged a jury rudder which enabled her to reach London only a week behind the *Thermopylae*. Credit for the race was given to the *Cutty Sark* on this account.

The *Cutty Sark* in the Pacific

This clipper's association with the Pacific began in 1872 when she started to carry outward cargo for Sydney before loading tea in China. Running her easting down in high latitudes from the Cape tested the racy clippers. The bird-tailed *Ariel* may have been overwhelmed on this passage but the *Cutty Sark* revelled in the conditions.

By the end of the 1870s the tea trade had been taken over by steamships to the extent that the clippers were hard put to find a cargo. In 1880 the *Cutty Sark*'s spars were reduced to ease the ship in the Southern Ocean, enabling her to carry topgallants in strong winds, a great advantage in those waters where even upper topsails could have the wind taken out of them by the massive seas.

For the next three years, however, the *Cutty Sark*'s story was dismal. Captain J.S. Wallace, a capable and kindly master, had the misfortune to ship a hard-case bucko mate who finally virtually murdered one of the crew. Wallace made another mistake by assisting the mate's escape and the worry and tension drove the captain to suicide. His position was filled by Captain W.H. Bruce, ex-mate of the *Halloween*, which ship's master was no doubt glad to get rid of him. Bruce was a hypocritical, sanctimonious Bible-thumper who drank and blasphemed at sea and played the saint ashore. He bullied the crew, preached against intemperance and lacked courage in handling the ship.

From the latter part of 1880 through to May 1882 both ship and crew were mismanaged by the Jekyll and Hyde master and a mate who became his crony and drinking companion. The *Cutty Sark* was never given her head and her maintenance was neglected. Her crew were alternately hazed and sweetened. Cholera in Shanghai brought work to a halt. On resumption, the desperately weak convalescent hands were driven to back-breaking labour cleaning the holds. For this Captain Bruce and the mate were officially censured by the Consul. Their drunkenness nearly lost the ship in the Sunda Straights. Only by plying Bruce with liquor until he passed out was the second mate able to take over command and save the ship. On that passage to New York food ran out and a seaman was lost when knocked from the main-shrouds by the mate letting go the clew garnet, an act which was incredibly careless, or perhaps deliberate, as the third mate, who would have supported the second mate in any report to the authorities, was working alongside the seaman. Fear of reports on the debacle in the Sunda Straits could have been a motive. On the *Cutty Sark*'s arrival in New York in April 1882, an investigation resulted in both the captain and the mate having their certificates suspended.

For the *Cutty Sark* the dawn of a new career was about to break. Under Captain E. Moore, previously master of the *Blackadder*, she made one voyage to the East before sailing in July 1883 for Newcastle, NSW, to load her first cargo of wool. The ship's gear was still in poor repair, Willis being unwilling to go to the expense of refitting. In spite of this, Captain Moore made good passages. On her second trip both the *Cutty Sark* and the *Thermopylae* led the wool fleet home in 79 days; the fleet included many fliers such as the *Patriarch* and the *Macquarie*.

Sailing from London on 1 April 1885, the *Cutty Sark* was commanded by her most renowned master, Captain R. Woodget. Willis was once more becoming interested in the little clipper's achievements, and apart from refurbishing her gear he appointed the able new captain with orders to drive the ship. Woodget drove her. He carried sail until the spars groaned, cracking on at every lull. He beefed up her running and standing rigging to withstand the punishment. On her first voyage home she made the English Channel in 67 days. Unfortunately she was delayed there for six days by adverse weather and lost her chance of setting a new record. She still beat her rival, *Thermopylae*, by a clear week. In 1889 on the New South Wales coast she passed and beat into Sydney the crack P & O liner *Britannia*, sailing 17 knots to the steamer's 16. The *Cutty Sark* made consistently fast passages, delivering her wool in first-class condition in spite of her mature age and hard-driving. In 1893 she made her last voyage from Sydney; Willis was once again scrimping on her expense. There followed one more voyage to Brisbane to load a record wool cargo before, in 1895 and to Captain Woodget's sorrow, the *Cutty Sark* was sold to the Portuguese shipowners, Ferreira and Company.

Renamed the *Ferreira* but nicknamed by the Portuguese sailors *El Pequina Camisola*, the old clipper survived the hazards of hurricanes and war, turning up occasionally in Great Britain where she revived interest in her past. After World War I she was cut down to a barquentine and later renamed the *Mario do Amparo*. In 1922 she put into Falmouth for repairs. She was observed by a retired master, Captain Wilfred Dowman, who decided to buy her and fit her out as a training ship for boys. It was his ambition to send her back to sea but this was not to eventuate. Captain Dowman died in 1936, but not before he had rerigged her and trained many a young lad. On his death, his widow, Catherine Dowman, presented the ship to the Thames Nautical Training College, where 16 years later I first stepped on her deck. She now lies restored in Greenwich, not to her original perfection, but near enough to stir anyone with an eye for beauty in a ship.

IMMIGRANT SHIPS

From about 1840 the flow of migrants from the United Kingdom to Australia and New Zealand gradually increased. At first the settlers were carried in ships which had changed little since the turn of the century; wooden, bluff-bowed small ships with stern windows and sometimes quarter-lights such as the *Jane Gifford* and the *Duchess of Argyle*, which made slow but reasonably safe voyages. The remains of one of these ships, the *Edwin Fox*, still lies in Marlborough Sounds in the South Island of New Zealand, and has just been refloated to undergo restoration.

After delivering their freight and passengers, as a full return cargo could not always be got in the young colonies, the ships would often sail to the Far East or India to pick up a return cargo. It was not many years, however, before the energetic pioneers began to produce worthwhile return freight by way of wool, grain, timber and later frozen meat. Larger vessels were employed and in the 1860s and seventies shipping lines specialising in the Australasian trade – often part-owned and manned by colonials – were established. R. & H. Green, Messrs Devitt and Moore, Shaw Savill and Albion, and the New Zealand Shipping Company were perhaps the most well known. The ships employed in this trade were in my opinion the finest passenger- and freight-carrying sailing ships ever. Their route was long and hard but ideally suited to wind-driven ships which could utilise the westerlies of the Southern Ocean as they stormed around the world. Powerful, immaculately maintained and fast, they held a place of affection in the hearts of established settlers and immigrants.

The New Zealand Shipping Company's fleet

The *Hurunui*, one of the New Zealand Shipping Company's vessels, is shown on p.163 berthing in Auckland in the 1890s. This ship was built by Palmers of Newcastle, England, in 1875. Grossing 1054 tons, she measured 204 ft (62.2 m) in length, with a beam and depth of 34 ft (10.4 m) and 20 ft (6.1 m) respectively. She is a good example of the large fleet of New Zealand Shipping Company ships which carried freight and passengers to Britain's distant colonies. The *Hurunui* broke no records as did some of the faster of the fleet, but she made nearly 20 voyages to New Zealand under the company's flag. Her best outward passage was 86 days; several passages exceeded 100 days.

The *Otaki*, homeward bound for London, made an extraordinarily fast time of 63 days land-to-land in 1877, and the *Rangitiki*, the largest owned by the company, made a record passage outwards of 67 days, land-to-land. All the New Zealand Shipping Company's ships were beautifully maintained and competently manned. In spite of this, accidents happened. The *Hurunui* and the *Waitara* left London together and while beating down the English Channel, the *Waitara*, on the port tack, failed to give way. The ships collided and within minutes the *Waitara* had sunk with the loss of 20 lives. The Channel was so hazardous that subsequently the company made a policy of embarking passengers at Plymouth. The *Hurunui* survived the disaster and was sold to the Russians in 1895. She was sunk by a German submarine in 1915.

The *Jane Gifford* and *Duchess of Argyle*, two ships which are representative of the earlier vessels which brought immigrants to Australia and New Zealand. They both arrived in the Waitemata, Auckland's lovely harbour, within hours of each other one evening in 1842. They were the first large ships to bring settlers to what is now New Zealand's biggest city.

The *Jane Gifford*, the first to arrive, was boarded by the harbourmaster who was to pilot her to anchor. Unfortunately he ran her aground off North Head and the *Duchess of Argyle*, piloted by his junior, sailed quietly past a few hours later. As the ships were companions in the venture, the comments passed between them would have been interesting.

Shaw Savill ships

Shaw Savill and Company and Patrick Henderson's Albion Line had been established in the New Zealand trade for more than ten years before the founding of the New Zealand Shipping Company. They provided the bulk of the competition and in 1882 amalgamated to become Shaw Savill and Albion Company Ltd. It was their ship, the *Dunedin*, which in 1882 carried the first shipment of frozen meat to the UK, closely followed by another experimental shipment in the New Zealand Shipping Company's *Mataura*.

The *Crusader*, an iron ship of 1058 tons, was one of Shaw Savill's most famous sailing ships. She made remarkably fast passages, averaging 91 days for her outward passages from the English Channel

to New Zealand and holding a record passage of 65 days from Lyttelton to the English Channel. She made 28 voyages to New Zealand and carried thousands of passengers before being sold to the Norwegians in 1898.

The *Macquarie*

Built by R. & H. Green of London, who had their own shipyard on the Thames and were well known for their line of 'Blackwall Frigates' in the India trade, the *Melbourne*, as the *Macquarie* was originally named, was specifically built for the passenger trade to Australia. She measured 1857 tons with a length, beam and depth of 269 ft (82.05 m) 40 ft 1 in. (12.23 m) and 23 ft 7 in. (7.19 m) respectively. She was built to be the finest iron passenger ship of her time. Under a 69 ft (21 m) poop she carried well appointed and ventilated first-class accommodation and retained a stern cabin with large windows, a relic of the old East Indiamen. Gilding and scroll work graced her stern and trailboards and her figurehead was a well carved bust of Queen Victoria.

The *Melbourne* was launched in June 1875 and sailed on her first voyage two months later. In spite of losing her foretopmast and main topgallant mast only 25 days out, she completed the voyage in 86 days from the English Channel. R. & H. Green made a policy of safety and comfort before speed, consequently the *Melbourne* proved to be very popular with passengers who preferred a more leisurely voyage to the discomfort and soakings of

The *Macquarie* was launched in 1875 as the *Melbourne*; her name was later changed. She carried passengers and freight from Britain to Australia during the last decades of the nineteenth century and was renowned for her comfort and safety.

hard-driving ships out to break records. One of her best times was 77 days out and between 90 and 100 days could normally be expected.

In 1887 she was bought by Devitt and Moore to join their ships in the Sydney trade and on her second voyage her name was changed to *Macquarie*, the name by which she was best known. In the mid 1890s sailing passenger ships were to find it hard to fill their berths due to the competition of steam and the opening of the Suez Canal in 1869. *Macquarie* replaced the company's cadet ship *Harbinger* in 1897 and made six successful voyages until in 1903 she was sold to the Norwegians who barque-rigged her, renamed the old ship *Fortuna* and used her in the timber trade. In 1909 she was sold for £3500 and became a coal hulk in Sydney.

The *Crusader*, an immigrant ship belonging to Shaw Savill and Albion Company, hove to

The *Harbinger*

Author Frank Bullen, who served in the *Harbinger* as second officer, was a great admirer of this fine vessel:

She was to my mind one of the noblest specimens of ship-building that ever floated. For all her huge bulk she was as easy to handle as any ten-ton yacht – far easier than some – and in any kind of weather her docility was amazing. She was so clean in her entrance that you never saw a foaming spread of broken water ahead driven in front by the vast onset of the hull. She parted the waves before her pleasantly, as an arrow cleaves the air. In a grand and gracious fashion she seemed to claim affinity with waves, and they in their wildest tumult met her as if they knew and loved her. She was the only ship I ever knew or heard of that would stay under storm staysails, reefed topsails and a reefed foresail in a gale of wind. In fact, I never saw anything that she would not do that a ship should do. She was so truly a child of the ocean that a bungler could hardly mishandle her – and she would work in spite of him. And lastly she would steer when you could hardly detect an air out of the heavens, with a sea like a mirror and the sails hanging motionless. The men used to say that she would sail a knot with only the quartermaster at the wheel for a wind.

The *Harbinger* was built by Messrs Steele & Co., Port Glasgow, and launched in 1876. Iron built, 1506 tons net, she was one of the loftiest ships of her time, measuring 210 ft (64.05 m) from her main truck to the load waterline. Her shrouds came down to outboard channels, a practice which was becoming unusual by that time. On the fore and main masts she crossed double topsails and topgallants, royals and skysails. On the mizzen her topgallant was single but she still had a royal and skysail on the mast. Aft of the mainmast was a spenser and she carried a flying jibboom not shown in the painting.

This vessel was one of the finest of the passenger-carrying sailing ships, providing for 30 saloon

161

passengers and up to 200 immigrants in the 'tween decks. She started her career under the Orient Line but came under the flag of Devitt & Moore in 1890 when, as well as shipping freight and passengers, she was employed as an officer-training ship for the Brassey Scheme.

The training of officers was, and still is, normally undertaken by an apprenticeship system. In the past, a young prospective officer could, on payment of a premium, sign indentures with a company and proceed straight to sea. Alternatively he could join training colleges such as HMS *Worcester* or HMS *Conway* for two years pre-sea training. In this case the four-year apprenticeship would be reduced to three, and cadets from the training ships were more likely to be selected for the 'brassbound' companies such as Orient and later Holts and P & O. (It was precisely this system I entered when, in 1951, I joined the tough but efficient HMS *Worcester* at the tender age of 15.)

Apprentices throughout the sailing-ship period and up to the 1960s continued to be used for every conceivable dirty job on the ship, and were generally worked harder than the seamen. Granted that an officer should have practical experience of every job in the ship – engines and galley usually excluded – this is not a bad start. However, in the sailing ships the premium-paying apprentices were often used as a source of cheap labour, and as they frequently became better and more conscientious seamen than the men, they were profitable to the company. Everything the apprentice learned was by practice and rarely was he lucky enough to sail under officers who would teach him the navigation, ship stability mathematics and principles required for his second mate's ticket.

It was to provide better training that the Brassey Scheme was introduced. Inaugurated by Lord Brassey in 1890, the first ships, the *Harbinger* and *Hesperus*, each trained 30 to 40 'cadets' as they came

to be called. The boys worked watches, four on and four off, were provided with the same food as the officers, and worked aloft and on deck in all weathers. In addition, they were given proper instruction in seamanship and navigation.

With regards to the *Harbinger* painting, I have used a bit of licence. In Sydney it was a harbour board regulation that the jibboom should be run in for berthing; I felt that this would have rather spoilt the graceful appearance of the ship.

(*Right*) The New Zealand Shipping Company's immigrant ship *Hurunui* berthing at Auckland, New Zealand, circa 1890.

The *Harbinger* berthing at Circular Quay, Sydney. Another famous Australian immigrant vessel, she was one of the loftiest ships of her time, measuring 210 ft (64.05 m) from her truck to her load waterline.

(*Below*) It was often the task of the apprentices to set up the standing rigging of the mizzen mast; sometimes the result was visible.

164

THE *LANCING*

This remarkable ship was built for the Compagnie Generale Transatlantique in 1865 and named *Pereire*. She was originally a screw steamer, but in contrast to the contemporary trend to powered ships, was converted and ended her days 60 years later as a very successful sailing ship.

She was built of iron and incredibly strong, her hull plating being 2 in. (5 cm) thick. This caused some problem in Tunis when, having an uncontrollable fire aboard, it was necessary to scuttle her. The French Navy resorted to using a spar-torpedo to open her hull to the sea. In her later years this strength was to save her life.

In 1888 *Pereire* was sold and converted at Blyth, Northumberland, into a four-masted full-rigged ship. Some idea of her size can be grasped from her dimensions. On a hull 356 ft (108.58 m) in length her main and mizzen masts rose 175 ft (53.38 m) from the deck. The main and mizzen yards were just short of 100 ft (30.5 m) and her 36 sails totalled nearly 2 acres (0.81 ha).

After her conversion she was renamed *Lancing* by her owner, G.A. Hatfield of Nova Scotia. She changed hands several times until purchased in 1901 by a Norwegian firm Act. Lancing, Johansen & Co.

of Kristiania. The Norwegians seemed to know how to get the best out of her and she claimed some remarkable records. In 1916 she crossed from Sandy Hook, New York, to the Orkney Islands in 6 days 18 hours. From Rio de Janeiro to Noumea, New Caledonia, she averaged 12½ knots, travelling at speeds up to 21 knots. While running her easting down to Melbourne she ran at 22 knots for 15 consecutive hours. She frequently showed a clean pair of heels to powered vessels and beat a Danish Mail steamer by one day on a passage from New York to Denmark.

The voyage from Rio to Noumea strikes me as the most extraordinary if it is true. To maintain an average of 12½ knots on such a long passage would demand consistently fair and strong winds, and fleeter ships than *Lancing* would be hard put to match

such an average. Granted, her route south of the Cape of Good Hope and Australia would provide her with the necessary winds to 'run her easting down', and she would not have had to pass through the doldrums, but even so. . . .

Towards the end of her days the *Lancing* ran at some speed into an iceberg, where she remained grinding against the ice. The crew, expecting her to sink, launched two boats, abandoned her and pulled clear. Instead of sinking, the ship cleared herself and sailed slowly away – the boats in frantic pursuit. On inspection later, the ship showed only a dented plate below the waterline, causing a weep in a ballast tank and a cracked yard truss. The crew must have blessed her 2-inch (5 cm) plate.

The *Lancing* was sold to an Italian shipbreaking firm in 1925.

The *Lancing*. This ship started her life in 1865 as a screw steamer named *Pereire* and was converted 23 years later to a very fast sailing ship. She claimed an average speed of 12½ knots from Rio de Janeiro to Noumea, attaining speeds of 21 to 22 knots at times. She was immensely strong, her hull plating being of 2 in. (5 cm) iron.

SHIPS PLYING THE AMERICAN WEST COAST

The 'Pacific Northwest', apart from describing a geographical area, was also the name of the first ship in which I sailed as a certificated officer in the 1950s. The name evokes a wealth of memories. My previous ship was the *Pacific Fortune*, a misnomer, for she seemed to have anything but fortune, having rammed wharves in various parts of the world and once sank in Manchester Docks. The stench of filthy canal water that impregnated the ship and the contrasting scent of fresh-sawn pine brings back memories of our visits to the lumber ports of British Columbia, Washington and Oregon. Here we would load lumber and pulp at tiny ports with names such as Port Albernie, Chemainus, Nanaimo, Bellingham and Coos Bay. Apart from lumber, these places have much in common; the scent of pine, the beautiful fall when the maple glows in the misty light, friendly people, fog and rain.

When I was an apprentice much of my time was spent in foggy weather riveted to the radar. I well remember the Puget Sound pilots, particularly the one who almost scorned the radar. He required silence on the bridge and would listen intently after sounding the whistle. We had seen nothing for hours and once again he sounded off. Out of the mist and drizzle and quite close a dog barked. 'W'aal, Cap'n', drawled the pilot, turning to the Old Man, 'that old hound, best foghorn round here. I knows where I am now.' Memory has possibly made this anecdote a little apocryphal.

Captain James Gaby, in his book *Mate in Sail*, compliments the Puget Sound skippers of that era. He was in a large, four-masted barque which had very nearly been run down in the sound by a

steamer. The steamers, he says 'maintained their schedules right through the fog season, partly by the aid of whistle echo, but usually by the steel nerves that enabled them to drive their ships'.

Captain Gaby gives his impression of Bellingham in Puget Sound.

Some places in the world are always remembered for their own particular smells. Bellingham had the pleasant, pervading medicated odour of the freshly sawn Oregon pine. It was a clean cargo to load, coming on board mostly in large flitches, thirty feet and longer, and from twelve to twenty-four inches square.

Bellingham was in every respect a Western town with its timbered foot-paths and pool rooms with space set aside for the gambling tables. Poker was the main gambling game, and the players obtained their chips from the bartender just inside the doorway. Alongside the cash register in the handiest position, standing out so everyone would see it, was the fully loaded Colt forty-five, a reminder to anyone who might get the wrong ideas about picking up some easy money.

Big men from the logging camps were the main ones found at the gambling tables, but their stakes were too high for a deep-waterman on five pounds a month and two dollars a week sub. It was a common sight to see a big back-woodsman striding along with a small tame brown bear trotting along like a dog at his heels.

In the picture theatre, I found it fascinating to rub shoulders with real live Red Indians, members of 'Alexa' Billy's Siwash tribe that often paddled past the ship in their birch bark canoes.

The *Falls of Clyde*

The *Falls of Clyde* was the first ship built for the Falls Line of Wright Graham and Company, who ran her in the Calcutta trade. An iron, four-masted ship of

Ships loading lumber at Port Blakely, Puget Sound

1748 tons, she made a name for speed but was unlucky in her passages. In 1898 she was sold to Captain William Matson, founder of the Matson Line, and until Hawaii became American territory, she flew the Hawaiian colours. She was reduced to a four-masted barque and her jigger mast lengthened by raising the heel on a wooden extension.

In 1907 the *Falls of Clyde* was turned over to the Associated Oil Co. of San Francisco, converted into a sailing tanker and painted the colours shown here. She loaded oil inside the kelp beds near Santa Barbara and transported it to Honolulu. From 1916 she loaded at San Francisco and after 1919, having been sold to George W. McNear, she made voyages to Europe with oil. After 1922 she was rigged down to a barge.

In 1963 a campaign was started to resurrect the ship, which was then a rusting hulk at Seattle, and she is now partly re-rigged as a museum ship in Honolulu under the care of the Hawaii Maritime Center.

Captain Fred K. Klebingat, one-time mate of the *Falls of Clyde*, is full of praise for the ship's handiness and the magnificent condition in which she was maintained when he sailed in her from 1916.

She was a handy ship; the mate and one watch could make her do their bidding; at no time did we ever call all hands. While in the Hawai'i trade she carried master, two mates, pumpman, carpenter, cook, cabin boy, and ten A.B.s. In the Atlantic she carried sixteen men before the mast. She handled like a boat, the mate and his five men on watch would have no trouble going about, but of course they had to step lively. Only beating in close quarters we would have steam up and haul the yards around with steam, and if it was night we used the electric decklights to make work easy.

When I was in her, the best day's run was 327 miles – that was running eastward. She had 11 days from Honolulu to San Francisco, and the days, of course, were less than 24 hours. Her best sailing point was with the wind on her beam. She travelled 12 knots very easily, and I have seen her logging 14 and over many a time. In the two years I was in the vessel I never saw a ship which could keep up with her. . .The Associated Oil Co., and its general manager, Mr Walter E. Buck, took great pride in the upkeep of their fleet, and especially of the *Falls of Clyde*, but nobody could have been more proud of the looks of his command than the captain [Captain William Smith]. He insisted that the mast trucks be finished in gold leaf; we not only had canvas bunt gaskets but they were lettered with the company monogram. The *Marion Chilcott* lost a skylight pane and replaced it with canvas; this would never do for Captain Smith. When the *Clyde* had a similar accident, he would not rest until a piece of fancy etched glass with the original curve was fitted again in the skylight.

The Alaska packers

In 1893 the Alaska Packers Association of San Francisco was formed by the merging of certain small Alaskan salmon canneries. The far north could supply enormous quantities of the fish but the season was short, starting in late spring and ending in late August. The grounds were inaccessible except by ships. It was necessary to carry in these the whole workforce and supplies for the summer. Initially the Association chartered vessels, but this was found to be unsatisfactory. The ships were only at sea for the 2,500 mile passage to Alaska and back; while in the north each lay to two anchors shackled to a swivel throughout the season and became a virtual floating warehouse. Chartered ships lacked the facilities required and within seven years the Association began to purchase vessels. Their first ships were American-built wooden vessels, many of them old 'down-easters', but by the turn of the century replacements were becoming hard to find. Some of these ships continued in service a further 20 years or more.

In 1900, two years after the annexation of the Hawaiian Islands by the United States, an act of Congress provided that ships of Hawaiian registry were entitled to full rights on the American coast, where foreign-built vessels were not permitted to engage in the coastal trade. Several British-built iron and steel sailing ships became immediately available. The first to grace the Packers' fleet was the small, one-time Shaw Savill immigrant ship *Euterpe*, already a veteran of 38 years. The fleet grew with the addition of other iron and steel ships, among them the *Balclutha* in 1902 and four crack Belfast fliers, the *Star of Bengal*, the *Star of Italy*, the *Star of France* and the *Star of Russia*. Subsequently the Packers applied the 'Star' prefix to their own ships, the *Euterpe* becoming the *Star of India* and the *Balclutha* the *Star of Alaska*. At the commencement of World War I, 16 iron and steel ships and about eight wooden ships were employed.

Every spring the fleet would put out from San Francisco, each ship manned mainly by Italian and Scandinavian fishermen. On board also were all the cannery hands, who were predominantly Chinese or Japanese, and inveterate gamblers. All up, there could be well over 200 men in a ship, and to provide room for them the tween-decks were made over to accommodation and galleys, and on some ships the fo'c's'le or poop was extended to make extra space. In the hold were all the stores, tin plate, box shooks and coal required for the season.

Although the voyage was short, it was not without risk. The hazardous channels, fogs and storms of the north caused the loss of several ships, the most disastrous of which was that of the *Star of Bengal* in September 1908. She was on her way to San Francisco under tow until she cleared the Alexander Archipelago when, during the night, the wind rose to gale force. The two tugs lost control and ran for shelter, leaving the ship to fend for herself on a lee shore. Captain Nicholas Wagner let go both anchors and for a while she brought up 50 ft (15.25 m) from a rocky beach where enormous waves were dumping. Attempts to get a line ashore succeeded, but before anything could be rigged to get the men ashore, the cables parted and the ship struck, immediately breaking up in a welter of spars, drums and boxed salmon. It is thought that 132 lost their lives; only 22 survived.

World War I saw a boom time for the Packers' fleet. The demand for shipping enabled the Association to charter many of their ships during the off season when the fleet would be laid up, forming a forest of spars, at Alameda, Oakland. The boom was not to last long after the war. Shipping slumped in 1921 and the following year saw most of the wooden ships go, followed by the less useful of the iron and steel sailing ships. Throughout the twenties the fleet dwindled, some off to find work in the Pacific under new ownership, others to provide props for the blossoming film industry. The *Star of Alaska* was the last of the sailing ships to go north, ignominiously towed there and back. During the thirties the sailing fleet was laid up, sold or scrapped. At the beginning of World War II the Packers' last remaining ship got a brief reprieve when she was recommissioned and chartered. She made a voyage carrying lumber from Grays Harbour to Durban. She then sailed to Hobart. In Australia the *Star of Finland* was sold to the United States Army, hulked and ended her days on a beach in the Philippines.

The *E. R. Sterling*

The *E.R. Sterling* was built in 1883 by Harland and Wolf of Belfast as a four-masted iron ship measuring 2518 tons. She was named the *Lord Worsley*, for Lord Lines of Belfast, who ran her successfully until the turn of the century, when she was sold to Tidemans of Bremen, who renamed her *Columbia*. In 1903, off Cape Flattery on a voyage from Japan to Puget Sound, she rolled her fore and main masts overboard in a heavy swell. She was towed to Victoria on Vancouver Island where surveyors wrote her off. At about this time there was a bad slump in shipping and there is little doubt that the ship had been allowed to get run down before the dismasting and the expense of refitting would not have been worthwhile.

The Victorian and Vancouver Stevedoring Company bought her and she was rerigged as a six-masted barquentine. The mizzen mast was shifted to replace the lost foremast and five other masts of the same height stepped. Steam winches were installed to hoist the huge gaff fore and aft sails and the upper topsail, upper topgallant and royal, allowing the crew to be reduced from 28 to 17. She was renamed the *Everitt G. Griggs* and was employed in the lumber trade between the American west coast and Australia.

Captain E.R. Sterling bought the ship in 1912 and named her after himself. He and his son were enthusiasts and innovators; electric light and radio were installed and the accommodation was improved considerably. In the 1920s there were virtually only two trades in which the large sailing ships could compete – the Chilean nitrate trade and the Australian grain trade. Both of these involved carrying a single cargo and avoiding the crippling cost of the Panama or Suez canals. The ships could also make good use of the powerful winds along their way.

In 1927 the *E.R. Sterling* took on a load of grain at Adelaide and sailed with the grain fleet for a winter passage round Cape Horn. All went well until she turned the corner and met up with icebergs and a series of storms. Near the Falkland Islands a severe gale tore out the second and third masts. After 122 days out she was still 600 miles south of the equator, creeping slowly northward under reduced sail. Another storm and the foremast went overboard; the mate died from injuries he received while clearing the shambles. The ship could hardly sail now, so an SOS was sent. This was received by the S.S. *Northern Monarch*, but by the time the steamship arrived some sail had been jury-rigged on the *E.R. Sterling* and an offer of a tow was refused. I do not know enough detail to give you the gist of the feelings of the captain of the *Northern Monarch* at this point, but it doesn't need much imagination.

The disabled *E.R. Sterling* now sailed 2200 miles to St Thomas in the West Indies, making a little over 50 miles a day. Two months later she left St Thomas under tow from the powerful Dutch tug *Indus*. She was towed clear across the Atlantic, arriving in the Thames on 28 January 1928. She was the last dismasted sailing ship into the Thames and was sold to the breakers for £4000.

The *E.R. Sterling* was a compromise between the square rig and the total fore and aft rig exemplified in the large American schooners, one of which had seven masts – each named after a day of the week. The schooners were never really successful; often they had to be towed and made poor passage times on ocean runs. Small schooners were ideal for coastal work, but when the rig was applied to larger ships, problems arose. While small schooners could carry a large spread of canvas for their size, it was impossible to set a similar proportion on a large ship, for the gaff fore and afts would have been just too large to handle. Consequently a multiplicity of masts were stepped, but still these ships could not set the sail area of a comparable square-rigged ship. Also, the centre of effort was reduced so that the higher and fairer winds undisturbed by the surface of the sea, were not utilised. This is a phenomenon which can be seen in the set of a gaff sail which lies freer at the head than the foot. Square-rigged ships screwed the columns of canvas by having each yard checked a little freer than the one below.

In addition to the lack of power on these ships, and probably more dangerous, was the unbalanced weight of the gear hinged like a door on the mast. Imagine gybing four, five or six huge gaff sails. In calm weather with a swell they would crash and

bang to the extent that preventers and vangs would be of little help and the sails would have to be lowered. The *Kineo*, a five-masted schooner, came in from a voyage without a mast-hoop left and the jaws of her gaffs wrecked – all caused not by storm, but by the combination of calm and swell.

(*Left*) The *E.R. Sterling*, a six-masted barquentine which sailed in the lumber trade between North America and Australia during World War I

(*Right*) The Alaska Packers Association ships *Star of Alaska* and *Star of India*, among others, beating up through the Unimak Pass in the Aleutians.

The *Star of India* is the oldest surviving merchant sailing ship still afloat, let alone occasionally sailing. In 1863 she was built in the Isle of Man as the *Euterpe*, 1318 tons, and ran to India and later to New Zealand as an immigrant ship under Shaw Savill of London. In 1901 she was the first British iron ship to come under the Alaska Packers house flag and, re-rigged as a barque, she ran annually to the canneries in the north until 1923. In 1927 she was purchased by the San Diego Zoological Society and languished in San Diego until the 1960s, when restoration began. She has now been beautifully restored by volunteer labour under the aegis of the Maritime Museum Association of San Diego. Now and then she even leaves the security of San Diego's Embarcadero for a sedate sail, as befits a lady of such advanced years and 22 world circumnavigations.

The steel *Balclutha* was built at Glasgow in 1886 for Robert McMillan of Dumbarton. At the end of the century she was sold, put under Hawaiian registry and carried lumber from Puget Sound to Australia until she was purchased by the Alaska Packers in 1902. After her last voyage in 1930 she was laid up until in 1933 she was bought by Frank Kissinger, renamed the *Pacific Queen* and toured the American west coast ports. She was rescued from the Sausalito mudflats in 1954 by the San Francisco Maritime Museum and restored; she now graces the waterfront of that port.

The setting for the painting is taken from a photo in possession of the San Francisco Maritime Museum.

The *Falls of Clyde*, once a sailing oil tanker and now being restored in Honolulu as a museum ship

THE NITRATE SHIPS

Nitrate from the dry and barren west coast of South America, along with Australian grain, were the last major freights carried by the large sailing ships. During the nineteenth century the increasing demand for fertilisers in Europe provided employment for ships carrying guano from the offshore islands of the west coast, and sodium nitrate or saltpetre, transported from the South American back-country, was shipped from a scattering of ports on the coast. Most of these ports were no more than bays sheltered from the usually light southerly-quarter winds. Periodically ferocious northerly gales would sweep into the crowded anchorages, causing anxiety and, not infrequently, shipwreck.

The bagged nitrate was lightered out to the ships which were usually moored in tiers with two anchors ahead and another astern, slowly rolling and pitching on the ever-present swell. From the lighters it was winched aboard in canvas slings; some care was taken in its stowage. The nature of the chemical required that it be stowed dry and fire was the greatest hazard. Once alight, only a solution of nitrate and water would extinguish it and barrels of nitrate water were kept in readiness by each hatch. In spite of all precautions, many ships were burnt while loading.

In the earlier days of the trade both guano and nitrate were considered poor cargoes and were usually carried by older and more decrepit ships. However, from the 1890s on, as demand grew and competition with steam increased, ships were designed with the cartage of nitrate in view, resulting in the building of some extremely sophisticated and powerful commercial sailing ships.

A young crew member taking part in the farewell to a nitrate ship homeward bound

Ships of every nation, size and description crowded the ports but there is little doubt that *the* clippers of the nitrate trade were the ships of Laeisz and A.D. Bordes.

The 'P' line of Laeisz, a German firm, had its beginnings in the early 1870s and by the mid eighties they were building their ships in iron and steel. All the vessels either built for the firm or bought by them were large powerful ships and soon developed a reputation for speed and efficiency. Apart from the *Henriette Vehn*, all the names of the Laeisz ships had the initial letter P, from their first ship, the *Polynesia*, to their finest, the 4026 gross ton five-masted barque *Potosi* and the 5081 gross ton five-masted ship (the only one of its kind), the mighty *Preussen*.

The names of many Laeisz ships evoke an immediate response in anyone remotely acquainted with sailing ships: the *Peru, Parma, Priwall* and ill-fated *Pamir*, the *Padua* and sisters *Peking* and *Passat*. The last three survive: the *Padua* is still sailing as the Russian training ship *Kruzenstern*; the *Peking*, which once existed as the *Arethusa*, a boys training ship on the Medway, England, now belongs to the South Street Museum, New York; the *Passat* is preserved at Travemünde in Germany.

The only company to rival Laeisz in the nitrate trade was that of Anton Bordes et Fils, a family firm founded in France in 1847 by A.D. Bordes senior, running passengers and general cargo to Valparaiso and returning to Great Britain with nitrate. It was not until 1870 that nitrate was shipped to France. Bordes' earlier ships were mostly under 1000 tons, many of them built in Britain, but as nitrate became more available during the late seventies, the size of their ships increased.

A.D. Bordes died in 1883, but 1882 saw his first four-master – the 2139-ton *Union* – launched at Greenock, Scotland. In 1880 Bordes ran 40 ships with a total capacity of 45,765 tons. At the outbreak of World War I their fleet consisted of 46 ships carrying in all 163,160 tons. These figures graphically illustrate the increase in the size of the ships.

The Bordes were astute businessmen and ran their company with foresight and efficiency; their ships were well built and maintained.

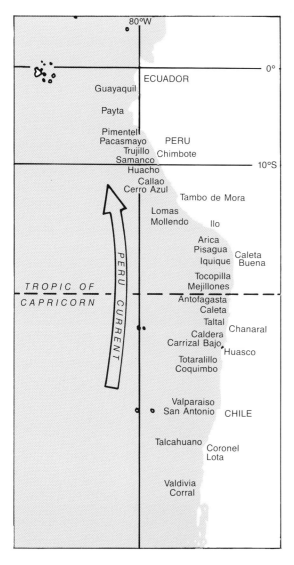

The French bounty system, established in the late 1890s, although subsidising the company to the tune of about 10 per cent, had its most obvious effect in the design of French ships. Building bounties were paid on gross tonnage which was worked out on the *volume* of all the spaces of a ship, as opposed to net tonnage, which is worked on the *paying* space, that is, cargo and passenger capacity only. Thus it was worthwhile for the French designers to increase their bounty by enlarging the superstructures to the benefit of the seaman. The long fo'c's'les and poops were characteristic of the bounty-assisted ships.

The navigation bounty was paid at the rate of 1 franc 70 cents per gross ton per 1000 miles, enabling French ships to be able to afford to sail in ballast if need be. There are stories of French ships deliberately taking longer routes so as to reap a greater bounty, even to the extent of running their easting down to the Pacific rather than making the difficult westbound rounding of Cape Horn. Hobart, Tasmania, was frequented by French ships calling for water, stores and orders. British sailing ships were unable to compete with this subsidised competition and in spite of the owners forming a union to fix minimum freights, British ships were sold off at an increasing rate. All French ships were generally better run and manned than their British competitors. Their seamen suffered less casualties and their ships were better designed and, on the whole, safer. The firm of A.D. Bordes ran the finest of the French ships and their success was aided by, but by no means solely due to, bounties on building and navigation.

Nitrate ships in port

The master of a sailing ship bound for a west coast nitrate port was careful not to get to the north of his destination, for the light southerly winds and Humboldt current off Peru make even a few miles of southing a lengthy and sometimes impossible business. Even with a good landfall, light winds and calms have prevented ships from getting into their anchorages and, driven north by the current, they have taken weeks to get back. Sometimes a ship would have to stand offshore and make south in more favourable conditions. An example was the *Lindisfarne*, which in 1903 drifted north of ther destination, Antofagasta, and had to stand off to the southwest for 1300 miles to make an approach from the south. The detour took her one month.

Once the ship, often laden with coal from Great Britain or Newcastle, Australia, was safely moored, the sails were unbent and the crew settled down to the lengthy process of discharging and loading. Sundays were a day of rest when regattas and fishing trips were enjoyed. The rare and valued leave ashore for the sailors usually resulted in sore heads from the fiery *aquardiente*, *anisardo* or *pisco*, if nothing worse.

The departure from the crowded anchorages of a ship homeward bound was an occasion for ceremony, as was customary in Shanghai, Sydney or wherever large numbers of sailing ships loaded for home. At the Peruvian and Chilean nitrate ports the simple cheering and saluting a homeward-bounder took on a ritual enthusiastically participated in by all sailing-ship crews. Basil Lubbock, writing first hand, best describes the sailing of a homeward-bound nitrate ship:

The usual custom when cheering the last bag was as follows: As the bag was hoisted over the rail, the youngest member of the crew, who was usually the smallest apprentice, jumped on to it with the national flag of his ship in his hand. He was then raised high enough for all the ships around to see, and proceeded to shout out at the top of his voice, 'Three cheers for the captain, officers and crew of – [the name of his ship].' Then he was lowered and hoisted again three times, whilst wildly waving the flag, and before he and the bag were lowered through the hatch he called for 'Three cheers for all the ships in the harbour,' which was responded to in stentorian tones.

That night at 8 p.m. the homeward bounder started to ring her bell. Immediately every ship followed suit until all the poop and foc's'le bells in port were ringing wildly.

The tones of the bells echoed amongst the hills and valleys ashore, and were often audible miles out to sea. This racket continued for ten or fifteen minutes, and whilst it was going on the homeward bounder proceeded to hoist a wooden frame-work aloft on the foremast, on which lighted riding lights were lashed in the form of the constellation of the Southern Cross.

A smart ship would go further than this by adding a long swinging outrigger which held two more lights, these being supposed to represent the Twin Centaurs. At the same time the captain who was not afraid of a little expense, and was jealous of his ship's reputation, would outline his rail and even his masts with coloured lights. The crew, too, of the homeward bounder would crowd on to the top of the midship-house and the foc's'le-head, each man holding a lighted torch of saltpetre. Some ships did not hoist the Southern Cross until the bell ringing had stopped, then sent it up to the strains of a favourite shanty, which, breaking out into the tropic night in the sudden deep hush which followed the din of the bells, was often extremely impressive, especially when well sung by a good deep-water crew.

As soon as the Southern Cross had been hoisted, the ceremony of cheering began. The man with the mightiest voice on the homeward bound ship sang out 'Three cheers for the *Pitlochry*'. (We will imagine that this is the name of the nearest vessel.) Immediately these cheers had been given, the *Pitlochry* replied with 'Three cheers for the homeward bounder!' It is noticeable here that the etiquette of the ceremony demanded that the name of the homeward bounder should not be given. That was only

The *Montmorency* the night before sailing, homeward bound from Iquique.

Built for A.D. Bordes by Ateliers et Chantiers de la Noir at Nantes, the *Montmorency* measured 322 ft 1 in. (98.24 m) length, 45 ft (13.73 m) beam, 25 ft 5 in. (7.75 m) depth, 3011 tons gross and 2376 tons net. She was launched in 1896 along with her sisters *Caroline* and *Madeleine,* and survived until Bordes ceased running sailing ships in 1926.

said when cheering the last bag, but in the evening performance the cheers were always given for 'the homeward bounder'. The ceremony then went on until every ship in port had been cheered and had given her cheers for the homeward bounder.

At some ports it was the custom to ring the ship's bell before each round of cheers. The din may be imagined, when, as often happened in one of the big nitrate ports, there were fifty or sixty ships in port and possibly two or three homeward bounders on the same night. When two homeward bounders were cheering each other, each tried to outdo the other in the various noises she could produce.

As soon as the last cheers had died down the captain of the homeward bound vessel had a further opportunity of doing his ship proud. Some homeward bounders then proceeded to give a very fine firework display, with rockets, Roman candles, etc. It was also the custom for her to send a boat round the nearest ships, and especially to her chum ships, with a bottle of grog aboard for each.

By 10 o'clock, as a rule, the fireworks had ceased, and the anchorage had quieted down except for spasmodic outbursts of song or cheering. By this time the homeward bounder was surrounded by a flotilla of boats, for her skipper was entertaining all the captains in port and their ladies, as well as many shipping people from on shore. Her half-deck, too, was flowing over with apprentices, most of whom had rowed their captains aboard, but many besides were there on leave or without leave bidding good-bye to their chums.

Last of all, before all hands turned in, and as soon as the Southern Cross and other lights had been lowered down, everybody aboard the homeward bounder joined in singing the 'Homeward Bound' shanty.

O fare you well, I wish you well!
Good-bye, fare you well; good-bye, fare you well!
O, fare you well, my bonnie young girls!
Hoorah, my boys, we're homeward bound!

– B. Lubbock, *The Nitrate Clippers.*

The *Preussen* carrying all sail

The *Preussen*

Built in 1902 by Teckenborg at Geesemunde for Laeisz, the *Preussen*'s statistics make impressive reading:

Length overall	433 ft (132.07 m)
Length reg.	407 ft 8 in. (124.34 m)
Breadth	53 ft 6 in. (16.32 m)
Depth (moulded)	32 ft 6 in. (9.94 m)
Draught loaded	27 ft (8.2 m)

The *Preussen* was the only five-masted ship-rigged vessel ever built and was a highly successful ship on the nitrate run, although she was often unable to load to her capacity of 8000 tons. Her spread of 48 sails had an area of 59,000 square ft (5481 m²) and her middle mast was 223 ft 1 in.(68.04 m) from keel to truck. The lower yards were 102 ft (31.11 m) long and royals 52 ft 6 in.(16.01 m). It is difficult to visualise the sheer size of these spars, but those lower yards were longer than *Bounty*'s masts were tall, and weighed 6.5 tons each.

To handle this gear the *Preussen* carried a crew of 48, who were aided by brace winches, capstans and steam which could work the anchor gear and, if required, the steering. The latter was usually managed by hand and, in heavy weather, sometimes up to eight men were needed to hold her on course. Her hull was strengthened in a manner unusual for her time, the framing and stiffening being designed to spread the enormous stresses from the rig.

The *Preussen* was no sluggard and kept her voyages to almost a steamship schedule. Her best day's run

The *Preussen* goes ashore in the English Channel

officers underestimated the speed of these ships.)

Although the *Brighton* survived, the *Preussen*, with all her headgear gone, her foremast in a parlous state and taking water forward, was in trouble. An attempt to anchor off Dungeness in rising wind carried away both cables and Captain H. Nissen put out to sea. The next day the gale increased and tugs which managed to get lines aboard could not handle her; she drove ashore under the cliffs of Dover at 4.30 in the afternoon.

During the next couple of days attempts to get a line aboard were frustrated by the weather. Heroic attempts by lifeboat-men to take off the crew were passed over until, on the third day after the collision, all hope of getting the *Preussen* off was abandoned and the crew were hauled ashore by breeches buoy.

Most of her gear and cargo were salvaged, but the hull, or at least half of it, was still there after World War I.

Had the *Preussen* survived the hazards of the sea and two wars, she could have been one ship that could have sailed economically and efficiently until the very end of the sailing-ship era, and perhaps beyond.

The *Pamir*

One bleak, cold, wet and windy morning, out of the vast reaches of the Southern Ocean the *Pamir* rolled into Cook Strait and Wellington Harbour. It was July 1941 and Captain V. Björkfelt was unaware that he was about to lose his ship.

In early June, under the Finnish flag, the *Pamir* had sailed from the Seychelles, taking the long lonely sailing-ship route south to New Zealand. While she reeled off her miles before the southern gales, her home country had been forced to declare war on the Soviet Union, consequently becoming an enemy of New Zealand. She entered Wellington displaying her name, flag and country along with the vertical blue

stripe on a white ground which was the declaration of a neutral ship; all this boldly painted along her sides. When she sailed again, eight months later, she was flying the New Zealand flag and was manned by New Zealanders and a few of the original Finnish crew.

The *Pamir* was built in 1905 by Blohm and Voss of Hamburg. She was destined to join the fleet of ships owned by Laeisz: *Preussen*, *Penang*, *Passat*, and all the other large and famous Cape Horners belonging to what became known among seamen as the 'Flying P Line'. She was a finely built ship, rigged as a four-masted barque, measuring 316 ft (96.38 m) in length and with a gross tonnage of 3020 tons. She sailed in the Chilean nitrate trade until the outbreak of World War I, when she was diverted on a passage from Chile to take refuge in the neutral Canary Islands. After the war, under the Treaty of Versailles she was assigned to Italy where she languished until bought back by Laeisz in 1923. She continued in the nitrate trade until 1931 when she was laid up but not for long, for she was soon bought by Gustave Erikson of Finland and it was under the house flag of Erikson, after years in the Australian grain trade, that the *Pamir* entered Wellington in 1941.

Ten voyages were made under the New Zealand flag, eight across the Pacific to the North American west coast, one to Sydney and the last to London and Antwerp. She was handed back to Finland in Wellington on 12 November 1948. Her old master, Captain Björkfelt resumed command and in Feburary 1949 *Pamir* sailed in ballast with a mainly New Zealand crew. Her destination was Port Victoria in the Spencer Gulf, South Australia, where she was to load grain for Europe. While lying in the roadstead there, her near sister, the *Passat*, arrived and when the *Pamir* sailed on 28 May 1949, shortly before her sister, the last grain race to Europe was begun. Not only was it the last grain race but the two ships carried the last commercial cargoes in sailing ships around the Horn.

The *Pamir* made good time, weathering the usual

was 368 miles by observation, during which she maintained a consistent 17 knots for four hours. With her rival, the *Potosi*, she was incredibly powerful and was able to carry all sail to lower topgallants in a gale of wind. Unfortunately, one November at midnight in 1910, this fine ship ran down the Channel ferry *Brighton*. (Collisions between the big Laeisz vessels and steamers were only too frequent, possibly because the steamer succession of gales running her easting down and surviving a hurricane near Cape Verde, until light variable winds baffled her in the North Atlantic. It took her all of September to work up the Atlantic to Falmouth where, on 2 October, she called for orders. (It was the practice of sailing ships not equipped with radio to anchor at either Falmouth in Cornwall or Queenstown in Ireland to collect their instructions as to where their cargoes were to be discharged.) The *Pamir* had been 128 days on passage from Australia. Her rival, the *Passat*, had beaten her by 18 days to Queenstown. Both ships discharged at Pennarth in South Wales.

No further profitable cargoes could be found for either ship and after an eighteen-month lay-up, the two were sold to shipbreakers in Antwerp in March 1951. Just before the vessels were to be dismantled, they were reprieved when a shipowner, Heinz Schliewen of Lubeck, purchased them to use as cargo-carrying sail-training ships.

Back under the German flag, the ships underwent a considerable refit at Kiel. Three watertight bulkheads and a centre-line bulkhead with shifting boards were built. A 750-ton water ballast tank was installed to do away with the necessity of loading solid ballast. Two deck-houses and other improvements were made to the accommodation, and the cargo-working gear was upgraded by fitting derricks, sampson posts and diesel winches. Two extra lifeboats were secured on skids over the foredeck and a 900 horsepower diesel auxiliary, driving a two-bladed propeller, was installed.

The *Pamir's* first voyage to South America with bagged cement and a complement of 91, including 46 cadets, got off to a bad start. She sailed from Hamburg in January 1952 but a strong gale forced her to shelter in the Thames Estuary. Requests were made for assistance and the Margate lifeboat stood by until the wind subsided. At the height of the gale when only her anchors lay between her and possible destruction, the port cable parted. Later in the voyage her propeller dropped off. Only two voyages were made before her owner went bankrupt and she was laid up in Hamburg. On 2 April 1954 the *Pamir* was auctioned to the Schleswig-Holsteinische Landesbank. The following year both the *Pamir* and the *Passat* were taken over by an association of 40 German shipowners and the ships were once more employed on the South American run.

In May 1957, after an overhaul at the yard of her builders, Blohm and Voss, *Pamir* sailed on what was to be her last voyage. In command was Captain Johannes Diebitsch who had sailed in *Pamir* before World War I and had spent 12 years in command of smaller sailing vessels. The mate, Rolf Koehler, had only the experience of the two previous voyages in sail. Fifty-two cadets, half of whom were first voyagers, brought the total complement to 86.

On 1 June 1957 the *Pamir* sailed in ballast for Buenos Aires, where 3525 tons of bulk and 255 tons of bagged barley were loaded. The ship sailed for Hamburg on 10 August. On the thirty-first she crossed the equator. Three weeks later three distress calls were received by vessels widely distributed throughout the Atlantic. At that time I was on watch as Third Officer of a ship in the Mediterranean and remember well the radio officer calling me with the SOS. We were off Tunisia and there was nothing we could do, but everybody in the ship lost sleep that night following the reports coming in from ships going to the *Pamir's* assistance. The first messages, at 1400 GMT, read: 'D.K.E.F. four-masted barque *Pamir* heavy seas at position 35°57'N, 40°20'W 35 degree stall [list] gaining stop ships in vicinity please communicate with master.'

Later calls informed the ships going to her assistance that she was in hurricane-force winds, all sails had been lost and she was listing 45 degrees and in danger of sinking. The last message from her was at 1501 GMT. When ships reached the area only six survivors were found.

The following quotes I have extracted from Jack Churchouse's well researched book *The Pamir Under the New Zealand Ensign*. One of the survivors stated:

It was dreadful. As the boats were launched they were caught by the mountainous waves and sent hurtling hundreds of feet away from the ship. The pounding of the seas . . . heeled the ship over further and further. It was now impossible to keep the *Pamir's* bows head on to those tremendous waves. She was lying broadside on. There was no time to send another SOS. The end was here. It took only thirty seconds. In the trough of a giant wave, she rolled right over and we last saw her bottom up and going down by the bow like a submarine slowly diving. The few men who were still on board when she capsized were struggling in the water. I don't know how we got away, but it seemed to me that our lifeboat was the only one successfully launched.

The following is the finding of the enquiry held in January 1958:

With a heavy NNE storm in the area of a tropical hurricane the four-masted barque *Pamir*, a cargo-carrying sail-training vessel, has capsized and sunk towards 16 o'clock GMT on 21 September 1957, in the Atlantic on position 35°57'N, 40°20'W, about 600 nautical miles WSW of the Azores. Only six men could be saved out of a crew of 86 men. They have been rescued in the following days from destroyed lifeboats. All the others have lost their lives.

The *Pamir* carried all topsails, the foresail and several staysails and sailed close-hauled on the starboard tack, when the wind in a short time increased severely after having blown with Force 9 Beaufort. With those sails set, the yards close-hauled, her state of loading and her ballast tanks not flooded, the stability was not sufficient, so that the vessel got a heavy list to port. Because the angle of slope was exceeded, the barley which for the greatest part had been loaded loose (i.e. unsacked) and had settled during the voyage, began to move in spite of the erected shifting boards and was going over to port in an increasing degree. Furthermore, water poured into the superstructures which were not closed everywhere and which were already immersed on the port side so that their buoyancy was lost. In this way the vessel capsized.

Difficulties, which have existed for many years, have influenced the manning of the vessel with master, officers and a nucleus crew. It is possible that an unfavourable effect was caused by the master's lack of thorough knowledge of *Pamir*'s special sailing qualities and her stability as well as by the chief mate's limited experience in sailing vessels...

After the loss of the *Pamir*, the *Passat*, which had also experienced difficulty through her barley shifting in heavy weather, was first laid up in Hamburg and then towed to Travemünde to serve as a youth hostel.

The *Pamir* was not the only commercially running sail-training ship to be lost. In 1928-9 the *Kobenhavn* vanished with all hands on a voyage from Buenos Aires to Australia. It is now a policy that all sail-training ships should be divorced completely from the role of carrying cargo.

The *Pamir*, originally one of Laeisz's 'Flying P' line and employed in the nitrate trade until 1931. She was sold to the Finns but came under the New Zealand flag when she unwittingly sailed into Wellington Harbour after Finland had been forced to declare war on the Soviet Union in 1941. In 1948 she was handed back to Finland and in 1951 came once more under the German flag. In 1957 she capsized with the loss of 80, many of whom were cadets in training.

THE SCOWS

Of the sailing vessels which worked in the Pacific, possibly the ugliest duckling of them all was the scow, a vessel peculiar to the North American and New Zealand coasts. Though not a clipper, it became the most practical and longest serving of most local craft. Perhaps I am being a little unfair as to its appearance, for from the original box-shaped hull of the first scows was developed such handsome sailing craft as the *Rangi* and the *Moa*. Nowadays some of these craft, although power driven and with the rig very much cut down, are still earning a living.

The prototype of the scow probably originated in the Baltic and Canada where they were used for hauling lumber; possibly the builders of the first New Zealand craft had experience of these vessels. In the 1870s the first small New Zealand scows were built to work the sheltered waters of Auckland's Hauraki Gulf. They were punt-bowed, flat-bottomed barges – as indeed they were at first called. To assist what little sailing qualities they must have had, they were equipped with leeboards and the huge rudder was hinged to allow beaching. Within a decade the leeboards were replaced by centreboards – up to three in line on the larger scows – and the bows were given some entrance and shape. They became superbly adapted to the tasks demanded of them such as mudholing up tiny estuaries, beaching and loading on and off sometimes not so sheltered shores, and freighting anything and everything around a coastline not then served by road. They could keep the sea, make long ocean passages and work the wild and dangerous bar harbours on the west coast of New Zealand.

Timber was the scow's first reason for existence in Canada and New Zealand. Pine on the Pacific west coast and kauri in New Zealand was rafted down rivers and streams to await shipment to the sawmills and nearly every suitable cove had its mill. Most of the scows were 'deck' scows; that is, there

The New Zealand scows *Rangi* and *Moa* beating up Auckland harbour

was no hold and the whole hull was watertight, or supposed to be. The logs would be loaded on deck by parbuckling up the side and jacking into position. Unloading was carried out by the simple expedient of jacking and rolling them overboard. Once the timber began to be worked out in New Zealand, the scows turned to carting sand and shingle, cattle and sheep, or any other freight they could get. Some, such as the *Echo* made themselves indispensible by serving a particular community. At present a scow serves Great Barrier Island in the Hauraki Gulf.

By the turn of the century some scows were making ocean passages to Australia and the Pacific Islands and were confidently working the aforementioned bar harbours. The sailing qualities of these craft should not be underestimated; some of the larger and faster scows could give the conventional schooners and ketches a run for their money. It appears that the skippers of the scows were a competitive lot and the annual scow or traders race on the Auckland harbour was enthusiastically attended. The press of sail they would carry was remarkable for they had enormous initial stability, although should they be knocked down, I imagine they would capsize very easily, as indeed happened to several craft.

The *Moa* and the *Rangi* were both 'hold' scows. In the painting I have depicted them beating up the Waitemata, Auckland's harbour, and obviously making a bit of a race of it. The event is fictitious and before starting on the painting I was told on good authority that it would be doubtful if they would be sporting their flying jibs in the confined waters of the harbour, especially with that big black southwesterly squall coming down. I hope my little bit of licence will be excused.

During World War I both these ships featured in the resourceful Count von Luckner's attempt to escape from incarceration on Motuihe Island near Auckland. The German Count had been captured in Fiji after making a long boat voyage from Mopelia in the Society Islands where his raider, the *Seeadler*,

had been wrecked. With splendid enterprise and determination he planned his escape, preparing maps, acquiring weapons and manufacturing anything he could not steal. A sextant was made from part of an old steering wheel from a launch. On 13 December 1917 they were away. . .in the camp commander's launch, the *Pearl*. The Count knew that the *Pearl* was incapable of making a long passage, so a larger seagoing vessel was required. To this end he took the *Pearl* out of the Hauraki Gulf to the Mercury Islands, not far offshore in the Bay of Plenty. Between the Mercurys and the mainland a narrow passage known as the Hole-in-the-Wall funnelled coasting traffic and cut miles off the run from the bay into the gulf. Hiding the *Pearl* in a cove, the fugitives kept watch. Sure enough, on the sixteenth, two sailing vessels hove into sight from the south. First came the *Rangi*, and four miles astern, the *Moa*. Count von Luckner boarded and took the *Moa*, hoisted the German ensign and bore away northeast for the Kermadecs, taking with him the *Moa*'s crew under Captain Bourke.

Captain J. Francis of the *Rangi*, who was aware of the Count's escape, saw what had happened and got into the nearest port with a telegraph where he alerted the authorities before carrying on to Auckland. On the way he intercepted the cable steamer *Iris*, which he boarded. The master of the *Iris* guessed that the Count would make for the Kermadecs and set off in pursuit. Von Luckner, his crew and captives, made Raoul in the Kermadecs where they raised the flag, made the Samoan plantation manager a naval officer, and raided the castaway stores kept on the island. Preparations were nearly complete to sail for South America when the *Iris* appeared. The Count sailed immediately, cracking on to a good breeze, but the *Iris* gradually overhauled them and they were retaken after a shot was fired across their bows. This time Count von Luckner was put away far from the sea.

The *Rangi* was lost in 1937 when she capsized.

Running before a fresh wind in the Hauraki Gulf with a deck cargo of logs, her weather main chain plates carried away, opening a bad leak and endangering the rig. Captain P. Peterson gybed and ran down under the partial lee of Motutapu Island, where he anchored. The wind rose to a full gale and her pumps could not cope with the leak. A decision was made to rid the *Rangi* of some of her logs. To right any ship with water in her by dumping loads from the lower side can be dangerous, for when the ship comes upright, the water in her will shift its centre of gravity more and more amidships. Finally, with a rush, it will flow to the opposite side where it adds its weight to the loads remaining on board, thus creating a worse list the other way. Dumping cargo is usually a last resort when the angle of heel becomes critical and there is a very real danger of capsizing. With the broad transverse section of the *Rangi*, this danger would be amplified. In theory, logs should have been jettisoned from the high side first but in Captain Peterson's case that would have been impossible as the enormously heavy logs would have to have been rolled uphill. Captain Peterson must have considered this, but he had no option but to attempt to lighten the ship. The worst happened and she went over on her other beam. Captain Peterson and the crew took to the boat and tried to steer to the island but could make no headway, so they ran off, heading for the mainland. Not far off their destination, the boat capsized. Of the complement of six, only one crewman and the ship's boy made it ashore. During the night the *Rangi* broke up.

The *Moa* was lost in 1935 when she stranded at Big Wanganui, south of Hokitika on the West Coast of the South Island.

THE INTERCOLONIAL SHIPS

During the first quarter of this century many fine small ships found employment in the trade between Australia and New Zealand. Most of these were British-built barques and barquentines. Handsome, sturdy and good sailers, they could be managed with a small crew and still cope with the stormy Tasman Sea. In a period when so many of the smaller sailing ships were lying rusting, unable to compete with steam, the intercolonial trade provided a good home for a handy barque whose new Antipodean owner often took an enormous pride in his vessel.

The *Polly Woodside*

The *Polly Woodside*, preserved in Melbourne, is typical of these intercolonial ships. She was built in Belfast by Workman, Clark and Co. Ltd in 1885, grossing 678.17 tons, with a length of 192 ft (58.56 m) and breadth of 30 ft (9.15 m). Until she came under New Zealand ownership in 1904, the *Polly Woodside* was mainly employed in carrying coal from south Wales to South America. She made one voyage which took her as far afield as Chittagong and in the first years of this century made two voyages to Australia and one to New Zealand. Her first New Zealand owner, Arthur Hughes Turnbull of Christchurch, renamed her the *Rona* after the daughter of the company's marine superintendent.

Until 1916 the *Rona* traded mainly in the Tasman Sea, but because of heavy shipping losses during World War I, from 1916 until 1920 she ran between New Zealand and California carrying mainly copra and coal out and returning with case oil. In this trade,

and during the last two years of her sailing life back in the trans-Tasman trade, she was owned by George Scales of Wellington. She made her last commercial voyage in September 1921 from Newcastle to Wellington. The same month she was sold to the Adelaide Steamship Company Ltd and sailed for Sydney where she was hulked. In 1925 she started her life as a coal-lighter in Melbourne and apart from one excursion to northern Australia during World War II, the Victorian capital has been her base.

Today she is one of several old sailing ships which have been, or are being restored around the Pacific shores. The *Falls of Clyde* in Honolulu, the *Star of India* in San Diego, and the *Balclutha* in San Francisco, have all been saved and preserved from the ignominy of hulk or scrapyard. Thanks to the efforts in 1961 of Mr Karl Kortum, director of the San Francisco Maritime Museum, and the late Dr E. Graeme Robertson, Captain Sir John Williams and others, steps were taken to save the *Rona*. In 1968 she became the property of the National Trust of Australia. Now, after years of hard, dedicated and painstaking work, the old barque, bearing her original name, is restored and graces an historical area on the banks of the Yarra which flows through Melbourne.

The *Huia*

A fast, handsome topsail schooner, the *Huia* was a good example of the many small traders which plied the coasts and islands of the southwest Pacific. Her measurements were: 165.89 tons net (250.78 gross) when built; length 115 ft 1 in. (35.10 m); beam 25

The *Huia*, a fine example of the schooners which traded in the southwest Pacific during the first half of this century. She was still trading in 1951 when she struck a reef and caught fire, becoming a total loss.

ft 2 in. (7.68 m); depth 11 ft 5 in. (3.48 m). She was launched in 1894 far up the Northern Wairoa River on the west coast of the North Island of New Zealand. Her builder, James Barbour, produced many fine small ships using no plans but developing their lines from half models. The *Huia* was the most famous and longest serving of his ships until, in January 1951, when on a voyage from Noumea to Vila she ran on a reef and later caught fire.

Most of the *Huia*'s life was spent on the New Zealand and Australian coasts, voyaging as far afield as Fremantle and Queensland, with one voyage in 1917 to San Francisco. In the last year of her life she came under Fijian registry and made one voyage to Pitcairn Island where she took the islanders to Henderson Island to get wood and coconuts.

The *Huia* was not the fastest of the New Zealand built schooners but although there is some doubt, she did claim the record for west to east crossing of the Tasman. In 1895 she put out from Newcastle, NSW, for the Kaipara on the west coast of the North Island of New Zealand, and ran straight into a gale. Under staysail, lower topsail and reefed foresail she roared off downwind across the Tasman. According to Captain George McKenzie, it was a matter of keeping going – conditions were so severe that they couldn't reduce sail. Apparently the watch had to sit astride the main boom to stop themselves being washed overboard, and the helmsman had a continuous struggle as the seas came aboard forward, swept aft and tried to take him with them over the

(*Top right*) The *Rona*, ex *Polly Woodside*, towing down the Yarra River, Melbourne

(*Right*) The *Polly Woodside* shortening down before a squall

stern. The galley, frequently a separate entity and not built-in on a sailing ship, broke adrift and the water tanks were washed over the side.

When the mate finally managed to get a sight, it put them 200 miles ahead of their dead reckoning and there was naturally some doubt about its accuracy until the Pouto Light at the entrance of the

Kaipara Harbour loomed on the horizon. With the prevailing conditions it was impossible to cross the bar so the *Huia* hove-to for two days until the weather moderated sufficiently to cross. Thus the time for the passage was for land-to-land, still an achievement even though I suspect the crew would have been thankful to have had a slower passage.

The wooden barquentine *Laura*. Built in Denmark in 1889, the *Laura* was later used in the intercolonial trade and registered in Suva, Fiji, in 1920

Glossary

AB (Able-bodied seaman): a senior deckhand.

Abaft: further aft or nearer the stern.

Aft: behind or near the stern of a vessel.

Aftercastle: superstructure aft; originally denoting a fighting platform, this term came to designate the poop deck and quarterdeck.

Aloft: up in the rigging.

Amidships: the middle of a ship, either along her length or across her breadth.

Ballast: any heavy material which is used to provide stability to a ship.

Bare poles: the state of a ship at sea with no sails set.

Beakhead: the ship's head forward of the forecastle, forming a small deck built forward of the stem.

'Before the mast': to sail as a seaman berthed in the fo'c's'le apart from officers who berthed aft.

Bend sail: to attach a sail to its yard, stay, gaff or boom.

Bent: to make fast with a bend (as in hitched).

Block: pulley used for various purposes, especially to increase the mechanical power of the ropes used in handling the sails.

Bluff bowed: said of a vessel with broad, rounded bows which push through the water rather than cut through it.

Boatswain (bosun, bo's'n): warrant officer responsible for handling the crew and the ship's general maintenance.

Bobstay: the stay leading from the end of the bowsprit to the stem.

Bonaventure: small mast and lateen sail set aft of the mizzen on sixteenth- and seventeenth-century ships.

Bonnet: additional piece of canvas laced to the bottom of a sail to give it more area.

Bower anchor: one of the two principal anchors of a ship, permanently attached to a cable. 'Best bower': anchor carried on the starboard bow of the ship; originally slightly larger than the port bower, known as the 'small bower'. Later both were the same size.

Bowline: line attached to the leech rope of a squaresail and leading forward.

Bowse: to tighten any line or tackle. Hemp shrouds and stays would often become slack after days at sea and as a temporary measure until conditions permitted the rig to be set up properly, the shrouds or stays were often bowsed by clapping on a tackle or lashing above the dead-eyes or hearts and leading it to a ringbolt inboard, tensioning the rigging by heaving on it like a bowstring.

Bowsprit: large spar projecting over the stem and carrying sail forward, in order to govern the fore part of the ship and counteract the force of the sails extending aft; it is also the principal support of the foremast, since the stays holding that mast are secured to it.

Brace: gear used to swing a yard in a horizontal plane.

Brail: rope used to gather in a fore-and-aft sail.

Bulwark: planking round the edge of the upper decks which stops the sea washing over the decks and prevents crew being swept overboard in high seas.

Buntline: rope attached to the foot of a squaresail, passing up in front of the sail to a block on the yard; used to pull the bottom of the sail up and spill the wind out of it.

Burden: number of tons of cargo which a ship can carry.

Cable: heavy chain or hemp rope to which an anchor is secured.

Cap: two-holed fitting which holds an upper mast in one hole against the top of a lower mast which fits in the other hole.

Capstan: apparatus enabling the anchor or other heavy lifts to be raised by hand. It consists of a strong upright cylindrical barrel revolving on a spindle. The capstan bars fit into sockets in the upper rim, while the base carries pawls which fit into the pawl rim beneath and prevent the capstan from slipping back and running out the cable.

Careen: to beach or haul a ship over to one side by means of tackles leading from the masts to the shore, in order to carry out caulking, repairing and cleaning work on the underwater part of her hull and on her bottom.

Catted and hung: to hoist an anchor by its ring and hang it to the cat-head ready for letting go or bringing inboard and on to the anchor-bed where the anchor is secured on deck.

Caulk: to make the seams of a wooden ship's decks or sides watertight by driving in oakum or some other fibre, and covering it with hot melted pitch or resin.

Channels (chain wales): broad, thick planks projecting horizontally from the side of a ship, used to spread the shrouds and thus provide better support for the masts.

Chock: a wooden wedge used to prevent any article stowed on board from shifting when the ship is in motion.

Clew: lower corner of a squaresail—usually to which the sheet is attached. Also, the after lower corner of a fore-and-aft sail.

Clew garnets: tackles attached to the clews of a course and running up towards the yard aft of the sail; used to pull the clews up to the yard when taking in the sail.

'Clew lines' perform the same function as clew garnets on squaresails other than the courses.

Close-hauled: the general arrangement or trim of a ship's sails when she is trying to sail as closely as possible towards the direction from which the wind is blowing.

Collar: eye in the end or bight of a shroud or stay looped over the masthead. Also, rope formed into an eye with a dead-eye inside.

Collier: vessel built to carry coal as cargo.

Concretions: marine growth and debris that accumulates on an underwater wreck.

Conning: guiding.

Cordage: rope.

Courses: the sails attached to the lower yards: the foresail, mainsail, and mizzen. Sometimes the staysails on the lower masts are included.

Crank: a ship which, due to her construction or the stowage of her ballast or cargo, cannot carry sail without danger of capsizing.

Cro'jack (cross-jack): lower yard on mizzen mast or the sail it supports.

Damped compass: a compass in which the card is suspended in some medium which prevents it from swinging wildly when the ship is in motion.

Davits: curved pillars fitted to the deck close to a vessel's sides and from which boats are lowered and hoisted.

Dead-eye: round or pear-shaped flattish wooden block pierced with three holes.

Derrick: form of crane used to hoist cargo or other weights.

Dodger: windshield spread to protect the man on watch from the weather.

Doldrums: area of low pressure near the equator between the trade winds alternating with squalls, heavy rains and thunderstorms.

Draught: depth of water needed to float a particular ship, measured from the bottom of the keel to the waterline.

Earring: short length of rope used to lash the upper corners of a squaresail to the yard.

Embayed: trapped inside a bay due to bad weather, currents or heavy seas and unable to get out.

Fairing: correcting a ship's plans before building begins, or the frames before planking.

Fathom: 6 ft (1.83 m).

Fid: square-section pin of wood or iron with a shoulder at one end inserted through a hole in the heel of the topmast on to the trestle-trees. The topmast is then said to be 'fidded' or fixed in place.

Fish: long convex piece of wood designed to reinforce

a damaged mast or spar. Usually fastened in pairs on both sides of the damaged section.

Flush deck: one continuous upper deck.

Fo'c's'le (forecastle): a space at the forward end of the upper deck covered by a short raised deck. In merchant ships, the seamen's quarters.

Forward: relating to that part of a ship which lies in or towards the bows and stem.

Founder: to fill with water and sink as a result of damage or flooding.

Furl: to gather in a sail, rolling it up and securing it with gaskets to the yard, boom, spar or mast.

Futtock: one of the sections making up a frame between the floor timber and the top timber.

Futtock shrouds: short lengths of rope, chain or iron bar supporting the tops or topmast crosstrees against the pull of the shrouds above them. They lead down and inward to join either the mast or lower shrouds at the level of the lower yard.

Gaff: spar to which the head of a four-sided fore-and-aft sail is attached. One end often has a jaw which fits round the mast.

Gammoning: tautened rope or chain lashing, staying the bowsprit to the knee of the head. It serves to hold the bowsprit down against the upward pull of the forestay.

Gasket: short line attached to the yard used to secure a furled sail.

Goose-winging: a topsail with its weather clew hauled up to the yard and its lee clew hauled down and spread. Goose-winging was used as an additional form of reefing in very severe conditions; the sail would be furled on the weather yard and lashed at the tie, only the lee clew sheeted out.

Gripes: wide plaited bands of rope used to secure the boats in their position on board.

Ground (aground): to bring a vessel's keel in touch with the bottom, usually by accident rather than intent.

Guano: excrement of sea fowl found in many small islands of the Pacific Ocean and western coast of South America, used as fertiliser.

Gunwales (gunnel): uppermost strake, or run of planking on a ship's side, in modern usage also the upper edge of the bulwarks.

Guy: general term usually applied to a line or tackle which is used for steadying a spar.

Gybe: to bring the wind on the opposite side of a fore-and-aft sail when running downwind.

Halliard (halyard): rope or tackle used to hoist or lower a sail, yard or gaff.

Hatch: rectangular opening in the deck of a ship, providing access from one deck to another, or to the hold.

Hawser: heavy line.

Helmsman: seaman who steers the ship.

Hold: internal cavity of a ship between lower deck and floor, where cargo, stores and ballast are kept.

Hounds: where the collars of the shrouds lie on the mast.

Hulk: olden-day name for a large merchant vessel; now means the hull of a vessel not fit or not used for sea service.

Hull: the body of a vessel, excluding masts, sails and rigging.

Jackstay: originally a line stretched along a spar or exposed deck to give a sailor something to hang on to. On a sailing ship's yard the jackstay became a bar to which the head of a squaresail was bent. Large ships in the latter days of sail often had two jackstays on their larger yards—the forward one, to which was bent the sail, and the after one forming a handhold. Applies generally to any rope or wire stretched to give support.

Jaw: pronged inner end of a gaff or a boom, shaped to fit into a mast.

Jeer tackle: tackles used for hoisting or lowering the lower yards.

Jibboom: spar extending from the end of the bowsprit on which the jibs are set.

Jigger tackle: light small tackle, comprising a single and double block, used on various occasions by seamen.

Jury rig: temporary rig created from materials to hand, used as a replacement in emergency.

Kedge: light anchor which can be laid out for warping.

Keel: principal length of timber in a ship, running fore and aft; usually the first component laid on the blocks, in shipbuilding and often comprises several sections scarfed together, bolted and clinched from above.

Keelson: an internal keel fastened above the keel to provide additional strength.

Knee: angled piece of timber generally used to connect the beams of a ship with her sides or frames.

Lanthorn: a lantern.

Lanyard: the short lengths of line securing shrouds and stays.

Lateen: triangular sail attached by its foremost edge to a long yard which is hoisted at an angle to the mast.

Latitude: angular distance of a place north or south of the equator, measured along the meridian of the place in degrees, minutes and seconds of arc.

Leadline: weight and line used for measuring depth.

League: 3 nautical miles or one-twentieth of a degree of latitude, and varies from country to country.

Lee board: heavy, ironbound, tapered board pivoted by its forward edge to the side of a flat-bottomed vessel. It is lowered by a chain to serve as a drop keel when the vessel is sailing and thus reduce leeway.

Leech: the side edges of a squaresail, also the after edge of a fore-and-aft sail.

Lighter: a barge or similar type of craft without its own means of propulsion, used for carrying goods to and from ships or shore.

Log or log book: official record of events on board ship as well as of the ship's movements.

Log: apparatus used for measuring a ship's speed.

Longitude: angular distance of a place east or west of a chosen prime meridian, today usually Greenwich.

Mast-hoop: sliding ring of wood or metal which attaches the edge of a fore-and-aft sail to the mast.

Maul: heavy wooden or iron hammer; usually leather covered when used for working on the rigging.

Meridian: a line running from pole to pole, crossing all latitudes at right angles; also known as a line of longitude.

Mizzen mast: third mast from forward in a vessel with 3 or more masts.

Monsoon: seasonal winds throughout Asia.

Parcel: to wrap fabric, such as canvas or hessian, round a wormed rope to prepare it for serving.

Parrel: rope or iron collar which attaches the centre of a yard to the mast and can slide up or down the mast as required. Also a rope which fastens the jaws of a gaff to the mast.

Pieces-of-eight: gold coins.

Pilot: a person qualified to navigate a vessel through intricate channels in or out of the harbour. Manila galleon pilots were ocean-going pilots.

Pink: a vessel with a high, narrow, overhanging poop, derived from and similar to the Dutch fluyt; commonly used as a merchantman.

Pinrail: long rack holding belaying pins to which lines are belayed.

Pirogues: canoes.

Poop: highest and aftermost upper deck of a ship.

Port: left-hand side of a ship, looking forward.

Preventer: any rope used as an additional security for another.

Reefband: narrow band of canvas sewn along the reef-line for reinforcement.

Rig: the distinctive arrangement of a vessel's masts, spars and sails.

Ring-bolt: type of bolt with an eye and ring in its head; used especially for hooking tackles.

Roach: the curve of the leech or foot of a sail.

Roundhouse: deck-house aft of the mainmast; also an old name for the poop.

Running rigging: moving rigging used for raising, lowering or adjusting yards and sails.

'Run the easting down': generally applied to the long sea route to Australia from the Cape of Good Hope.

Scantlings: any piece of timber of a particular standard square-section.

Scend: the movement of a vessel in a heavy sea when her stern falls into a trough and her bow is thrown violently upwards.

Scudding: running before a gale with minimum sail set or under bare poles.

Scupper: channel cut through a ship's side or waterway in order to carry water off the deck into the sea.

Scurvy: disease caused by the lack of vitamin C.

Scuttle: to purposely sink a vessel by opening its side or bottom to let in the sea.

Sea-kindly: ability of a vessel to cope well with different conditions, particularly heavy weather.

Seizing: means of binding 2 ropes together or binding 1 rope to a spar or similar fitting.

Sheathing: covering nailed over the outside of a ship's bottom below the waterline to protect it against marine growth and worm.

Sheer: the longitudinal vertical curve of a ship's deck or sides.

Sheet: wire, rope or chain attached to one or both of the clews of sails to extend them or hold them in place.

Shoals: shallow water.

Shoe: point where the stem meets the keel.

Shorten sail: reduce the sail area set.

Shrouds: ropes or wire rigging supporting a mast laterally.

Skids: beams on which boats are carried.

Sling: strop attached to the centre of a yard by which it is suspended.

Spanker: fore-and-aft sail set aft of the aftermost mast on a square-rigged ship; the foot is extended by a boom.

Spencer: a sail laced to a gaff and set on the after side of the fore or main lower mast of a square-rigged ship.

Spirketting: heavy plank in ship's side to provide extra strength at the level of the deck beam or immediately above.

Splice: general term for the technique of joining two ropes or forming an eye in one by tucking or re-laying the separated strands into the lay of the rope according to the nature of the splice.

Sprung: said of a wooden mast or spar which is fractured.

Standing rigging: fixed rigging used to support the masts.

Starboard: right-hand side of a ship, looking forward.

Stay: rope or wire that supports a mast in a fore-and-aft direction.

Stem: upright component uniting the sides of a vessel at the fore end, rising from the keel.

Stern: the rear end of a vessel.

Sterncastle: the same as 'aftercastle'.

Sway: another word for haul, but applies particularly to the raising of masts and spars.

Sweeps: long, heavy oars.

Swifters: the foremost shrouds of each lower mast.

Tackle: pulley or purchase created by running a rope through one or more blocks.

Teredo: a marine worm that bores into wood.

Tiller: wood or iron bar fitted in the head of the rudder for the purpose of moving it from one side to the other in order to steer the ship.

To beach: to run a ship ashore in order to prevent her foundering in deeper waters or repair her underwater hull and bottom.

Topsides: hull above the waterline.

Trades: consistent wind which, within the tropics, blows usually from the northeast quadrant in the Northern Hemisphere and the southeast quadrant in the Southern Hemisphere.

Transom: one of the beams fastened across the stern-post, strengthening the stern and giving it shape.

Trenails: wooden pins used in fastening the planks to the timbers and beams (pronounced 'trunnels').

Truck: round cap that goes over the very top of the mast.

Truss: rope binding securing the lower yard to the mast; generally replaced in later years by metal fittings.

Tumblehome: inward slope of a ship's sides as they rise from the broadest point to the upper deck.

Tye (tie): leads from the halliard through a sheave to the yard and is attached to the slings of the yard.

Typhoon: tropical storms in the China seas and western north Pacific.

'Under canvas': propelled by sail.

Vangs: lines leading from the end of a gaff down and out to the ship's sides, steadying the gaff when under sail and keeping it amidships when no sails are set.

Waist: that part of the ship between the quarter-deck and forecastle.

Wales: a number of strong planks extending the entire length of a ship's side at different heights, reinforcing the decks and forming the distinctive curve of the ship.

Warps: heavy rope used for towing, mooring, etc.

Weather-deck: any uncovered deck which is not protected from the weather or the sea.

Weigh: to lift the anchor out of the ground by its cable.

Williwaws: very violent squalls in Magellan Strait which blow in any direction.

Winch: a horizontal revolving barrel used to give mechanical advantage.

Windlass: a device similar in principle to a capstan but rotating on a horizontal axis.

Wolding: rope binding placed at intervals around the mast, the purpose of which was to strengthen the spar and prevent splitting.

Work: said of a vessel straining her timbers when labouring in a heavy sea.

Wormed: to pass spun yarn along the lay of a rope to strengthen it, or to make a smooth surface preparatory to parcelling or serving it.

Yard: spar used to stretch the head of a squaresail.

Yardarm: outer part of a yard between the lift and the tip of the yard.

List of references

ASHBY, TED. *Phantom Fleet*. Reed, Wellington, 1975.

BAKER, MATTHEW, *Fragments of English Shipwrightry*. Publisher unknown. c. 1586. (Now in Pepys Library, Magdalene College, Cambridge University Cambridge.)

BARRATT, GLYNN, *Russia in Pacific Waters, 1715-1825*. University of British Columbia Press, Vancouver, 1981.

BATESON, CHARLES, *Gold Fleet for California*. Minerva, Auckland, 1963.

BATHE, B.W., G.B. RUBIN DE CERVIN, E. TAILLEMITE ET AL., *The Great Age of Sail*. Edited by Joseph Jobé, translated by Michael Kelly. Crescent Books, New York, 1977.

BEAGLEHOLE, J.C., *The Exploration of the Pacific*. A. & C. Black, London, 1966.

BLIGH, WILLIAM, *A Voyage to the South Sea*. George Nicol, London, 1792.

BOTT, ALAN, *The Sailing Ships of the New Zealand Shipping Company (1873-1900)*. Batsford, London, 1972.

BROSSE, J., *Great Voyages of Exploration*. Bateman, Australia, 1983.

BULLEN, F. T., *The Cruise of the Cachalot*. Smith Elder, London, 1897.

CHAPELLE, H.I., *History of the American Sailing Ship*. Bonanza Books, New York, 1982.

CHAPMAN, DON, *1788 The People of the First Fleet*. Cassell, Australia, 1981.

CHARLTON, WARWICK, *The Voyage of the Mayflower II*. Cassell, London, 1957.

CHICHESTER, F., *Along the Clipper Way*. Pan Books, London, 1967.

CHURCHOUSE, JACK, *The Pamir Under the New Zealand Ensign*. Millwood, Wellington, 1978.

CHURCHOUSE, JACK, *Sailing Ships of the Tasman Sea*. Millwood, Wellington, 1978.

CONNER, D., AND MILLER, L., *Master Mariner Captain J. Cook & Peoples of the Pacific*. University of Queensland Press, Brisbane, 1978.

COOK, CAPTAIN J., *The Journals of Captain James Cook on his Voyages of Discovery Vol. II. The Voyage of the* Resolution *and* Adventure *1772-1775*. Edited by J.C. Beaglehole. Cambridge University Press for the Hakluyt Society, Cambridge, 1961.

COOK, CAPTAIN J., *The Journals of Captain Cook on his Voyages of Discovery Vol. III. The Voyage of the* Resolution *and* Discovery, *1776-1780*. Edited by J.C. Beaglehole. Cambridge University Press for the Hakluyt Society, Cambridge, 1961.

COURSE, A.J., *Painted Ports*. Hollis & Carter, London, 1961.

CRAIG, GAVIN, *Boy Aloft*. Lymington Nautical Publishing, Hampshire, 1971.

DAMPIER, WILLIAM, *A New Voyage Round the World*. Dover, New York, 1968.

DANA, R.H., *Two Years Before The Mast*. P.F. Collier & Son, New York, 1969.

DARROCH, V., *Barque Polly Woodside (Rona)*. Lowden, Australia, 1978.

DARWIN, C., *A Naturalist's Voyage Round the World*. John Murray, London, 1901.

DOW, G.F., *Whale Ships and Whaling*. Argosy Antiquarian, New York, 1967.

EADDY, P.A., *'Neath Swaying Spars*. Reed, Wellington, 1954.

FALCONER, R., 'Shortening Sail' in *The Eternal Sea*. Edited by W.M. Williamson, Books for Libraries, Freeport, New York, 1969.

FITZ-ROY, CAPTAIN ROBERT, R.N., *Narrative of the Surveying Voyages of HMS* Adventure *and* Beagle . . . . , *Vol. 2*. Henry Colburn, London, 1839.

GABY, CAPTAIN J., *Mate in Sail*. Antipodean, Artarmon, Australia, 1974.

GIBBS, JIM, *Pacific Square Riggers*. Superior, Seattle, 1969.

The Golden Hinde. A Jarrold & Sons colour publication, Norwich, 1973.

GREENHILL, B., AND GIFFARD, A., *The Merchant Sailing Ship*. David & Charles, Devon, 1970.

HARLAND, J., *Seamanship in the Age of Sail*. Conway Maritime, London, 1984.

HAWKINS, C.W., *A Maritime Heritage*. Collins, Auckland, 1960.

HAWKINS, C.W., *Out of Auckland*. C.W. Hawkins, Auckland, 1960.

HENDERSON, D., 'Nantucket Whalers' in *The Eternal Sea*. Edited by W.M. Williamson. Books for Libraries, Freeport, New York, 1969.

HILDER, BRETT, *The Voyage of Torres*. University of Queensland Press, St Lucia, 1980.

HURST, ALEX A., *Square-Riggers: The Final Epoch 1921-1958*. Teredo, Sussex, 1972.

HUTCHINSON, WILLIAM, *A Treatise on Practical Seamanship*. Scolar Press, London, 1979.

HUYCKE, HAROLD D., 'The Great Star Fleet', in *Yachting*, February and March issues, New York, 1960.

INGRAM, C.W., *New Zealand Shipwrecks 1784-1982*. Reed, Wellington, 1984.

KANE, HERB KAWAINUI, 'The Manila Galleons', in *Honolulu*, November 1982.

KEMP, P., *The Oxford Companion to Ships and the Sea*. Oxford University Press, Oxford, 1979.

KEMP, P., AND LLOYD, C., *The Brethren of the Coast*. Heinemann, London, 1960.

KENNEDY, GAVIN, *Bligh*. Duckworth, London, 1978.

KLEBINGAT, CAPTAIN F.K., 'The Falls of Clyde in the Days of Sail' in *Historic Hawaii News*, April 1985.

LANDSTROM, B., *The Ship*. Allen & Unwin, London, 1961.

LANGDON, R., *The Lost Caravel*. Pacific Publications, Sydney, 1975.

LEES, J., *The Masting & Rigging of English Ships of War 1625-1860*. Conway, London, 1979.

LEVER, DARCY, *Lever's Young Sea Officers Sheet Anchor*. Sheetman, London, 1819.

LITTLE, B., *Crusoe's Captain*. Odhams Press, London, 1960.

LLOYD, C., *Ships and Seamen*. Weidenfeld & Nicholson, London, 1961.

The Lore of Sail, Nordbook Facts on File, New York, 1983.

LUBBOCK, BASIL, *The Last of the Windjammers, Vol. 2*. Brown Son & Ferguson, Glasgow, 1929.

LUBBOCK, BASIL, *The Log of the Cutty Sark*. Brown Son & Ferguson, Glasgow, 1924.

LUBBOCK, BASIL, *The Nitrate Clippers*. Brown Son & Ferguson, Glasgow, 1932.

McGOWAN, ALAN, *THE SHIP Tiller and Whipstaff*. National Maritime Museum HMSO, London, 1981.

McINTYRE, K.G., *The Secret Discovery of Australia*. Picador/ Souvenir Press, South Australia, 1977.

McKAY, RICHARD C., *Some Famous Sailing Ships and Their Builder Donald McKay*. 7Cs Press, Connecticutt, 1969.

MASEFIELD, JOHN, 'The Tarry Buccaneer' in *Collected Poems*. Heinemann, London, 1925.

MAY, W.E., *A History of Marine Navigation*. Norton & Co., New York, 1973.

MITCHELL, W., 'Reefing Topsails' in *The Eternal Sea*. Edited by W.M. Williamson. Books for Libraries, Freeport, New York, 1969.

MOOREHEAD, ALAN, *Darwin and The* Beagle. Hamish Hamilton, London, 1969.

MORRIS, R., *Sail Change*. David Bateman, Auckland, 1981.

MORRISON, J., *Journal of James Morrison*. Published by the author, London, 1798.

MORTON, H., *The Wind Commands*. University of British Colombia Press, Vancouver, 1975.

PARSONS, R., *Sail in the South*. Robert Hale, London, 1975.

RAWSON, G., *Pandora's Last Voyage*. Longmans, London, 1963.

REYNARD, KENNETH D., 'The *Star* is Reborn!' in *Sea History* No. 5, New York, Fall 1976.

RIESENBERG, FELIX, *Cape Horn*. Robert Hale, London, 1941.

ROGGEVEEN, JACOB, *The Journal of Jacob Roggeveen*. Edited by A. Sharp. Oxford University Press, Oxford, 1970.

ROYAL NAVY, THE, *Ocean Passages of the World.* Hydrographic Dept., Somerset, 1973.

SCHURZ, W.L., *The Manila Galleon.* Dutton, New York, 1959.

SHAPIRO, I., *The Story of Yankee Whaling.* American Heritage, New York, 1959.

SPURLING, J. AND LUBBOCK, B., *The Best of Sail.* Grosset & Dunlap, New York, 1972.

TASMAN, ABEL, *The Journal of Abel Tasman.* Edited by G.H. Kenihan. Australian Heritage Press, Adelaide, 1965.

THOMSON, G.M., *Sir Francis Drake.* Book Club Assn., London, 1973.

Voiage Round The World by Willem C. Schouten. Author unknown. London, 1619. Translated by W.P.[hillips]. Da Capo Press, New York, 1968.

WAFER, L., *A New Voyage and Description of the Isthmus of Panama.* Hakluyt, London, 1934.

WALLIS, HELEN, *Carteret's Voyage Round the World.* Cambridge University Press for the Hakluyt Society, Cambridge, 1965.

WALTER, RICHARD, *Anson's Voyage Round the World.* Hopkinson, London, 1928.

WOODES ROGERS, CAPTAIN, *A Cruising Voyage Round the World.* Cassell, London, 1928.

WORSLEY, FRANK, *First Voyage in a Square-rigged Ship.* G. Bles, London, 1947.

WYCHERLEY, G., *Buccaneers of the Pacific.* Rich & Cowan, London, 1935.

Acknowledgements

I would like to thank the staff of the following institutions for their generous assistance:

The Auckland War Memorial Museum Library; National Museum, Wellington; the Auckland Central Library; the Warkworth Library, Auckland; the Dana Point Maritime Museum, California; the Mitchell Library, Sydney; the National Maritime Museum, Greenwich; and the Naval Museum, Madrid.

For kind permission to reproduce copyright material, I acknowledge the following:

K.G. McIntyre and Picador/Souvenir Press, S.A. for extract from *The Secret Discovery of Australia* (p 35); Robert Langdon and Pacific Publications, Sydney, for extract from *The Lost Caravel* (p 36); G.H. Kenihan (ed.) and Australian Heritage Press, Adelaide, for extracts from *The Journal of Abel Tasman* (pp 61, 63); The Society of Authors as literary representative of the estate of John Masefield, and Wm Heinemann, London, for verses from *The Tarry Buccaneer* by John Masefield (p 64); Dover Publications Inc, New York, for extracts from *A New Voyage Round the World* by Wm Dampier (pp 66, 67, 68, 69); Glynn Barratt and the University of British Columbia Press, Vancouver, for extracts from *Russia in Pacific Waters 1715-1825* (pp 89, 92, 94, 95, 96); Jacques Brosse and David Bateman Ltd, Australia, for extract from *Great Voyages of Exploration* (p 103); Scolar Press, London, for extracts from *A Treatise on Practical Seamanship* by William Hutchinson (pp 117-18); Putnam Publications, New York, for the poems *Shortening Sail* by William Falconer (pp 122-3), and *Reefing Topsails* by Walter Mitchell (pp 123-4); G. Bles, London, for the extract from *First Voyage in a Square-rigged Ship* by Frank Worsley (pp 128-9); P.F. Collier, New York, for extracts from *Two Years Before the Mast* by Richard Henry Dana (pp 137, 138-9); Putnam Publications, New York, for the verse from the poem *Nantucket Whalers* by Daniel Henderson (p 142); Richard McKay and 7Cs Press, Connecticutt, for the extracts from *Some Famous Sailing Ships and Their Builder Donald McKay* (pp 150, 151, 153); Grosset & Dunlap Inc, New York, for the *Flying Cloud* extract from *The Best of Sail* by J. Spurling and B. Lubbock (p 150-51); Captn J. Gaby and Antipodean Press, Australia, for the extract from *Mate in Sail* (p 166); Brown, Son & Ferguson, Glasgow, for extracts from *The Nitrate Clippers* by Basil Lubbock (pp 173-5); Jack Churchouse and Millwood Press, Wellington, for extracts from *The Pamir Under the New Zealand Ensign* (pp 177-8).

Although every effort has been made to establish copyright for the material published here, the author would like to apologise for any contravention which may have occurred without his knowledge and invites holders of copyright in such cases to advise him or the publishers.

For their companionable and personal help in their own particular fields I would also like to thank: Clifford Hawkins, marine historian and author of Auckland, and a seemingly inexhaustible source of information; Herbe Kane, historian and artist of Hawaii, for his help with research into the Manila galleons; Noel Hilliam, director of the Northern Wairoa Museum, New Zealand, for enabling me to print some details of his archeological finds and research; Jack Churchouse, curator of the Wellington Harbour Board Museum, and Don Hamer of Whangarei, for assisting with research; Timothy Morris for assistance with maps and for casting his critical seaman's eye over the scripts and paintings; Grey Hutchinson and Paul Leppington for the loan of some valuable books.

Finally, a special thanks to the editor, Joy Browne, for her meticulous attention to detail, and to my wife, Kathleen, who has supported and helped me throughout the three years it has taken to produce this book.

ROGER MORRIS
April 1987
Auckland

NOTE: In the index commencing opposite, the italicised page numbers refer to illustrations throughout the text.

Index